D1191564

THE HARP RE-STRUNG

Richard Fallis, *Series Editor*

The Harp Re-strung

The United Irishmen and the Rise of Irish Literary Nationalism

MARY HELEN THUENTE

SYRACUSE UNIVERSITY PRESS

Copyright © 1994 by Syracuse University Press,
Syracuse, New York 13244-5160

ALL RIGHTS RESERVED

First Edition 1994
94 95 96 97 98 99   6 5 4 3 2 1

The paper used in this publication meets the minimum requirements of American
National Standard for Information Sciences—Permanence of Paper for Printed Library
Materials, ANSI Z39.48–1984. ∞™

Library of Congress Cataloging-in-Publication Data

Thuente, Mary Helen.
    The harp re-strung : the United Irishmen and the rise of Irish
literary nationalism / Mary Helen Thuente.
        p.   cm. — (Irish studies)
    Includes bibliographical references and index.
    ISBN 0-8156-2616-9 (cloth)
    1. English literature—Irish authors—History and criticism.
    2. English literature—18th century—History and criticism.
    3. English literature—19th century—History and criticism.
    4. Politics and literature—Ireland—History—18th century.
    5. Politics and literature—Ireland—History—19th century.
    6. Nationalism—Ireland—History—18th century.   7. Nationalism—
Ireland—History—19th century.   8. Nationalism in literature.
    9. United Irishmen.   I. Title.   II. Series: Irish studies
(Syracuse, N.Y.)
    PR8749.T48   1994
    820.89'9415—dc20   93-37453

Manufactured in the United States of America

DISCARDED WIDENER UNIVERSITY

WIDENER UNIVERSITY
WOLFGRAM
LIBRARY
CHESTER, PA.

For David, Danny, and Michael Patrick

Mary Helen Thuente is Professor of English at Indiana University–Purdue University at Fort Wayne. She has contributed articles to many scholarly journals and is the author of *W. B. Yeats and Irish Folklore* (1980). She is President of the American Conference for Irish Studies and a member of the Executive Committee of the International Association for the Study of Anglo-Irish Literature.

Contents

Preface

This book had its origin in two research projects, one on the Young Ireland movement suggested by Maurice R. O'Connell (Thuente 1985), the other on the "folklore" of Irish literary nationalism suggested by Lawrence J. McCaffrey (Thuente 1989). Research for both projects revealed the United Irishmen's major but unexplored influence on the development of Irish literary nationalism. A preliminary version of my research on the United Irishmen appeared as an essay in *Irish Literature and Culture*, edited by Michael Kenneally (Thuente 1992).

As always, Maureen Murphy's incomparable expertise in Irish folklore, history, and literature was an indispensable resource in the course of my research. I am also deeply indebted to John Killen of the Linen Hall Library and to Christopher Woods of the Royal Irish Academy, who generously shared their unpublished research on Thomas Russell with me, and to James Ford for his assistance in providing me with essential information about a copy of *Paddy's Resource* in the Boston Public Library. Richard Fallis's editorial advice was invaluable as I prepared the original manuscript for publication.

I am very grateful for the research assistance provided by my friends and colleagues in the American Conference for Irish Studies and the International Association for the Study of Anglo-Irish Literature, and most especially to: Anthony Bradley, John Brennan, Martin Croghan, Kevin Danaher, James S. Donnelly, Tom Dunne, Marianne Elliott, Charles Fanning, Joyce Flynn, John Gray, John C. Greene, Thomas Hachey, Maurice Harmon, Michael and Rhona Kenneally, Frederick Kirchhoff, Emmet Larkin, Robert Lowery, Lawrence McCaffrey, Eilis McDowell, James MacKillop, Lucy McDiarmid, David

Miller, Maurice O'Connell, Harold Orel, Richard Ramsey, Robert Rhodes, Catherine Shannon, A. T. Q. Stewart, Blanche Touhill, and Robert Welch.

My research for this book owes a great debt to the efficiency and initiative of Marilyn Grush and Cheryl Truesdell, the Document Delivery Service librarians at the Helmke Library at Indiana University-Purdue University at Fort Wayne. I would also like to express my appreciation to the Boston Public Library; the Kenneth Spencer Library at the University of Kansas; the Lilly Library of Indiana University, Bloomington; the Linen Hall Library, Belfast; the National Library of Ireland; the Presbyterian Historical Society of Northern Ireland; the Public Record Office of Northern Ireland; the Royal Irish Academy; the State Paper Office of Ireland; the Trinity College Dublin Library; and the library of the University of Wisconsin-Madison.

My research has been generously supported by Indiana University, Bloomington, and Indiana University-Purdue University, Fort Wayne. Indiana University awarded me two Hewlett Foundation Summer Faculty Fellowships. Indiana University-Purdue University provided two summer research grants and a sabbatical. Special thanks are due to Gladys Thiele of the Department of English for her invaluable secretarial support.

Finally, I would like to thank my family for their patience and support. The hospitality of the Richard O'Neill family of Convabeg, Ballyhooly, has been the highlight of my many research trips to Ireland, and their knowledge and library have greatly enriched my understanding of Irish literature and history. My parents, Frank and Helen Mulcahy Ernst, my brother and sister-in-law, Frank and Rebecca Ernst, and my aunt and uncle, Jack and Helen Hendricks, have encouraged and sustained me in numerous ways during the writing of this book. My greatest debt is to my husband David and to my sons, Danny and Michael, for without their love and patience I would never have completed this book.

                                          Mary Helen Thuente

Fort Wayne, Indiana
July 1993

THE HARP RE-STRUNG

· 1 ·

Who Fears to Speak of Ninety-Eight?

"Who fears to speak of Ninety-Eight?," the opening line of the popular Young Ireland poem "The Memory of the Dead" (*Nation*, 1 April 1843), today could be asked of scholars who have generally ignored important literary and cultural dimensions of the United Irishmen's activities in the 1790s. The long-recognized contribution of the United Irishmen's political ideology to the development of Irish nationalism is certain to be reassessed as we mark the United Irishmen's bicentenary. Their contribution to the development of Irish literary nationalism also deserves to be finally recognized and explored. My analysis of the cultural and literary dimensions of the United Irish movement will demonstrate how their written works represent an important phase in a literary tradition that originated in the eighteenth century and continued in the nineteenth century in the songs and satires of Thomas Moore and in the writings of the Young Ireland movement of the 1840s.

The United Irish Society, founded in Belfast and Dublin in the autumn of 1791, was originally dedicated to achieving civil rights for Catholics and parliamentary reform through a "Union" of Irishmen of all religious persuasions. But the United Irishmen's original constitutional focus was transformed during the 1790s into a movement seeking separation from England by means of physical force. In 1791, the society was largely composed of middle-class radicals who wished to build upon the concessions from England achieved by the Volunteers and other patriotic reformers during the 1780s. The founders of the United Irish Society included William Drennan, Thomas Addis Emmet, Henry Joy McCracken, Samuel Neilson, Thomas Russell, and

Wolfe Tone. The majority of the original Belfast United Irishmen were Presbyterian merchants, whereas the Dublin branch included many Catholics who were acquiring control of the Catholic Committee from older, more conservative members.

The government's response to the United Irish reform efforts and their alliance of Presbyterians and Catholics was a policy of limited concessions to Catholics offset by legislation reducing general civil liberties. Government efforts to suppress the United Irish movement included the passage of restrictive legislation, prosecution for sedition, an extensive spy network, and a military reign of terror. In addition, the Catholic hierarchy urged Catholics not to become Irish "Jacobins" who would bring the violence and anticlerical dimensions of the French Revolution to Ireland. After the government officially suppressed the United Irish Society in 1795, an increasingly militant core of United Irishmen reorganized as a secret society, adding a military organization in 1796. Wolfe Tone was sent to France to seek military assistance, but attempted French invasions failed in 1796, when bad weather aborted a planned assault off Bantry, and in August and October of 1798 in Mayo and Donegal.

After the government arrested many United Irish leaders in March 1798, poorly organized United Irish uprisings in Wexford, in Antrim and Down, and in Mayo in the spring and summer 1798 were brutally suppressed after temporary initial successes. Ironically, a movement aimed at "Union" among all Irishmen generated a series of uprisings characterized by bitter sectarian and social division and precipitated the legislation that brought about the Act of Union with Britain in 1800. This event was opposed to the republican principles of the many United Irishmen who had preached a very different kind of "Union" throughout the 1790s. Although the United Irish movement failed in its efforts to bring about peaceful constitutional reform and to achieve an Irish republic through violent revolution, it bequeathed a revolutionary republican ideology to later generations of nationalists. United Irishman Robert Emmet's attempted uprising in Dublin in 1803 was a failure, but songs celebrating it glorified the United Irishmen and their violent campaign for an independent Ireland.

From the beginning, the United Irishmen sought to educate and influence public opinion. In addition to numerous pamphlets and resolutions, they published at least five songbooks, several prose satires, and four newspapers. Political poems and songs were regular features in their newspapers, the *Northern Star* (Belfast), the *National Journal* and *The Press* (Dublin), and the *Harp of Erin* (Cork). The four United Irish songbooks entitled *Paddy's Resource* included 160 different songs in successive editions in 1795, 1796, 1798, and 1803. (See appendix A for an annotated bibliography of these United Irish "literary" publications.)

The United Irishmen's literary nationalism was part of their larger cultural nationalism, which included their support for the Belfast Harp Festival in 1792 and the publication of a Gaelic magazine entitled *Bolg an tSolair* in 1795. United Irish songs, drawing upon diverse sources, generated what have become the stereotypical images of Irish nationalism: bards, harps, shamrocks, green flags, political martyrs, and blood sacrifice. Contrary to popular belief, Irish literary nationalism originated with the United Irishmen rather than with Thomas Moore or the Young Ireland poets.

Not surprisingly, historians have largely been concerned with analyzing the political activities and ideology of the United Irishmen and have either ignored the literary and cultural dimensions of the movement or dismissed them as insignificant.[1] The attitude of most historians about political songs is typified in the annotation "unimportant" written next to the entry for a document in the State Paper Office of Ireland at Dublin Castle (SPOI) that is described as a "pamphlet of songs" (SPOI 620/20/35). The pamphlet is actually quite significant because it is a 1793 songbook once owned by United Irishman Thomas Russell that provides important evidence regarding Russell's authorship of several poems.

The historians' myopia about the literary activities of the United Irishmen has fostered a distorted view of the movement's cultural dimensions, which were largely expressed in literary productions. R. B. McDowell does not even admit a cultural dimension to the movement. He sums up the position of most historians in his assertion that, despite the fact that all the materials for a cultural nationalism existed in Ireland in the 1790s, "very little was done by Irish radicals to link their political strivings with a national cultural movement" (1986, 301). In *Modern Ireland, 1600–1972* (1988), Roy Foster reiterates the standard historical perspective that the United Irishmen were of purely political and ideological significance in the history of Irish nationalism: " 'Nationalism' as such had not been part of the original United Irish package. They were internationalist liberals, anti-government rather than anti-English. Even when anti-Englishness took over, they had little time for ethnic considerations; recent fashions for traditional music and poetry, and archaeological divinations of the Celtic past, seemed to middle-class radicals at best silly and at worst savage" (269–70).

On the contrary, the United Irishmen had a great deal of time for such endeavors from the beginning. Eighteenth-century scholarly and literary antiquarianism, with its incipient cultural nationalism, was one of many aspects of eighteenth-century culture upon which the United Irishmen drew when creating the first songs and poems of the literary tradition of Irish nationalism. To date, A. T. Q. Stewart is the only historian to challenge the established view that the United Irish movement embodied no cultural nationalism. Although he does not consider either their literary productions or their cultural activities, Stewart argues that the political implications of the late eighteenth-century interest in Irish antiquities, music, and language were not lost on the United Irishmen (1986, 258–69). Similarly, literary historian Robert Welch, in his discussion of the Belfast backgrounds of Samuel Ferguson in *Irish Poetry from Moore to Yeats* (1980), observes without elaboration that "in late eighteenth-century Belfast, there was a strong connection between the tradition of Protestant Dissent, the radical republicanism of Wolfe Tone and the United Irishmen, and Gaelic song and culture" (123). That connection remains to be explored.

First, however, the arguments behind the historians' consensus that the United Irishmen were not cultural nationalists must be considered. Foster argues that as "internationalist liberals" the United Irishmen had no interest in Irish antiquities, music, and language. On the contrary, the United Irishmen did not see their advocation of universal liberty and an interest in Irish culture as mutually exclusive. Indeed, as they saw it, the high degree of culture in Irish antiquity, especially as regarded literature, music, and language, lent support to their claims for civil and political freedoms. Moreover, the songs in *Paddy's Resource* demonstrate that an "internationalist" liberal philosophy and a pride in an Irish cultural heritage went hand in hand among United Irishmen.

Historians frequently quote two passages from the *Proceedings of the Dublin Society of United Irishmen* (1795) as evidence of a lack of interest in Irish antiquities, and consequently in Irish culture as a whole. According to R. B. McDowell: "Far from being anxious to stress the continuity of national tradition stretching back to the Gaelic past, they were inclined to think 'mankind have been too retrospective, canonized antiquity and undervalued themselves.' 'In associating,' the Dublin society of United Irishmen declared, 'we have thought little about our ancestors and much of our posterity' " (1979, 371).

The two passages that McDowell quotes do not necessarily represent a wholesale rejection of Irish cultural tradition. The United Irishmen certainly intended to distance themselves from the exaggerated and romantic descriptions of ancient Ireland that had characterized some antiquarian writing. But their refusal to go along with the canonization of Irish antiquities did not mean that they categorically rejected all antiquarianism or the literary and political implications of the eighteenth-century interest in Irish culture. Indeed, their frequent use of images of harps, bards, and the other iconography bequeathed to them by Irish antiquarianism proved that their poetry, and the messages it propagated, owed a large debt to a romanticized image of early Ireland. Moreover, their declaration that they thought "little about our ancestors" (1979, 371) was more likely a rejection of the polemical sectarian controversies of more recent centuries of Irish history than of Irish antiquarianism.

Wolfe Tone's journal has provided the cornerstone of the argument by historians that cultural nationalism played no part in the United Irish movement. Tone's supposed lack of interest in the music performed at the Belfast Harp Festival in July 1792 has been the major evidence, and in some cases the only evidence cited, that the United Irishmen were immune from the enthusiasm for Irish antiquities, music, and language which raged in late eighteenth-century Ireland. The assumption that Tone represents the movement is surprisingly naïve, though it is one that is made frequently in Irish historiography about the United Irishmen. This interpretation of Tone's attitudes about Irish music and culture is also mistaken.

A single quotation from Tone's journal concerning the Belfast Harp Festival of 1792 is repeatedly cited as evidence of his lack of interest in Irish music: "The harpers again. Strum. Strum and be hanged" (1826, 2:157). This passage must be considered in context, however. The comment was clearly made in the tone of playful sarcasm that characterizes so much of Tone's journal. Moreover, the entry was for 13 July, a day when Tone was missing his dear friend

Thomas Russell deeply, had risen with a severe headache for the third straight day, and was experiencing a great deal of stress because of the lively debate over whether his resolutions concerning the Catholic question would be adopted the next day. The entry for 13 July depicts Tone in an uncharacteristically unhappy mood and is intensely sarcastic, even for Tone. Tone notes his "grievous want of P. P." (Tone's nickname for Russell), laments that Belfast was "not half so pleasant this time as the last," and records that he was "generally sulky" and "came home in not the most amiable temper" (1826, 2:156–58). Tone was clearly not in the frame of mind to be positive about much of anything when he recorded the day's events in his journal.

Here is the section of the entry for 13 July, actually one of the wittiest in Tone's entire journal, in which the "strum and be hanged" remark occurs:

> Weather bad. Afraid for tomorrow every way; generally in low spirits. Hear that the Tribune [Tone's nickname for Napper Tandy], with his suite, is arrived; go to the Donegal Arms and say O to him, (vide Robinson Crusoe.) The Harper's again. Strum strum and be hanged. Hear that several Catholics have been seen; run to try; find Magog, Weldon, and others, to a large amount. The hair of Dr. Haliday's wig miraculously grows grey with fear of the Catholics. Several comets appear in the market place. Walk the Catholics about to show them the lions. See a figure of Commerce at the insurance office; the Catholics mistake it for an image, and kneel down, take out their beads, and say their prayers before it. (1826, 2:157).

Despite the "strum and be hanged" remark, Tone returned to hear the harpers again later that day. Moreover, other comments in Tone's journal suggest a strong interest in traditional music. For example, a journal entry for 11 July recounts how he and a group of his fellow United Irishmen attended a performance by the harpers. Tone's comments evaluating that performance suggest a familiarity with and an appreciation of traditional Irish music: "All go to the Harper's at one; poor enough; ten performers; seven execrable, three good, one of them, Fanning, far the best. No new musical discovery; believe all the good Irish airs are already written" (1826, 2:155–56). Judging several of the harpers to be poor performers was not necessarily a blanket condemnation of Irish music. The remark actually suggests a discriminating taste and thus a familiarity with Irish music. Tone, an avid flute player whose fondness for music is well known, would have been familiar with the various collections of Irish music published during the eighteenth century that adopted old Irish airs to the flute. Tone was clearly a man who knew his Irish music. He punctuated his entire journal with snatches of traditional and popular songs. His journal entries for December 1796 tell how he amused himself singing the airs his wife loved, and how he wrote out "about thirty airs" for the band of his anticipated regiment during his dispiriting wait in Bantry Bay.

Like many other United Irish leaders, Tone composed at least one song to a traditional Irish melody. On 18 July 1792, the *Northern Star* printed a song entitled "Ierne United" by "Counsellor Tone" and reported that it had been sung at the dinner concluding the Belfast Harp Festival and the Belfast celebration of the third anniversary of the fall of the Bastille, just one day after Tone's flippant journal entry about the harpers. Tone's song was to be sung to the popular eighteenth-century tune "Ballinamoney."[2] (See appendix B for the text of the song.) The lyrics indicate that Tone was quite familiar with the contemporary debates concerning early Irish history and was willing to use recent antiquarian research to support his arguments for political freedom. In opposition to David Hume's influential *History of England . . .* (1754–1762), which argues that Ireland remained in a state of barbarism because it had never been conquered by the Romans, Tone's song counts the absence of Roman influence on Irish culture as a blessing.

The song's reference to the harp made it an appropriate song to be sung at a dinner marking the close of the Belfast Harp Festival and the commemoration of the anniversary of the French Revolution. All those present at the dinner, many of whom were United Irishmen, would have been well aware that a harp with the motto It Is New Strung and Shall be Heard was the insignia of the United Irishmen, who sought to infuse the popular mind with French revolutionary principles. In any event, Tone was clearly not immune from the romantic nationalism from which McDowell, Foster, and even Marianne Elliott, in her recent biography of Tone, try to disassociate him.

Even if Wolfe Tone had appreciated neither the cultural significance nor the propagandistic value of the eighteenth-century enthusiasm for Irish antiquities, music, and language, other United Irishmen, such as Whitley Stokes, who accompanied Tone to Belfast in July 1792, and Thomas Russell, Tone's closest friend, certainly did. Stokes was a noted scholar of the Irish language and of Irish antiquities. Russell studied Irish harp music and the Irish language, and translated Irish poetry into English.

The newly founded United Irish Society supported the Belfast Harp Festival, which it publicized and promoted in the United Irish newspaper the *Northern Star*. All four organizers of the festival—James McDonnell, Henry Joy, Robert Bradshaw, and Robert Simms—had close ties with the United Irishmen. Indeed, Robert Simms was a founding member of the Belfast Society of United Irishmen, one of the original proprietors of the *Northern Star*, and a close friend of Tone's. Henry Joy was the first cousin of Mary Ann and Henry Joy McCracken. James McDonnell was a friend of the McCrackens, of Tone, and of Thomas Russell. The latter lived with McDonnell intermittently in the early 1790s and had access to McDonnell's library of Irish manuscripts and books on Irish culture and history.

The announcement of the harp festival that was published and circulated in Belfast in December 1791 makes it clear that the organizers' goals had literary and political as well as musical dimensions. The organizers declared their intention was to assemble the harpers, whom they described as the "descendants of our Ancient Bards," to "revive and perpetuate the ancient Music and Poetry of Ireland . . . as monuments of the refined taste and genius of their ancestors." The following sentence from the festival announcement suggests the political significance of the event: "And when it is considered how intimately the spirit and character of a people are connected with their national Poetry and Music, it is presumed that the Irish patriot and politician will not deem it an object unworthy of his patronage and protection" (Fox 1911, 97–98).

Edward Bunting (1773–1843), who had come to live with the McCrackens in 1784 at the age of eleven and remained a member of the family for thirty years, was chosen to transcribe the music performed at the festival. Mary McNeill's *The Life and Times of Mary Ann McCracken, 1770-1866* (1960) recounts the close ties between Bunting, the McCrackens, and Thomas Russell. The McCrackens, who themselves collected airs for Bunting during the 1790s, gave

emotional and financial assistance to Bunting's continued collection
of music after the festival and to the publication of his first book, *A
General Collection of the Ancient Irish Music* (1796). The journals of
Thomas Russell demonstrate the close relationship between Russell
and Bunting, who taught Russell to play the harp. Bunting was indebted to Russell for helping to convince the Belfast Society for Promoting Knowledge, to which many Belfast United Irishmen belonged
and for which Russell was librarian, to underwrite Bunting's work
collecting Irish music. In 1803, when Russell was in hiding in the
hills outside Belfast, Bunting went to see him, though he did not
share Russell's revolutionary goals.

   Many United Irishmen shared Russell and Bunting's enthusiasm
for the Irish language and Irish music. Bunting's manuscript books of
Irish songs include translations by Thomas Russell, William Drennan,
Robert Emmet, and Thomas Stott (Fox 1911, 45). Several prominent
United Irishmen spoke Irish, including William James MacNeven,
Thomas Addis Emmet, and Robert Emmet. While MacNeven and
Thomas Addis Emmet were imprisoned in Fort George, MacNeven
compiled an Irish grammar for the use of Emmet's children, who were
taught Irish by the United Irish prisoners there (Ryan 1939, 65–66;
Webb 1878).

   The United Irish movement actively promoted the study of the
Irish language. In 1795, the office of the United Irish newspaper the
Northern Star published *Bolg an tSolair: or, Gaelic Magazine*, which
contained an Irish grammar, prayers, a glossary, and a selection of
poems from Charlotte Brooke's *Reliques of Irish Poetry.* (see chap. 3).
It was edited by Patrick Lynch, who taught Irish in Belfast and who
had been funded by the McCrackens to go to Connaught to gather
the words for the airs Bunting had already collected. Lynch's connections with the United Irishmen of Belfast were strong enough for him
to be suspected of being a United Irish emissary during his folksong
collecting expeditions (O Casaide 1930, 29; Fox 1911, 244, 254).

   Bolg an tSolair's seven-page preface declared Irish to be "the mother
tongue of all the languages in the West" and Ireland to be "the seat of
the muses from times of remotest antiquity" because "no nation ever
encouraged poets and music more than the ancient Irish" (1795, vii,
iv). The preface extolled the contemporary as well as the ancient
dimensions of Irish, promising to publish songs and airs of the present

as well as compositions from Ireland's ancient past. The United Irishmen were well aware of the contemporary relevance of the Irish language. On 20 April 1795, the *Northern Star* published an editorial entitled "The Irish Language" that praised Patrick Lynch's efforts to teach Irish. The editorial, probably written by Lynch's pupil Thomas Russell, claimed that Irish was of use to scholars, merchants, and artists, and declared that Irish would help communicate "our sentiments and instruction" with "our countrymen."

This contemporary focus in the late eighteenth-century interest in Irish music, literature, and language is important. For example, although Bunting's collections of Irish music include the word "ancient" in their titles, the airs were not found in ancient manuscripts; most of them were collected from the harpers at the festival in 1792 or during Bunting's subsequent collecting expeditions. These contemporary as opposed to ancient dimensions of Irish antiquarianism, largely ignored by scholars today who stress the backward-looking focus of antiquarianism, were exploited and politicized by the United Irishmen in the 1790s. Moreover, eighteenth-century antiquarianism did not necessarily involve revivalism. The antiquarian interests of the United Irishmen certainly did not. For the United Irishmen, antiquarian research bolstered their political arguments for social and civil parity. The literary productions inspired by antiquarianism also provided convenient images through which the United Irishmen could communicate with the middle- and upper-class portions of their audiences. Although the cultural nationalism generated by eighteenth-century antiquarianism did assume greater and greater revivalist implications in the course of the nineteenth century, such was not the case in the 1790s.

Unfortunately, twentieth-century historians too often presume that cultural nationalism necessarily involves the doctrine of political separation and that all antiquarianism is revivalist by its very nature. For example, Tom Dunne, defending the United Irishmen against the charge that they were cultural nationalists, declares: "The claim that the early United Irishmen were interested in a form of Gaelic revivalism seems unconvincing" (1990, 143). Similarly, Marianne Elliott argues in her recent biography of Tone that the "Gaelic Revival" in the late eighteenth century "seems entirely to have bypassed Tone" (1989, 173). Dunne and Elliott are correct in asserting that the United

Irishmen and Tone did not promote the revival of the Irish language. Few people at the time did. Yet the United Irishmen, individually and as a movement, had no qualms about combining politics and literature and drawing upon the images popularized in scholarly and literary antiquarianism in order to propagate their political principles in song.

Literary scholars, the most likely investigators of the literary dimensions of the United Irishmen, have obviously not been encouraged by historians to pursue such studies. Indeed, the reservations about mixing politics and literature, and about the artistic merit of popular political literature, are even stronger among literary historians than among political historians. Influenced by William Butler Yeats's diatribes against Thomas Moore's *Irish Melodies* and the poetry of Thomas Davis and the Young Irelanders, literary critics have disdained popular political poetry.[3] Yeats wrote a great many essays delineating a particularly Irish literary tradition, but he claimed that the tradition had originated with the poetry of Davis, Mangan, and Ferguson, or, at the earliest, with Thomas Moore. The argument that Irish literary nationalism originated with Thomas Moore or in the poetry of the Young Irelanders ignores the large debt that both owed to the United Irishmen (see chap. 6 and 7).

Yeats's definition of popular poetry as carelessly written, rhetorical, and lacking in true poetic substance and style, despite its undeniable energy and emotion (1961, 3–12), is to some extent true. But Yeats's focus on popular poetry's aesthetic value obscures its cultural significance and the nature of the discourse it embodies. Political songs were never meant to be high art. The usual standards of literary criticism do not always apply to the combination of song and verse in political "poetry." As John Hewitt shrewdly pointed out in a 1958 article entitled "Irish Poets Learn Your Trade," "it is easy to dismiss the sheaves of patriotic balladry by Thomas Davis, Charles Gavan Duffy, and T. D. Sullivan as rhetorical in thought, commonplace in image, conventional in decoration and mechanical in metre; but taken outside the limits of literature and looked at as political journalism, slogan-inventing, opinion-forming, they had their swift and, for a surprisingly long while, memorable value" (1987, 79).

The absence of any mention of a United Irish poet in Hewitt's list of "popular poets" illustrates the typical neglect of the United Irishmen's popular poetry. The only scholar to examine the literary dimensions of the United Irish movement has been R. R. Madden (1798–1886), a friend and associate of Thomas Davis and other Young Irelanders. Madden accumulated extensive information and primary materials from surviving United Irishmen and from the relatives of those who had died. Madden's *United Irishmen, Their Lives and Times* (published from 1842 to 1846), and his *Literary Remains of the United Irishmen of 1798, and Selections from Other Popular Lyrics of Their Times* (1887) remain the primary and in many cases the only sources of information about the literary activities of the United Irishmen. However, both works are incomplete as regards the literary works of the United Irishmen, and *Literary Remains of the United Irishmen* is disorganized and at times inaccurate. This is partly owing to the fact that *Literary Remains of the United Irishmen*, although published under Madden's name, was actually compiled posthumously from the materials he had accumulated.[4]

Although scholars have ignored the literary works of the United Irishmen, the English authorities in Ireland, who carefully monitored the activities of the United Irishmen, took their songs and satires very seriously indeed. Reports from various government "secret committees" in the late 1790s and surviving informers' reports in the State Paper Offices in Dublin and Belfast indicate that the officials considered the United Irish songs and satires to be a significant threat. The Rebellion Papers, now in the State Paper Office of Ireland in Dublin Castle, include many of the literary works of the United Irishmen and other materials associated with their cultural pursuits and activities.[5] The government's anxiety about United Irish songs and satires is well-portrayed in two United Irish satires, James Porter's *Billy Bluff and the Squire* (1796) and William Sampson's *Faithful Report of the Trial of Hurdy Gurdy* (1794), both of which make clear that the United Irishmen reveled in their songs as much as the authorities feared them.

Porter's *Billy Bluff and the Squire* first appeared in the *Northern Star* from May to November 1796 as a series of letters to the editor from an anonymous United Irishman. It recounts the conversations between an Ulster Protestant landlord, Squire Firebrand, and his spy Billy Bluff, who informs the squire about the local United Irishmen's seditious activities—they "read newspapers" and "sing songs." The songs that Billy accuses the United Irishmen of singing had all appeared in the *Northern Star* or in *Paddy's Resource*. According to the squire, "Tis songs that is most to be dreaded of all things. Singing, Billy is a d___d bad custom; it infects the whole country, and makes them half mad; because they rejoice and forget their cares, and forget their duty, and forget their betters." Billy tells the squire that the songs "are all put into one book, your honour, and they are called PADDY'S RACE-HORSE. ["Paddy's Race-Horse" became the popular name for *Paddy's Resource* throughout the nineteenth century owing to the immense popularity of Porter's *Billy Bluff*.] Such a parcel of lies and rebellion was never seen in a Christian country. *Teague and his Comrade digging Potatoes*, the very first; *Ierne United*, the last." (Songs of those titles are indeed the first and last in the 1795 *Paddy's Resource*.) The squire responds, "The world will come to an end unless such practices are put a stop to," and tells Billy that the title of the songbook is really *Paddy's Resource*, explaining that the Irishman "formerly had his Beila Bat—then he had his Irish Oak Stick—lastly his Volunteers—and now his last resource is singing patriotic lies, national impudence, and united treason" (*Northern Star*, 26 May 1796).

The other popular United Irish prose satire, William Sampson's a *Faithful Report of the Trial of Hurdy Gurdy*, was published anonymously in the *Northern Star* in July and August 1794. It is a parody of the trial of United Irishman Thomas Muir in Scotland at which the music of a hurdy gurdy had been "a material point of evidence to support his banishment to Botany Bay." Sampson's "Hurdy Gurdy, alias Barrel Organ, alias Grinder, alias the Seditious Organ" is tried and convicted on ninety-three counts for "playing as a symphony and as a country dance" and for publicizing "a certain false wicked malicious and scandalous noise . . . known by the name Ça Ira, Anglice, that will go (meaning thereby, that the constitution of this kingdom in church and state, will go)," which "promotes far and wide, the principles of anarchy and fanaticism" (Sampson 1806, 5–6). English translations of the popular French Revolutionary song "Ça Ira" were published in the *Northern Star* in April 1792 and in the 1795 *Paddy's Resource*.

Jurors in Sampson's satire have names like "Croucher Toryman of Sly-mount" and "Tyrant Cali-ban of Fleeced Island." Hurdy Gurdy uses titles of United Irish tunes and songs as answers during his interrogation. His accusers declare that "every mischief in the world had been occasioned by the *Northern Star*." Evidence against Hurdy Gurdy includes examples of bardic poetry from Joseph Cooper Walker's *Historical Memoirs of the Irish Bards*, which are labeled "effusions of ignorant and heated fanatics." The bards are also described as "a race of Rhapsodists . . . expert in satire and invective" whose harp music and rhymes had had an "astonishing" influence (Sampson 1806, 31–39). Sampson and his fellow United Irish songwriters and satirists were clearly emulating the example of such bards and hoping to have a similar influence.

Although the United Irishmen published numerous nonfictional prose works, such as the proceedings of the society's meetings, resolutions, declarations, letters to the people, and accounts of trials, they obviously considered songs and satires major tools in their campaign to capture the heads and the hearts of the Irish people. Prosaic publications could argue the United Irish agenda and appeal to the people's reason, but the United Irishmen recognized the greater appeal of songs and satires from the beginning. In *O'Halloran; or, the Insurgent Chief, An Irish Historical Tale of 1798* (1824), James McHenry, who was an eyewitness to the United Irish propaganda campaign before he emigrated to America, describes the public response in Belfast in 1797 to a ballad singer performing the United Irish ballad "Blaris Moor," which recounts the execution of four militiamen accused of being United Irishmen:

> Of this elegiac composition of some rustic political bards, whose numerous effusions were then so prevalent and so eagerly sought after in the country, it may not be amiss to give the reader a few stanzas, as a specimen of those lyrical productions, which, although utterly destitute of the graces of fine writing, yet being adapted to popular airs, being in unison with the popular feelings, and containing sometimes a great deal of simplicity and nature, were altogether suited to the taste of the lower orders, and produced in their minds a wonderful degree of political enthusiasm. It has been asserted that the prevalence of those songs did more to increase the numbers of conspirators than all the efforts of French emissaries, or the writings and harangues of all the political philosophers, and age-of-reason men of the times. (1824, 63)

When William Drennan, whose seminal role in the founding of the United Irish Society has been eclipsed by that of Wolfe Tone (Stewart 1976), circulated a paper in Dublin in 1791 containing the original plan for the society, he clearly wanted to appeal to more than reason. Drennan justified his preference for secrecy and ceremonial within the proposed "Irish Brotherhood" by citing the need to "strike the soul through the senses" and thus address the *"whole* Man" by "animating his philosophy by the energy of his passions" (Drennan 1844, 155–56). The popular success of Drennan's Volunteer pamphlet *Letters of Orellana . . .* (1785), in which he assumed the role of an "Irish helot" preaching an impassioned sermon filled with references to adding "new strings to the Irish Harp," demonstrated to Drennan and others the effectiveness of using literary devices as well as discursive prose arguments to convince an audience.

For Drennan, who in his *Second Letter to the Right Honourable William Pitt* (1799) described "that instinctive sentiment of country . . . which I often hear with strange delight in the wild and almost savage melancholy of native music," song was to be as central to the new movement as it had been to the success of the Volunteer movement in the 1780s (36). In May 1791, Drennan wrote to his brother-in-law Samuel McTier, a Belfast United Irish leader, "without enthusiasm nothing great was done, or will be done" (1931, 55). Like secrecy and ceremonial, song and satire would generate the enthusiasm necessary to transform rational principles into actual reforms.

Both informally and formally, music and song animated the United Irish Society, whose meetings were generally held at Belfast taverns. Even the selection of a "captain" within a local United Irish Society was evidently at times determined by a man's singing ability. Former United Irishman William Farrell recalled in his autobiography *Carlow in '98*: "A man remarkable for speaking with great warmth in praise of literature was considered a very proper person for captain. At another time, a man who had the greatest number of United Men's songs and could sing them best was chosen" (1949, 50).

Appropriately, a harp with the motto "It is new strung and shall be heard" was adopted as the official insignia when the first United Irish Society was founded in October 1791. The United Irishmen, many of whom had been Volunteers, thus appropriated the symbol and slogan of the Volunteers, and almost immediately began to publish newspapers and songbooks modeled upon those of the Volunteers. However, the significance of the harp antedates the Volunteer movement and indicates the complex eighteenth-century cultural backgrounds that must be considered before analyzing the United Irishmen's newspapers and songbooks.

◦ 2 ◦

The Eighteenth-Century Backgrounds

Literary, Antiquarian, Political, and Musical

The cultural and literary dimensions of the United Irish movement and its important transitional role in the development of Irish literary nationalism cannot be understood without first surveying the eighteenth-century backgrounds. Just as Wolfe Tone's contribution to the political ideology of Irish nationalism was largely a matter of consolidating and effectively articulating much previous eighteenth-century political thought, the United Irish movement's poetry and prose satires blended multiple aspects of eighteenth-century culture, including English literature, Celticism and Irish antiquarianism, political literature, music, popular culture, and periodical literature.

Most of the United Irish leaders and the chief writers for the movement were men of broad interests in a culture that did not segregate politics and literature into separate intellectual endeavors. Moreover, elite culture and popular culture were not mutually exclusive in the eighteenth century. As J. R. R. Adams has demonstrated in *The Printed Word and the Common Man: Popular Culture in Ulster, 1700–1900* (1987), this was especially true in eighteenth-century Ulster, the home of the majority of the United Irish poets and satirists. The diverse nature of the United Irishmen's audience also made it necessary that their writings appeal to a wide range of tastes. Not surprisingly then, the origins of United Irish literary works can be found in many places: in eighteenth-century English, Anglo-Irish, Irish and Scottish literary traditions; in the Celticism of the third quarter of the century; in the scholarly and literary antiquarianism of Irish Catholics and Anglo-Irish Protestants; in the pamphlets and

17

songs of the Volunteers; in the revival of English, Scots, and Irish traditional music; in the Gaelic song traditions of the rural Catholic peasantry; in the lowland Scots poetry of the Ulster Presbyterians; and in the lively drinking songs and street ballads, whether sentimental, satiric, or bawdy, that were enjoyed by all classes and sects.

The more elite literary tastes and the broad intellectual interests of the United Irishmen are illustrated by the books listed as being in the library of the Belfast Society for Promoting Knowledge in a 1795 catalogue compiled by the United Irishman Thomas Russell, who was the society's librarian. The Belfast Society for Promoting Knowledge was founded in 1788 and many of its earliest members were political radicals. Eight of the twelve original United Irish proprietors of the *Northern Star* newspaper belonged to the society: Samuel Neilson (editor of the *Northern Star*), Robert Caldwell, John and Henry Haslett, William Magee, Robert and William Simms, and William Tennent. Other prominent Belfast United Irishmen were also members: Henry Joy McCracken, William Sampson, Samuel McTier (William Drennan's brother-in-law), and Sinclare Kelburn (*Catalogue* . . . 1795, 27–29).

The society's 1795 catalogue listed over three hundred titles, including James Boswell's *Life of Samuel Johnson*; a six-volume edition of Johnson's works; Johnson's *Lives of British Poets*; a six-volume edition of Alexander Pope's works; and an eight-volume edition of Jonathan Swift's works. The library also included numerous histories of Ireland and England; Charles Smith's histories of counties Cork and Waterford; and the two major works of Irish literary antiquarianism: Joseph Cooper Walker's *Historical Memoirs of the Irish Bards* (1786) and Charlotte Brooke's *Reliques of Irish Poetry* (1789). Radical works such as William Godwin's *Political Justice* and Mary Wollstonecraft's *Vindication of the Rights of Women* were also listed. The broad interests of the members were attested to by numerous volumes concerning music, philosophy, and foreign countries, including China, Africa, America, the Artic, India, Japan, and Turkey. The sciences were represented by works about optics, chemistry, ornithology, physiology, and zoology.

The society's librarian, Thomas Russell (1767–1803), typifies the broad literary tastes of the United Irishmen. For many reasons, Russell is the quintessential and thus most representative United Irishman. Russell was a Protestant whose mother was a Catholic, and, according to one account, he became a Presbyterian during the years he spent in

Belfast. He had close personal and political ties in both Belfast and Dublin. Surviving letters and memoirs of the period repeatedly praise Russell as a person and as a political activist. Tone declared repeatedly that Russell was his dearest friend. Mary Ann McCracken's letter to the imprisoned Russell on 18 July 1798 to inform him of her brother Henry Joy McCracken's execution begins: "In obedience to the last request of a much loved brother, I wish to inform you who were his dearest and most valued friend . . . " (SPOI 620/16/3). William Sampson recalled Russell as follows: "With him [Robert Emmet] too fell Russell, whom to know was to love. Gentle of heart and merciful in nature, faithful and brave, with every grace of mind and person, and every charm of virtue" (W. C. Taylor, *History of Ireland* 1833–1839, 325).

Russell's own journal illustrates his close ties with persons representing all shades of United Irish opinion. He was a friend of the politically conservative James McDonnell and of younger more radical United Irishmen such as Thomas Storey, as well of many mainstream United Irish leaders and writers. Russell participated in the founding of the United Irish societies in both Belfast and Dublin and remained much more involved than Tone in the day-to-day activities of the movement. Russell wrote prose pamphlets, prose satires, and poetry, including some translations from the Irish, and he studied both Irish music and the Irish language before and during his imprisonment. That he was imprisoned without trial from September 1796 until June 1802, longer than any other United Irishman, suggests how dangerous (that is, how important and effective within the movement) the authorities considered Russell to be. Moreover, Russell was one of the few United Irishmen whose involvement spanned the founding of the movement in 1791 through his participation in Emmet's uprising in 1803, for which Russell was executed.

Russell's journals indicate that he was well-versed in the variety of subjects represented by the library of the Belfast Society for Promoting Knowledge. Russell's surviving papers demonstrate his familiarity with less elite kinds of literary culture as well. When he was arrested in 1796, government officials confiscated not only a Latin pamphlet by Whitley Stokes (inscribed by the author to Russell, who read both Greek and Latin), but also an eight-page songbook, published in Belfast in 1793, that contained a typical assortment of popular songs of the day (SPOI 620/20/35). The opening stanza of the first song, a bawdy ballad entitled

"The Sporting Plowman; or, Bartly M'Cuskers Frolick" illustrated the tenor of the stanzas that followed: "You lasses fair to me repair / And hear my declaration O, / I'm ready now your lands to plow, / That's fit for cultivation O" (*A New Song in Praise of the Sporting Plowman* 1793, 1). The lyrics went on for four pages to recount the hero's amorous adventures in every county and most major towns in Ulster.

The second song, by contrast, is a tender love song entitled "Answer to the Farmer's Daughter" about a happy elopement (*New Song* 1793, 4–5). The third song, "The Negro's Lament," was an antislavery song typical of numerous such songs published in the 1780s, except for this one purportedly being in African dialect (*New Song* 1793, 6–7). Interestingly, the same song had been published in London in *The Gentleman's Magazine* for August 1793 under the title "The African's Complaint on Board a Slave Ship," another indication of the close ties between popular and elite culture at this time. The songbook concluded with a rowdy "Drinking Song," the message of which is summed up in the chorus: "Then drink and sing, pang pain and sorrow, / The halter was made for the neck, / He that's now live and lusty—tomorrow / Perhaps may be stretch'd on the deck" (*New Song* 1793, 8). "Pang" is an eighteenth-century Scots word meaning to squeeze, press, or pack one thing into another.

Those four very different songs interestingly parallel the diverse aspects of Russell's own personality. His journal recounts both his tender love for a young impoverished gentlewoman, Bess Goddard, and his visits to Belfast prostitutes. Tone's journal frequently refers to Russell's love of drink. Their evenings at taverns and at United Irish dinners and meetings involved rowdy drinking songs, and probably bawdy ballads, given the large number of United Irish political songs that were set to tunes originally associated with some of the coarser Scots and Irish folk songs. Russell was also a strong opponent of slavery, even to the point of refusing to eat sugar, a commodity which depended on the slave trade. The papers and memoirs of other United Irishmen suggest equally "eclectic" literary tastes.

LITERARY BACKGROUNDS

My survey of the literary origins of the United Irish songs and satires will begin with their debt to English literary works such as those in the library of the Belfast Society for Promoting Knowledge. Paradoxically, Irish literary nationalism, which in the nineteenth century would become so vehemently anti-English, originated in the writings of a group of United Irish radicals who were deeply indebted to English and Anglo-Irish literary tradition for models in both prose and poetry. The *Northern Star* published poems by English poets such as Jonathan Swift, William Cowper, Oliver Goldsmith, and Samuel Taylor Coleridge. Russell's journal recounts his reading of Milton, Dryden, and Swift.

Tone had written and published essays of literary criticism and had coauthored a novel entitled *Belmont Castle* while he was a student in London (O'Kelly 1935, 47–48). Marianne Elliott's summary of Tone's literary tastes could apply to many United Irish leaders. According to Elliott, in addition to Shakespeare and Anglo-Irish dramatists such as Sheridan, Tone's journals, which abound in references to and quotations from literary works, "read like the Top Twenty of the eighteenth-century educated man's reading list, Pope, Swift, Defoe, Richardson, Goldsmith, Sterne, Smollett, Fielding" (1989, 145).

Jonathan Swift's works were held in especially high regard by United Irishmen. The sixth issue of the *Northern Star* (25 January 1792) prefaced a quote by Swift against religious prejudice with a reference to Swift as a patriot whose thoughts had been "sublimely animated" by "those generous convictions which dignify human nature." Excerpts from Swift's works were published in the *Northern Star.* Tone compared his journal to Swift's, and many of the quotations and nicknames in it are derived from Swift. For example, Tone's nickname for Belfast, "Blefescu," is from *Gulliver's Travels.* When Russell described his earliest literary ambitions in his journal, he recalled, "My wish was to write like Swift or at least as near" (Woods 1991, 179). Russell's prose satires, like the prose satires and satiric songs composed by other United Irishmen, owe a large debt to Swift. Moreover, like Swift, Tone, Russell, and many United Irishmen wrote political songs to traditional tunes. In 1720, Swift had even written English lyrics for the famous harper Carolan's tune "Plearaca na Ruarcach," which began: "O'Rorke's noble feast will ne'er be forgot / By those who were there and those who were not."

The tune "Plearca na Ruarc" had been one of the tunes reported in the *Northern Star* to have been played at the Belfast Harp Festival in

July 1792. The United Irishmen were familiar with Swift's English version of that Irish song because the first two lines of the Swift's lyrics,
citing Swift as author, were printed as the epigraph to a satire on a
recent government dinner in the *Northern Star* on 19 October 1793.
Swift thus provided a model for the two chief kinds of literary works
produced by the United Irishmen, prose satires and songs set to traditional tunes.

United Irish literary works were indebted to diverse English literary modes and theories. (Their debt to the literary cult of the "noble
savage" is discussed in chap. 3.) The exalted and elaborate lyricism
and the intellectual tone of some lyrics in United Irish songbooks
resemble earlier eighteenth-century odes. William Collins's "Ode to
Liberty" is one of many poems that prefigured United Irish songs
celebrating Liberty, Equality, Unity, and other abstract entities. Eighteenth-century English verse also offered models for combining elite
and popular literary styles. The English pastoral mode, which had
already infiltrated Scottish poetry in Ulster and street ballads throughout Ireland, also influenced some United Irish songs. Daithi O hOgain
has shown that a conflation of "elite" and "popular" styles occurred in
Irish tradition in the course of the eighteenth century (1990, 2–6).

A similar combination of elite and popular styles characterized
political verse. Political poetry became increasingly popular in England in the late eighteenth century and its songlike qualities were
emulated by the United Irishmen. For example, a poem entitled "The
Trumpet of Liberty" by John Taylor, published in the *Norfolk Chronicle*
on 16 July 1791, was probably written for a celebration of the fall of
the Bastille similar to the one organized by the United Irishmen to
coincide with the Belfast Harp Festival in July 1792. The opening
stanza of Taylor's radical poem is indistinguishable from much early
United Irish verse, except for its lack of specifically Irish references:

> The trumpet of Liberty sounds through the world,
>   And the universe starts at the sound;
> Her standard Philosophy's hand has unfurled,
>   And the nations are thronging around.
>   *Chorus*: Fall, tyrants, fall! fall! fall!
>   These are the days of liberty!
>   Fall, tyrants, fall!
>   (John Taylor 1984, 782–83)

Fortunately, the influence and conscious imitation of popular songs gradually made United Irish songs more songlike and less literary. Nevertheless, the first edition of *Paddy's Resource* in 1795 contained songs such as "Liberty's Call," which echoed the literary rhetoric of English radical verse:

> Come cheer up, my countrymen, ne'er be dismayed,
> For Freedom's great banners will soon be display'd,
> Be staunch for your Rights—Hark 'tis Liberty's call;
> For Freedom, dear Freedom, stand up one and all!
> *Chorus*: With heart and with hand,
>   Steady boys, steady,
>   We are always ready,
>   To banish Oppression from our native land.

The name of the tune for "Liberty's Call" was "Hearts of Oak," which was a sailors' song from David Garrick's popular musical *Harlequin's Invasion* (1759). The lyrics and tune for "Liberty's Call" thus represented the combination of elite and popular tradition common to much eighteenth-century verse in the British Isles.

Many of the songs in the first edition of *Paddy's Resource* were clearly part of a larger tradition of English radical verse. I am indebted to the detailed bibliography in Ray Browne's essay "The Paine-Burke Controversy in Eighteenth-Century Irish Popular Songs" for calling my attention to several English and American political songbooks of the day (1964, 95–97). One such English songbook served as an important model for *Paddy's Resource*. Nine of the sixty songs in that first edition of *Paddy's Resource*, including "Liberty's Call," were taken from a collection of English radical songs entitled *A Tribute to the Swinish Multitude: Being a Choice Collection of Patriotic Songs*, edited by "R. Thompson" also published in London and New York in 1794 and 1795, and in Philadelphia in 1796. In December 1792, William Drennan wrote to his sister and her husband, the United Irishman Samuel McTier, that Samuel Neilson was modeling himself on "Robert Thompson" (Drennan 1931, 112). As editor of the *Northern Star*, Neilson very likely was involved in the publication of the 1795 *Paddy's Resource*. The full title of the United Irish songbook, *Paddy's Resource: Being a Select Collection of Original and Modern Patriotic Songs, Toasts and Sentiments, Compiled for the Use of the People of Ireland,* echoed the title of the English songbook. Just as the English radicals had reveled in Burke's infamous appellation for the Irish, "the swinish multitude," the United Irish "editors" of *Paddy's Resource* proudly brandished the negative stereotype of "Paddy" in their title.

Some of the songs from *A Tribute to the Swinish Multitude* were printed verbatim in *Paddy's Resource;* others were modified to make them more Irish. For example, the concluding lines in "Liberty's Call" in the English songbook had been: "The just RIGHTS OF MAN, may we never forget; / For they'll save Britain's Friends from the bondage of Pitt." The United Irishmen changed the last line to "For they'll save Ireland's Sons from their bondages yet." A satiric seven-stanza song that had appeared in *A Tribute to the Swinish Multitude* as "Song— Composed by the Celebrated Capt. Morris, an Irish Gentleman," to the tune "Ballinamona," appeared almost verbatim in the 1795 *Paddy's Resource.* The latter version differed in that the title was changed to "The Red Night Cap," the tune became "Derry Down," and the word "heel" replaced "arse" in the opening lines: "Sure, Master John Bull, I shan't know till I'm dead, / Where the devil you're driving to, heel over head!" Such colloquial language indicates the range of styles in political poetry. The United Irishmen would use both the eloquent language of the ode and the colloquial dialect of popular songs in their political verse. Even they had allowed "arse" to remain when a twenty-five stanza version of the song appeared in the *Northern Star* on 29 September 1794, prefaced by the note that it had been "pub-lished in London, on Monday last."

The same "R. Thompson" who edited *A Tribute to the Swinish Multitude* had edited a similar songbook in 1793, *A Tribute to Liberty: or, a New Collection of Patriotic Songs, entirely Original, . . . together with a Collection of Toasts and Sentiments Sacred to the Rights of Man,* that also prefigured *Paddy's Resource.* A lurid and very popular later United Irish ballad, variously titled "The Maniac" or "Mary Le More," was ascribed to one of the contributors to that collection, Edward Rushton, a Liverpool poet and bookseller who claimed some Irish ancestry and published radical verse and prose. The fact that both William Drennan and R. R. Madden, the nineteenth-century histo-rian of the United Irishmen, accepted the claim by Rushton's son that his father had written "The Maniac," suggests the larger context in which United Irish verse must be considered (Madden 1887, 1–5). Although their message and their poetry became increasingly national, the literary traditions upon which the United Irishmen drew extended well beyond Ireland.

United Irish writers were also influenced by literary theories concerning the sublime, such as had been articulated in Edmund Burke's influential *A Philosophical Enquiry into the Origin of Our Ideas of the Sublime and the Beautiful* (1756), although they delighted in mocking Burke's political doctrines. Thomas Russell told a Belfast friend that he had once preferred Burke's essay on the sublime to the political ideas of Thomas Paine (Madden 1860, 2:149). Russell used the word "sublime" frequently in his journals to describe his response to the "solitude, silence and wildness" of the scenery he enjoyed on his frequent walking tours of Ulster. For example, in September 1793, during a walking tour of County Down with John Templeton, who shared his enthusiasm for the natural sciences, Russell described the Mourne Mountains as "all sublime" (Woods 1991, 111–12). Similar descriptions of "sublime" scenery, especially associated with ancient ruins, recur in Charles Hamilton Teeling's memoirs about the United Irishmen (1828, 225). The word "sublime" occurs frequently in United Irish verse, as it did in late eighteenth-century poetry. For example, John Corry's "Ireland, An Ode," (*Northern Star*, 22 August 1796), began: "Sublime, above the circling sea, / Ierne's pict'resque mountains rise." When Corry published a collection of his poems the following year, most of the United Irish leaders and writers, including some who were imprisoned, were listed as subscribers.

The momentary suspension of rational activity that was a part of the experience of the sublime parallels other irrational elements, such as millenarianism, in the literary backgrounds of the United Irishmen, who have too often been portrayed simplistically as pure rationalists. The ecstatic state of passionate and prophetic rapture that had supposedly characterized the ancient Irish bards, who were both a model and a popular literary motif for many United Irish writers, also suggests the attraction that both the sublime and the irrational had for the United Irishmen and their audience.

Burke's theory of the sublime included the idea that a painful thought can create a sublime passion. That idea and the lurid irrational elements of the Gothic novel certainly influenced the popular

United Irish songs, such as "The Maniac," which portrayed murder, rape, arson, and mad violated maidens. A letter to William Drennan from his sister, Martha McTier, on 17 March 1797, describes Thomas Russell's passion for Gothic novels and how John Chambers, a Dublin printer and United Irishman, provided Russell with such novels in Newgate: "I had a long letter from Russel [sic] . . . I was going to purchase Mrs. Radcliffe's last new novel as a present for him, knowing how high a relish he has for that particular kind of writing—but I hear the good-natured Mr. Chambers provides him with Books—tell him to send Russell *The Italian* which will reconcile him to his present situation" (Public Record Office of Northern Ireland, Drennan Letters, no. 652). Russell's intense interest in prophecy and the apocalyptic dimensions of political revolution further demonstrates the nonrational dimensions of the United Irish activities, as does the publication of such materials by United Irish presses, which will be considered in the analysis of the popular literary and cultural backgrounds of the United Irishmen.

CELTICISM AND ANTIQUARIANISM

The United Irishmen were greatly influenced by the intense interest in Celtic literary materials that had developed in the second half of the eighteenth century. Although the Irish dimensions of Celticism would assume greater and greater political overtones, especially in the hands of the United Irishmen, initially Celticism was of purely antiquarian and literary dimensions. One indication of English literary enthusiasm for things Celtic, and even Irish, is Samuel Johnson's letter to the distinguished Irish antiquarian Charles O'Conor of Belanagare in 1757:

> I have long wished that Irish literature were cultivated. Ireland is known by tradition to have been once the seat of piety and learning; and surely it would be very acceptable to all those who are curious either in the original of nations, or the affinities of languages, to be further informed of the revolutions of a people so ancient, and once so illustrious. . . . I hope you will continue to cultivate this kind of learning, which has lain too long neglected, and which, if it be suffered to remain in oblivion for another century, may, perhaps, never be retrieved. (Boswell 1934, 1:321–22)

Johnson's remarks elsewhere in the letter indicate that he was familiar with the works of O'Conor and other Irish antiquarians. Such studies had been inaugurated by Roderick O'Flaherty who, according to Joseph Leerssen, "embodies the final emergence of postbardic, autonomously Gaelic scholarship into the context of established Anglo-Irish domination, into a society on the threshhold of the Enlightenment" (1986, 321). A bardic scholar and chieftain of his Galway clan, O'Flaherty wrote a history of Ireland in Latin, *Ogygia, seu rerum Hibernicorum chronologia*, published in London in 1685. When an English translation of *Ogygia* was published in Dublin in 1793, the subscribers included not only Henry Grattan and Charles O'Conor, but also the United Irishmen Archibald Hamilton Rowan and Napper Tandy.

The publication in 1723 of Dermod O'Connor's translation of Geoffrey Keating's famous seventeenth-century history of Ireland, *Foras feasa ar Eirinn*, provided materials for the deepening interest in Irish antiquities. The scholarly Anglo-Irish interest in such materials was further encouraged by the publication of Francis Hutchinson's *Defense of the Antient Historians of Ireland and Great Britain* (1734), which staunchly defended the value of Keating's largely legendary history. By contrast, in *Dissertations on the Antient History of Ireland* (1753), Charles O'Conor criticized Keating for letting the fabulous part of his work degrade the historical part. Such objectivity on the part of the Catholic O'Conor, who was a founder of the Catholic Committee and who wrote anonymous pamphlets against the penal laws, partially explains the interest with which Samuel Johnson and amateur Anglo-Irish antiquarians greeted his work.

The interest of Samuel Johnson and of Anglo-Irish gentlemen in Irish antiquarian research indicates that it was part of a larger cultural and literary movement. The literary, as distinct from antiquarian, "Celtic Revival," described in detail by Edward Snyder in *The Celtic Revival in English Literature, 1760–1800* (1923), originated at midcentury. Earlier English literature had contained only scattered references to Druids and Celtic matter, as in Milton's allusion in "Lycidas" to Britain's "old bards, the famous Druids" (Snyder 1965, 3). Snyder claims there were fewer than a dozen such passages written before 1760 (1965, 3). A notable example that Snyder does not list, however, is William Collins's elegy for the English poet James Thomson,

"Ode Occasioned by the Death of Mr. Thomson" (1749). Collins portrayed Thomson as a "Druid" and "bard" whose "airy harp" was silent
(Collins 1937, 291–93).

Although Collins's bardic imagery in that poem amounted to
little more than a new ornament for the traditional pastoral elegy,
the figure of the bard contained political implications that would
appeal to later eighteenth-century patriots, including the United
Irishmen. An example is provided in one stanza of another poem
by Collins, "Ode on the Popular Superstitions of the Highlands of
Scotland; Considered as a Subject of Poetry," which was written in
1749 but not published until 1788 when it appeared posthumously
in four different publications. The passage that follows illustrates
two important aspects of the figure of the bard: first, his poetry had
supposedly played a crucial role in celebrating and inspiring events;
second, modern-day "bards" could be found in remote areas such as
the Scottish Highlands which had "preserved" the ancient bardic
tradition:

> Ev'n yet preserv'd, how often may'st thou hear,
>   Where to the pole the Boreal mountains run,
> Taught by the father to his list'ning son
>   Strange lays, whose power had charm'd a SPENSER's ear.
> At ev'ry pause, before thy mind possest,
>   Old RUNIC bards shall seem to rise around,
> With uncouth lyres, in many-coloured vest,
>   Their matted hair with boughs fantastic crown'd:
> Whether thou bid'st the well-taught hind repeat
>   The choral dirge that mourns some chieftains brave,
> When ev'ry shrieking maid her bosom beat,
>   And strew'd the choicest herbs his scented grave;
> Or whether, sitting in the shepherd's shiel,
>   Thou hear'st some sounding tale of war's alarm;
> When, at the bugle's call, with fire and steel,
>   The sturdy clans pour'd forth their bony swarms,
> And hostile brothers met to prove each other's arms.
>   (Collins 1937, 299)

When the enemies were outside conquerors, rather than "brothers,"
the bard became the champion of national liberty, whether Scottish,

Welsh, or Irish.

Collins's source for most of the material in that ode, Martin Martin's *A Description of the Western Isles of Scotland Circa 1695* (1703), had been even more explicit about the political role of the bards:

> Before they engaged the enemy in battle, the chief Druid harangued the army to excite their courage. He was placed on an eminence, from which he addressed himself to all of them standing about him, putting them in mind of what great things were performed by the valour of their ancestors, raised their hopes with the noble rewards of honour and victory, and dispelled their fears by all the topics that a natural courage could suggest. After this harangue, the army gave a general shout, and then charged the enemy stoutly. (Sigworth 1965, 175)

The political and martial implications of the literary image of the bard would not be lost on Irish political activists, including the United Irishmen.

Thomas Gray's "The Bard: A Pindaric Ode," published in 1757, was a major influence in the popularization of the bard as the champion of liberty against tyranny. Gray's poem is the imaginative reconstruction of the death song of a Welsh bard who, to escape the massacre of the bards ordered by Edward I during the subjugation of Wales in 1283, flung himself from the top of a precipice into the River Conway. Gray's bard, with his harp, curses, and prophesies, prefigures bards in many later poems. Standing on a rocky crag, "robed in the sable garb of woe" with streaming "hoary hair," the bard lamented his slaughtered fellow bards as he "struck the deep sorrows of his lyre" with "a master's hand and prophet's fire." He eulogized the massacred bards whose spirits joined in his curse on Edward and his descendants, whom he prophesied would be cursed with "despair and sceptered care" (Thomas Gray 1937, 55–64).

Gray's poem inspired his friend William Mason to write his influential verse tragedy *Caractacus* in 1759. Like Gray's "The Bard," *Caractacus*'s extensive use of Celtic myth and Druidical elements, the lyrical charm of many passages sung by a "chorus of bards," the powerful romantic scenery, and the celebration of the ancient Britons' Celtic love of liberty made the play enormously popular (Snyder 1965,

53–60). By 1760, Celts and bards clearly had literary potential as well as antiquarian significance. According to Edward Snyder, Gray's poem had very few admirers when it was first published, "but before the end of the century the poem was praised and quoted to an extent that baffles belief" (1965, 194).

There is no doubt that the United Irishmen were familiar with Gray's poem. Thomas Russell and William Sampson allude to Gray's bard in their satire *Review of the Lion of Old England . . .*, which was serialized in the *Northern Star* in late 1793 and published by the Northern Star press as a pamphlet in 1794. Several United Irish poems about bards, which will be discussed in detail later, indicate United Irish poets used Gray's poem as a model. The most significant example is a poem by "Rev, James Glass" published in the *Northern Star* on 16 May 1792 entitled "The Irish Bard," which opened with a description of how "an aged Bard, with locks like driven snow, / With trembling fingers tun'd his HARP OF WOE" and recounted how "Ierne drops the tear of woe" for her "ravaged" country and "slain warriors." However, this Irish bard rejected the passive despair evoked by the weeping figure of Ierne and urged active defiance through literary means:

> But rouse my Harp, let ev'ry daring String,
> Our dauntless heroes to remembrance bring—
> Oft did their foes their dreaded vengeance feel,
> Their crimson gore distain the sparkling steel.
> O cou'd I glow with Ossian's living fire,
> I wou'd a thousand warriors yet inspire,
> With all their father's love of deathless fame,
> While tyrants trembled at their awful name,
> Their valiant deeds should fire the Poets song
> Their glories live on his immortal tongue.
> Must you Hibernians ever wear the chain?

In a prophetic frenzy this new Irish bard then described an apocalyptic battle in which "Tyrant Ambition" would become a "beggar's skeleton of state." Unlike Gray's bard, who jumped to his death after prophesying how poetic genius would challenge tyranny, this United Irish version of a bard did not commit suicide. Instead he closed his oration with a defiant poetic agenda: "Proclaim to ev'ry land, this glorious theme, / The rights of man alone, shall reign supreme." In the United Irish poetic imagination, "bards" never committed suicide, although many were martyred victims of tyranny.

The "Irish Bard's" wish to "glow with Ossian's living fire" suggests the important influence that Celticism had on United Irish literary propaganda. James Macpherson's Ossianic translations greatly intensified the scholarly, literary, popular, and political fascination with bards and other Celtic materials. Macpherson published *Fragments of Ancient Poetry, Collected in the Highlands of Scotland, and Translated from the Galic* [sic] *or Erse Language* (1760); *Fingal: An Ancient Epic Poem in Six Books, Composed by Ossian the Son of Fingal* (1761); and in 1763 *Temora: An Ancient Epic Poem, in Eight Books, together with Several Poems, compiled by Ossian, Son of Fingal, Translated from the Gaelic Language* (all three are reprinted in *The Poems of Ossian*, 1857). In *Fragments of Ancient Poetry*, which was clearly influenced by Gray's poem, bards singing and playing harps mourned the fate of Celtic heroes and inspired young warriors with tales of ancient glory. Although Macpherson claimed the chief bard, Ossian, was Scottish, his "translations" inevitably contained material about Irish events and heroes. In *Fingal*, the Scottish king of Caledonia, Fingal, is married to the daughter of Cormac, King of Ireland. When Cormac's Irish general, Cuthullin (the Irish Cuchulain) is defeated by the Danes, Fingal and his Scottish warriors come to Ireland's rescue. All of Macpherson's warriors, Scottish and Irish alike, are inspired by the war songs of the bards and eulogized to the strings of their harps.

The harps and battle shields which adorn the walls of Ossian's hall in *Temora* represent the close connection between poetry and war in the Celticism popularized by Macpherson. That connection between poetry and the political life of a nation continued as a literary image and became a literary model for Irish political activists, Volunteers and United Irishmen alike, in the last three decades of the eighteenth century. Macpherson's recurring image of harp music, created by the wind or spirits, inspiring the words of the bards' songs, prefigured a major mode in Irish nationalist poetry: the writing of new political words to old melodies. Moreover, Macpherson's bard was a satirist and poet who provided a literary model for the United Irish writers who specialized in prose satire and poetry. Macpherson's images, especially those of the bard and his harp, reverberated in United

Irish verse. Even Macpherson's florid style would be influential. Thomas Moore published an Ossianic effusion in two United Irish newspapers. Likewise, United Irishman John Daly Burk's major poem "Erin" was in the Ossianic mode (1899, appendix, 9).

The controversy that ensued from Macpherson's claim that his Ossianic materials were of Scottish origin had important repercussions in Ireland where antiquarians were indignant at what they considered his appropriation of Irish materials. According to Macpherson, "the chimera that Ireland is the mother country of the Scots" was false; the Irish bards had simply "appropriated" the Scottish bards and heroes; and "it would be as ridiculous to think that Milton's *Paradise Lost* could be wrote [sic] by a Scottish peasant, as to suppose that the poems ascribed to Ossian were to be written in Ireland" (1857, 76–77). Macpherson criticized Keating and O'Flaherty as "idle fabulists" who were "credulous and peurile" and responsible for "improbable tales" (1857, 67). Interestingly, evidence suggests that Macpherson used materials from Keating and O'Flaherty in fabricating his Ossianic translations. Nevertheless, Macpherson dismissed eighteenth-century Irish antiquarians and what he referred to as "the pretended antiquities of Ireland" (1857, 66). He claimed Ireland had no history as such until the arrival of St. Patrick.

Among the first to respond to these charges was Sylvester O'Halloran. He wrote an anonymous letter entitled "The Poems of Ossine, the son of Fionne MacComhal Reclaimed," published in the *Dublin Magazine* in January 1763, that declared Macpherson's *Fingal* to be the worst instance to date of "Caledonian plagiary" (Leerssen 1986, 401–2). The second edition of Charles O'Conor's 1753 history, published in 1766 and retitled *Dissertations on the History of Ireland, to which is subjoined a Dissertation on the Irish Colonies established in Britain with Some Remarks on Mr. MacPherson's [sic] Translations of Fingal and Temora*, also contained a stinging rebuttal of Macpherson. Literary rebuttals of Macpherson by Joseph Cooper Walker and Charlotte Brooke would appear during the 1780's.

The 1778 publication of Sylvester O'Halloran's *General History of Ireland from the Earliest Accounts to the Close of the Twelfth Century* continued the Irish rebuttal of Macpherson and announced a younger generation of antiquaries who were as much concerned with vindicating Ireland's national reputation as elucidating its ancient history.

O'Halloran's book, which represented a confluence of Irish and Anglo-Irish antiquarianism, retold ancient Irish legends that, unlike more modern Irish history, were devoid of political and sectarian controversy and presented heroic examples of Ireland's ancient greatness in the actions of characters such as Deirdre and Cuchulain. O'Halloran thus offered a reason for patriotic pride in being Irish to the Anglo-Irish political activists and propagandists and to creative writers such as his goddaughter Charlotte Brooke. Macpherson's forgeries thus unleashed a significant scholarly, literary, and political response in Ireland. As Joseph Leerssen has noted, "the Gaelic past is no longer just a Gaelic, but rather a national Irish concern" (1986, 402).

The Irish response to the Celticism fostered by Macpherson included literary works with important political overtones. Dramatic productions in Dublin acquired new national implications under the influence of the vogue for Celtic materials and the growing Anglo-Irish political consciousness. Earlier in the century plays had used early Irish history as a vehicle for pro-English propaganda. For example, in 1722 William Phillips's historical drama in blank verse, *Hibernia Freed*, which depicted the Irish defeat of the Vikings, contained anachronistic eulogies on the benefits of English rule and an Irish bard who prophesied the Normans' glorious arrival in Ireland (Leerssen 1986, 378–79).

By the 1770s, the influence of Gray's "Bard," Mason's *Caractacus*, and Macpherson's Ossian, as well as the growing Anglo-Irish sense of an Irish identity fostered by economic problems and antiquarianism, could be seen in Dublin drama. But the new Celt who appeared on the Dublin stage was Irish, unlike Gray's Welsh bard, Mason's ancient Briton, or Macpherson's Scottish Ossian.

Georges Howard's tragedy *The Siege of Tamor* (1773), which he based on the works of Keating and O'Conor, presented the Irish defeat of the Danes in Ossianic images of "our antient Druids" and in a new patriotic political context. The play's presentation of Irish bards as "our" ancestors invited Dublin audiences to identify with ancient Ireland. When the king lamented his valiant dead sons in Ossianic style, the traditional Celt's championship of liberty had clearly acquired new contemporary patriotic resonance. The play's prologue, which referred to the "patriot spirit" of the play and to Howard as "a native bard" who heralded the rebirth of ancient literary and political greatness, declared:

Here too, of yore, stupendous deeds were done,
High conquests enterpriz'd, high honours won.
To the famed facts ten thousand harps were strung,
And what our sires achiev'd, their poets sung,
The circling nations listen'd and admir'd,
But with the closing age, the tale expir'd.

(Leerssen 1986, 431)

Francis Dobbs, a member of the family of United Irishman William Sampson's mother, wrote a historical tragedy entitled *The Patriot King; or, Irish Chief*, which was printed in Dublin in 1773 and in Lisburn in 1775. Not surprisingly, the play, which identified the Irish expulsion of the Danes with the contemporary Irish patriotic agenda, was rejected by the main London theaters before being performed in Dublin 1774 (Leerssen 1986, 431–32). When the Volunteers were founded four years later, the new literary images fostered by Celticism and antiquarianism would assume political significance. Later in the century the Irish Celt would be portrayed as confronting the English rather than the Viking invaders.

Many United Irishmen in Belfast were deeply interested in antiquarianism and perceived its political significance. On 23 October 1793 an announcement in the *Northern Star* concerning the Belfast Society for Promoting Knowledge, to which so many United Irish leaders belonged, declared that the society would "revive and encourage all communications concerning the antiquities of Ireland" and would publish Edward Bunting's collection of Irish music as "new and decisive proof of the existence of a high degree of civilization among our ancestors, at a period when the greatest part of Europe was buried in the deepest barbarity and ignorance." The society's museum, of which the librarian Thomas Russell was in charge, included specimens of Irish antiquities (Killen 1990, 28).

POLITICS: PATRIOTS AND VOLUNTEERS

The United Irishmen were not the first political activists inspired by Celticism and antiquarianism. The political activities of the Anglo-Irish patriots and Volunteers, which had culminated in England's granting legislative independence to Ireland in 1783, had been accompanied by a quickening of interest in native cultural traditions and the popularization of images fostered by Irish antiquarianism. Henry Grattan, Henry Flood, and other leading political figures had encouraged the founding in 1785 of the Royal Irish Academy, which from its origin emphasized the study of Irish antiquities.

This new enlightened Anglo-Irish attitude toward Irish antiquities marked not only a new rapport with Catholic antiquaries such as O'Conor and O'Halloran, but also the rejection of standard arguments among English historians that early Ireland had been barbaric. This standard English historical view had been articulated in David Hume's massive *History of England from the Invasion of Julius Caesar to the Revolution of 1688.* According to Hume, "the Irish, from the beginning of time, had been buried in the most profound barbarism and ignorance; and as they were never conquered, or even invaded by the Romans, from whom all the Western world derived its civility, they continued still in the most rude state of society" (1754, 1:424).

Anglo-Irish opposition to such a view of ancient Ireland is illustrated in the popular and influential works of Colonel Charles Vallancey, the English-born military engineer and surveyor whose work in Ireland introduced him to Irish antiquarian research. A founding member of the Royal Irish Academy, Vallancey popularized a romantic and often inaccurate portrait of early Ireland as editor of *Collecteana De Rebus Hibernicus* (1770–1804). Vallancey's central theory, now completely refuted but in his day accepted by many scholars, was that the Celts, including the Irish, were of Phoenician and Carthaginian origin. Not only was this theory popular, but it also had important political overtones. Just as the Phoenicians had been defeated by the Greeks, and the Carthaginians by the Romans, the Irish Gaels had been subdued by England. Vallancey argued that the fact that the Irish had never been conquered by the Romans was a cultural advantage because, contrary to Hume's view that the Romans had civilized barbaric peoples, Irish culture had never been corrupted by Roman influence. Such was the view of Irish history that Tone presented in his song "Ierne United" in which the absence of Roman influence allowed Ireland to remain united, happy and free—until the coming of the English. Tone, who planned to write a history of Ireland, was familiar with antiquarian research.

Publications by Vallancey, O'Conor and other antiquarians in the 1780s all listed leading Anglo-Irish politicians among their subscribers. Evidence of civilization among the ancient Irish had become a matter of patriotic pride among prominent Anglo-Irish families. Charles Rawdon, later Earl of Moira, and his mother, the Countess of Moira, patronized the study of Irish antiquities and their library had many books and manuscripts on the subject. The memoirs and papers of many United Irish leaders and writers, including Wolfe Tone, Thomas Russell, Edward Fitzgerald, William Sampson, and Thomas and Robert Emmet, recounted visits to the Rawdons. Charles Rawdon, the godfather of one of Tone's children, was later the patron of Thomas Moore. Although the Rawdons did not share the democratic and revolutionary principles of the United Irishmen, they did share with many of them an interest in Irish antiquities.

Henry Flood had certainly been inspired by Irish antiquarian research. When he died in 1791, his will (dated 27 May 1790) bequeathed a large portion of his estate, worth several thousand pounds, to Trinity College to establish a professorship of Irish, to endow prizes for the best composition in the Irish language on a subject concerning Irish culture, and to purchase manuscripts and printed books in Irish (Parsons 1795, 14–15). Flood's will requested that Vallancey be appointed to the Trinity professorship; however, Flood's family succeeded in having the will invalidated.

As part of the controversy over Flood's will, Sir Lawrence Parsons, a friend of Tone's, issued a pamphlet entitled *Observations on the Bequest of Henry Flood to Trinity College Dublin with a Defense of the Ancient History of Ireland* in 1795. Citing Samuel Johnson's letter to Charles O'Conor, which was quoted earlier in this chapter, and publications by Irish antiquarians as evidence, Parsons argued that the ancient Irish had been a civilized people who were especially skilled in music and poetry (1795, 67, 40). Parsons's "defense" pointed to the "great antiquity of the Phoenician settlement in Ireland" and the similarity of the Irish and Phoenician language, alphabet and numbers (158, 174, 228). Parsons declared his design was "not to put Irish again into general use," only to have it "studied by men of letters" (24). Moreover, he distanced himself from the more excessive antiquarian enthusiasts when he noted that "some over-zealous modern writers have, by pompous descriptions of a state of magnificence which never existed, cast a false glare over the whole" (228). The writings of the United Irishmen indicate that they were familiar with and shared many of the ideas of writers like Vallancey and Parsons. When Tone claimed that Parsons had been a formative influence in his early adulthood, he was no doubt referring to Parsons' literary and cultural as well as his political activities. Even Marianne Elliott, who elsewhere in her biography of Tone downplays any romantic nationalism on his part, claims that, under Parsons's influence, Tone's early essays displayed a "romantic attachment to things and people Irish" (1989, 104). In addition to his political speeches and pamphlets, in which he displayed a pride in Irish culture such as he had evidenced in his pamphlet about the Flood bequest, Parsons had written an influential satiric poem in heroic couplets entitled "Poem on the State of Ireland, 1791." Tone's son William included the entire eighty-four–line poem by Parsons at the end of the first volume of his father's autobiography (Tone 1826, 1:564–65).

William Tone also listed the poem and a pamphlet by Parsons among the surviving productions of the political and literary club Tone had formed in Dublin in 1790 (1:545). Tone's son did not include Parsons's name on the list of members of the club, which included Thomas Russell, Thomas Addis Emmet, William Drennan, Joseph Pollock, who had been a noted literary propagandist for the Volunteers, and Whitley Stokes, whose scholarly pursuits focused on Irish language and antiquities. However, the list of club members ended "&c., &c." and presumably Parsons had some association with the group, given his friendship with Tone and the fact that Tone preserved Parsons's poem and one of his pamphlets among the literary productions of the club (1:545). Moreover, Parsons's poem was dated 1791, the active period of the club.

In the course of his defense of Flood's bequest for the support of the study of the Irish language and ancient Irish culture, Parsons referred to a work that is almost unknown today but was influential in its day: William Hamilton's *Letters Concerning the North Coast of Antrim, containing a Natural History of its Basaltes: with an Account of such Circumstances as are worthy of notice respecting the Antiquities, Manners, and Customs of that Country* (1786). Hamilton, a member of the Belfast Society for Promoting Knowledge and a founding member of the Royal Irish Academy, argued for a high level of civilization among the early Irish. For evidence he cited round towers, an eighth-century colliery at Ballycastle, and "our ancient buildings" at Glendalough and Clonmacnoise (1786, 38).

The fact that a Protestant clergyman like Hamilton used the pronoun "our" in such a context illustrates the cultural identity that both Anglicans and Presbyterians were coming to have with early Irish culture. Such architectural monuments, according to Hamilton, "disproved" the arguments of English writers that early Ireland had been a country of barbarians; on the contrary, "many and unequivocal circumstances prove that during the barbarous ages this sequestered island enjoyed the blessings of peace, learning and religion" (46). As proof, Hamilton quoted an English translation of a ninth-century poem by St. Donatus from the Vide Hibernia Dominicana (46–47). The argument of the poem bears an interesting similarity to Tone's "Ierne United." Hamilton's book was certainly known to Wolfe Tone because it was among the works in his personal library when it was given to the New York Irish Historical Society (O'Reilly 1924, 13).

The final section of Hamilton's book, entitled "Instances of Wisdom in the Structure of the Earth, and Proofs favourable to natural and revealed Religion, derived from the History of the Earth and Its Inhabitants," exemplifies the belief shared by a small number of United Irishmen, including Thomas Russell, and a large portion of their lower- and middle-class audience, that the scientific study of the natural world revealed religious and millenarian significance. Ironically, Hamilton was killed by United Irish rebels during the 1798 rebellion because as a magistrate he had been active in rounding up insurgents in Donegal (Stewart 1977, 118–19).

Hamilton's Antrim Letters were also in the library of William Sampson (O'Reilly 1924, 13), whose daughter married Tone's son and who, like Tone, was a friend of the Rawdons and familiar with Vallancey's and other antiquarian work. Sampson, a lawyer who represented United Irishmen in court on many occasions, once defiantly took the United Irish oath in public at a United Irish trial. Sampson typified the broad intellectual interests of the United Irishmen. A Presbyterian from Derry, he wrote several United Irish prose satires, including The Trial of Hurdy Gurdy (1794) and, with Thomas Russell, Review of the Lion of Old England (1794). Sampson has also been credited with some of the verse that appeared anonymously in United Irish newspapers and songbooks.

Sampson's memoirs, written in 1807, declared that the "vindication" of his motives for joining the United Irishmen "rested" on his views of Irish history (1832, 204). Sampson included in his memoirs, a thorough summary of Irish history from ancient times to the present, in which he cited major works by Irish antiquarians and, like Vallancey, Parsons, and Hamilton, agreed with the theory about the Phoenician origins of the Irish. Sampson argued that the music and songs of the Irish bards were proofs of ancient Irish civilization, claimed that Irish language and culture were superior to those of England when Strongbow arrived in Ireland, and cited modern contributions by Irish writers to English literature (206–9).

In 1833, Sampson wrote a lengthy "Conclusion" to W. C. Taylor's *History of Ireland, from the Anglo-Norman Invasion till the Union of the Country with Great Britain* in which he discussed his views of Irish history and the various eighteenth-century antiquarian and historical works from which they were derived. Sampson's view of Irish history represented a synthesis of Gaelic Catholic and enlightened Protestant perspectives. He defended his United Irish associates such as Tone, Russell, and Robert Emmet as "martyrs" who, he claimed, had been "lured to revolt" but whose principles were true and imperishable (W. C. Taylor 1833–1839, 2:325, 342). He quoted Parsons's poem on Ireland, cited antiquarians like O'Flaherty, gave examples of English violence and barbarity, and praised the glories of early Ireland and the Irish language, which he claimed had affinities with that of Moses and the prophets (2:322, 298, 295, 298–301). Yet Sampson, like Parsons before him, distanced himself from "over-zealous advocates" who had exposed Ireland's "cultural monuments of high antiquity" to derision by "too passionately adopting as literal truths the allegorical fiction of poetic annals and rhapsodies of enthusiastic bards" (2:292-93).

The Anglo-Irish patriots bequeathed more than an interest in Irish history and antiquities to the United Irishmen. The United Irishmen inherited a literary tradition as well as political principles from the Irish Volunteer movement, which had been founded in Ulster in 1778 as a citizens' militia to defend Ireland during the American war. The Volunteers became a powerful element in the effort by Irish patriots in the early 1780's to achieve greater political and economic independence from England. Lord Moira, Sir Lawrence Parsons, Charles Vallancey, Henry Grattan, and Henry Flood had been actively involved in the Volunteer movement before its demise in the early 1790s, which, not coincidentally, coincided with the rise of the United Irish movement. Many early groups of United Irishmen originated in radical sections of the Volunteers. United Irishmen Wolfe Tone, Napper Tandy, William Drennan, Samuel Neilson, William Sampson, James Porter, Thomas Addis Emmet, James "Jemmy" Hope, and many others had been Volunteers. Two important tools in the Volunteers' propaganda had been newspapers and songs, the success of which provided an example that was not lost upon the United Irishmen as they organized their own movement.

The *Volunteers' Journal; or, Irish Herald,* published from 1783–1786, was founded by Mathew Carey in October 1783 (Bradsher 1966, 2). Carey emigrated to America in September 1784 to escape arrest for an especially vitriolic attack on the government that he had published (Casteleyn 1984, 52). During the 1790s Carey was associated with exiled United Irishmen and their publications in the United States. Like later United Irish newspapers, the *Volunteers' Journal* printed songs and poems, often sent in by its readers and usually anonymous, that represented a wide range of literary styles and tastes: odes on love, liberty, or Ireland; satiric songs about elections or royalty; inflammatory songs threatening violence; humorous songs on politics and other topics. Songs far outnumbered the more formal odes in the pages of the *Volunteers' Journal.*

One ode, entitled "Ode in Imitation of Alcaeus," which appeared in two successive issues of the journal in November 1783, posed the question, "Shall fair Ierne's sons be MEN no more?" and included the following address by "Hibernia":

> My sons attentive hear;
> If close united, you'll prevail;
> If not—the moral's clear:
> "While Flood and Grattan rail and scold,
> And Patriot views disjoint;
> The venal herd will vote for gold,
> And Britain gain her point."

The images of Ireland as a woman named Ierne or Hibernia, reminiscent of the Irish aisling or vision poem, and of political activists as her
"sons" would become standard motifs in later nationalist verse. Likewise, references to the need for "manly" behavior would become a
common image in United Irish writings and reach a floodtide in those
of the Young Irelanders in the 1840s. The ode's satire resembled the
topical references common in political songs and street ballads and
illustrates how more popular and informal styles would influence even
poems labeled "odes" as Irish political verse developed.

Another poem that appeared in the *Volunteers' Journal* in November 1783 began "Awake Hibernia!" The motif of Ireland as a sleeping
woman who must awaken would continue in United Irish verse and
in Thomas Moore's *Irish Melodies* (1808–1834). Harps also appeared
in Volunteer songs, not surprisingly because one of the most popular
Volunteer mottos called for stringing the Irish harp anew to the tune
of liberty. In the tradition of the Volunteers, the official symbol of the
United Irishmen would be a harp on a field of green with the motto It
Is New Strung and Shall Be Heard. When the *Volunteers' Journal* for
13 February 1784 published "Favourite Airs in the New Masque of the
Genius of Ireland," the lyrics described the tuning and striking of
harps. The image of attuning harps to liberty was realized in the
Volunteers' practice of setting new words to traditional tunes, a technique they had adopted from eighteenth-century broadside ballads
that had set topical verses to popular melodies. That technique would
also become standard practice in United Irish and Young Ireland
songbooks and newspapers.

Like later nationalist verse, Volunteer verse could be solemn or
comic. The eloquent, inflammatory rhetoric of a poem published in
the *Volunteers' Journal* on 9 February 1784 declared:

> Rouse, then, Hibernians, rouse each latent flame;
> Stand firm, resolv'd, all tyranny disclaim:
> Force base usurpers to restore your right,
> And teach those men who've dared your voice to slight,
> That if they dare refuse your just demands,
> You have the means of freedom in your hands;
> Arm'd to promote your injur'd country's good,
> And in her cause prepar'd to spill your blood.

In a less serious vein, the Irish Volunteer depicted in a poem published on 22 December 1783 declared, "For Ireland and freedom I bellow'd and roar'd, . . . I'll kiss the king's hand, / And let them kiss my asse."

Volunteer military marches had lyrics, few of which have survived, largely because they were supplanted by new lyrics written by United Irishmen whose songbooks contain several songs to be sung to a tune entitled "The Volunteer's March." Jonah Barrington described Volunteer songs being sung to traditional tunes such as "God Save the King," "Patrick's Day in the Morning," and even "Lullibulero" (1833, 2:176–77). Samuel McSkimin described the Volunteers marching to "The Boyne Water" and "The Prussian Drum" (1906, 3). With the exception of "Lullibulero," all those tunes would be used by United Irishmen for their songs.

A recruiting song used for a Volunteer regiment in America in 1779 demonstrates how the practice of writing new lyrics to old tunes generated literary motifs that could be used for a variety of political messages. In 1778, before he became Earl of Moira, Francis Rawdon had recruited for a regiment called the Volunteers of Ireland in New York. After duty in the American South, during which time young Edward Fitzgerald served as Rawdon's aide-de-camp, the regiment returned to Ireland in 1782 where they were disbanded in 1784. The regiment used a broadside ballad entitled "Patrick's Hearty Invitation to His Countrymen," printed in New York in 1779 to the tune of "Paddy Whack," as a recruiting song that spoke of shamrocks and Paddies:

> Each Son of St. Patrick, each true-hearted Fellow,
> Come Join in our March, and bear Part in our Song;
> . . . .
> The Harp of sweet Ireland has called us together,
> The Rights of our King and our Country to shield
> . . . .
> And now my brave Boys, let us toast our Commander,
> The gallant young Rawdon, our Chief of Renown.
> (Mitchell 1976, no. 4, x)

The song's refrain, "St. Patrick's the Word, and each Fist to the Can," reiterates its many references to drinking and toasts, bumpers and cans. Many United Irish songs would be drinking songs, but they would toast "the Rights of Man" rather than "the Rights of our King."

In the 1780s the Irish Volunteers in Ireland used the same tune of "Paddy Whack" and images of shamrocks, St. Patrick, Paddies, and harps in songs questioning the rights of the king, especially in Ulster where many people had relatives who had emigrated to America. In the 1790s the United Irishmen used the same images and the same tune in songs calling for an Irish revolution. When the United Irishman James Porter satirized the English government's fear of United Irish songs and tunes in *Billy Bluff and the Squire*, the old tunes of "Patrick's Day in the Morning" and "Paddy Whack" were listed as two of the four "impudent, national, seditious songs" that the English authorities feared the most. The United Irish song entitled "Granu's Advice to Her Children," printed to the tune "Paddy Whack" in the 1796 edition of *Paddy's Resource*, exhorted the "sons of Granu" to rouse from their slumbers and fight taxation. The tune and many of the images remained the same, but the message of the 1779 recruiting song had been radically transformed.

"Patrick's Day in the Morning" was an old Irish tune that had been played by Irish pipers at the Battle of Fontenoy in 1745 before it was adopted by the Volunteers. The song and its tune were popular among Irishmen who served on both sides in the American Revolution (O'Neill 1910, 174). In 1783 a group of Irish in Philadelphia had cheered loudly for the toast: "The friends of liberty in Ireland. May the harp be tuned to independence and touched by the skillful hands," as a band played "Patrick's Day in the Morning" (Doyle 1981, 148–49). "Patrick's Day in the Morning" was performed at the Belfast Harp Festival in 1792 and used for several United Irish songs.

Volunteer songs often appeared in popular songbooks known as garlands. One such song, "Ireland's Glory, or a Comparative View of Ireland in the Years 1776 and 1783," was published in a garland in Newry in 1783 to the tune of "Derry Down." The song declared "From a nation of slaves we've emerged into glory," and praised the practical benefits of taking muskets in hand, of national pride, and of religious toleration (Zimmermann 1967, 123–24). Slavery would be denounced and guns and religious toleration would be celebrated in United Irish songs, many of which would be set to the same tune of "Derry Down."

The slavery motif was central to two enormously popular and influential Volunteer pamphlets: Joseph Pollock's *Rights of Ireland Asserted, in the Letters of Owen Roe O'Nial* (1779) and William Drennan's *Letters of Orellana, an Irish Helot* (1785). Pollock's and Drennan's rhetoric and their literary images prefigured United Irish writing, including that of Wolfe Tone. Pollock and Drennan were friends of Tone's who joined his political and literary club in 1790, and Tone was so familiar with their Volunteer pamphlets that, according to Marianne Elliott, ideas and phrases from both writers echoed throughout Tone's writings (1989, 103–04). Pollock's and Drennan's pamphlets would also influence Thomas Davis, who wrote on the title page of his personal copy of Pollock's *Letters of Owen Roe O'Nial*: "Boldest and ablest of Volunteer pamphlets. But its doctrines are not stronger than those printed at the same time by Dr. Drennan in his *Orellana, or the Irish Helot*" (Noonan 1913, 40).

Joseph Pollock, barrister and Ulster Presbyterian, under the pseudonym of the famous Irish general Owen Roe O'Nial *[sic]* had exhorted Irishmen not to be "slaves." According to Pollock, "the Spartans had their Helotes, and the English have their Irish," and English insults to the Irish character were as severe as barbed arrows (1779, 11–12). Pollock's argument that the rebuttal of the English defamation of the Irish national character was a top priority, because English "art has been exhausted to make us appear contemptible both to others and ourselves," illustrates why the Irish antiquarian portrait of the high civilization of ancient Ireland offered an important political weapon to the Volunteers and the United Irishmen (45). Implicit also in Pollock's argument was the suggestion that the Irish must counter English stereotypes of them as barbarians and as "blunderers and blockheads" with positive images in both life and literature. Pollock labeled England as a "sinking nation" who should not be allowed "to grasp us in her dying convulsion and pull us with her to the bottom" (47). Recent antiquarian research offered the basis for the new images of Irish culture necessary to help Ireland assert her true identity and become what Pollock called "a nation of heroes" (47).

Pollock, like Tone and other United Irishmen would, traced Ireland's problems to the connection with England: "If we can trace all our misfortunes, the destruction of our liberty and the failure of every public scheme, to the power of England and our unfortunate connection with her, we must throw off her power and abjure her connection, before we can either be free or happy" (41). Pollock's political radicalism waned during the 1790s. By 26 September 1796 a song published in the *Northern Star* rebuked him as follows: "See *Owen Roe O'Neill*, like Burke, become wise, / Now a pension he loves and can Freedom despise."

Pollock's *Letters of Owen Roe O'Nial* had also advocated religious toleration, such as the Ulster Volunteer Convention at Dungannon in 1783 would endorse. In June 1784, the *Volunteers' Journal* began using the following passage from Pollock's *Letters of Owen Roe O'Nial* as an epigraph below the title of every issue: "When the Men of Ireland forget their destructive religious prejudices, and embrace each other with the warmth of genuine philanthropy, then, and not until then, will they eradicate baneful English influence, and destroy the aristocratic tyrants of the Land." The epigraph bore the signature "O'NIAL." Religious toleration, of course, became one of the central tenets of the United Irishmen.

Drennan's *Letters of Orellana, an Irish Helot*, first published in 1785 in the *Belfast Newsletter* and then as a pamphlet, used the same letter format and slavery imagery that Pollock had. Drennan's letters were addressed to his "Fellow-Slaves," a form of address that Wolfe Tone, Samuel Neilson, and other United Irishmen would frequently use in their letters to each other. Echoing the imagery of Volunteer songs, Drennan depicted Ireland as a woman in a trance and called upon her children, now slaves, to "add new strings to the Irish Harp" and to "awake, arise,—for if you sleep you die!" (1785, 6, 74, 9–10). Drennan's images would be repeated in innumerable United Irish and Young Ireland songs.

When Drennan told his readers, "You are all native Irish," he was clearly appealing to the new identity with Irish culture that had been developing among Protestants and Presbyterians alike (8). As he would in his *Letter to His Excellency Earl Fitzwilliam, Lord Lieutenant of Ireland* in January 1795, Drennan presented a central argument behind the Volunteer and later the United Irish efforts at propaganda: the public education of the people of Ireland about all aspects of Irish culture could transform their negative self-images derived from English oppression and prejudice into positive new images that would encourage new social attitudes and reform. Drennan's fifth letter from "Orellana"

envisioned "a republic of letters arising to illuminate the land" (38).
Drennan's active career as a United Irish poet and pamphleteer was
clearly intended to make such a vision a reality. Even after the demise
of the United Irish movement, Drennan wrote poetry and prose aimed
at "educating" the people of Ireland according to the program he had
first outlined in *Letters of Orellana*.

THE MUSICAL BACKGROUND

Drennan, the Volunteers, and the United Irishmen all subscribed
to the idea that the songs of a people were a more powerful social
force than any laws. They were all well aware of the powerful effect
that political verse set to traditional melodies could have. The power
that "Lullibulero" had in 1688 was common knowledge. According to
one eyewitness account of the song's effect: "The whole army, and at
last all the people both in city and country, were singing it perpetu-
ally. And perhaps never had so slight a thing so great an effect"
(Simpson 1966, 449).

Drennan's exhortation to "the Men of Fermanagh and of Cavan"
in his *Letters of Orellana* had called upon them to "add two new strings
to the Irish Harp, and it will then, in rich and deep variety of tone,
resound throughout the nation" (74). His allusion to the Volunteer
slogan about restringing the Irish harp underscored the antiquarian
and popular dimensions of the effort to educate the Irish people. Both
the harp, a major motif in Celticism and in Irish antiquarianism, and
songs and music from popular tradition were central to the effort to
politicize the people.

The growing eighteenth-century interest in Irish antiquities had
been accompanied by an enthusiasm for traditional Irish music. The
one thing all antiquarians agreed on was that song and music had
been the two major productions of the Irish bards. Although some
questioned Macpherson's claim that ancient poetry had survived until
the present in rural areas, all agreed that ancient music had survived.
That surviving music, a living link with a heroic past, was a source of
cultural pride and national identity. Indeed, the loss of the poetry in
itself proved a blessing because the old tunes were like empty slates
upon which Anglo-Irish dramatists, or Volunteer or United Irish writers, could impose new words and meaning.

Thomas Percy's landmark study *Reliques of Ancient English Poetry* (1765), demonstrated the close connection between antiquarianism and the study of eighteenth-century music and song as the survival of ancient culture. The subtitle of Percy's collection, *Consisting of Old Heroic Ballads, Songs, and Other Pieces of Our Earlier Poets, Together with Some New Pieces*, indicates that songs and ballads, and implicitly music, were integral to his antiquarian researches. Most of the lyrics in Percy's collection are songs and ballads rather than poems. Although Percy did not publish the music of the songs he anthologized, their musical dimensions were central. He had acquired some of his materials from old manuscripts, but he "heard" many others. With few exceptions, most of Percy's pieces had originally been intended to be sung. Percy had not escaped the Celticism that raged in Europe, and he appropriated "bards" to English literary tradition by claiming that the Anglo-Saxons, like all early Europeans, had had bards (Percy 1876, 1:xvii–xxi). The tradition defined by Percy was as much musical as it was literary. He claimed that the ancient Anglo-Saxon bards had been succeeded by medieval "minstrels" whose songs and harp music had performed the same function as that of the bards. Next in succession had been the ballad writers of Elizabethan England who, according to Percy, were "an inferior sort of minor poets," and who had written narrative songs for the press and songbooks known as garlands (1:xxxiv).

As evidence of the literary worth of his materials, Percy quoted the high praise that Philip Sidney had for the old Scots ballad "Chevy Chase," about the rivalry of the families of Percy and Douglas (Percy 1876, 1:lxxi), and that Joseph Addison had for more recent peasant songs and ballads (2:vi). Percy's materials had political as well as literary significance, as the story told in "Chevy Chase" suggested. Many of Percy's ballads pertained to the history and politics of recent centuries, thus making their "bardic" function quite contemporary. He cited the seventeenth-century Irish song "Lilli Burlero" as an example of the emotional and political power that even a mediocre song or tune could produce (2:43). Percy's demonstration of the survival of ancient tradition into modern times and the political potential of old tunes set to new lyrics was as important as the pride in national antiquities that he and other antiquarians offered to readers.

Although Irish materials make up only a small portion of his *Reliques*, Percy's activities in Ireland while he was Bishop of Dromore from 1782 until 1811 and his surviving letters indicate his strong interest in Irish subjects (Green 1970, 224–32). Irish antiquities were the subject of some of Percy's correspondence with his neighbor, the Countess of Moira, Francis Rawdon's mother, who collected Irish manuscripts and was an amateur antiquarian. In 1785, at the invitation of her husband, Percy became a member of the Royal Irish Academy, and actively participated in the society. Although he questioned some of the theories of Vallancey, Percy carried on an extensive correspondence with Irish antiquarians and historians such as Thomas Campbell, Edward Ledwich, and Joseph Cooper Walker in which he demonstrated a strong interest in Irish antiquities. Charlotte Brooke, the title of whose *Reliques of Irish Poetry* was clearly modeled on that of Percy's *Reliques*, wrote to Percy acknowledging his inspiration and asking him for any Irish manuscripts he had, as well as for his help in her application to become the housekeeper for the Royal Irish Academy (Nichols 1817–1858, 8:250–51).

Percy was also a close friend of Thomas Stott, a wealthy linen manufacturer who was his neighbor at Dromore. In the early 1790s Stott had close ties with the Belfast United Irishmen and contributed several songs and poems to the *Northern Star*. Stott's "Liberty and Equality; or, Dermot's Delight" appeared anonymously to the tune "Patrick's Day in the Morning" as the first song in the 1795 edition of *Paddy's Resource*. Stott's revolutionary fervor dwindled, however, and by 1798 he was an ardent loyalist. Even so, Stott retained the interest in Irish antiquities that he shared with both Percy and many United Irishmen; in 1825, at the age of seventy, he published *The Songs of Deardra*, which retold the Deirdre legend in verse.

By the turn of the century, Percy was a friend of the clergyman, poet, and former United Irishman William Hamilton Drummond, whose verse had appeared in the *Northern Star* and whose poems, *Hibernia* and *The Man of Age*, had been published in pamphlet form by the Northern Star press in 1797. Drummond was one of many links between the literary nationalism of the United Irishmen and that which developed in the course of the nineteenth century. He contributed a number of translations to James Hardiman's *Irish Minstrelsy; or Bardic Remains of Ireland* (1831). Drummond's own anthology, *Ancient Irish Minstrelsy*, appeared in 1852.

Percy also contributed money in 1807 to the founding of the Belfast Academical Institution, a project launched by William Drennan. Drennan's *Letter to His Excellency Earl Fitzwilliam* (1795) had recommended "a plan of national information" and that the government "establish parochial or county libraries, endow a professor's chair in every province, for giving lectures gratuitously, on a single subject—Ireland—its history, natural philosophy, politics—its present state—its possible improvements" (15). Daniel O'Connell's Repeal Reading Rooms and similar Young Ireland projects thus had a United Irish precedent. The young Samuel Ferguson attended the Belfast Academical Institution, which fostered the study of Irish culture and the Irish language. Percy and many United Irishmen clearly shared an interest in cultural and literary antiquarianism if not a political ideology.

Ireland provided abundant materials for proof of Macpherson and Percy's theory that ancient music survived into the present in rural areas. The music and songs of the Irish harper Carolan (1670–1738) represented the survival of what many believed was an ancient bardic tradition, as well as a popular living musical tradition that appealed to all classes and religions. Carolan embodied the antiquarian, the elite, and the popular dimensions, as well as the potential political significance, of the eighteenth-century interest in Irish music. Oliver Goldsmith, an Irishman in London, wrote an essay entitled, "The History of Carolan, the Last Irish Bard," published in the *British Magazine* for July 1760, that recognized Carolan's significance:

Irish Bards, in particular, are still held in great veneration among them; those traditional heralds are invited to every funeral, in order to fill up the intervals of the howl with their songs and harps. In these they rehearse the actions of the ancestors of the deceased, bewail the bondage of the country under the English government. . . .

Of all the Bards this country ever produced, the last and greatest was CAROLAN THE BLIND. He was at once a poet, a musician, a composer, and sung his own verses to his harp. The original natives never mention his name without rapture, both his poetry and his music they have by heart; and even some of the English themselves, who have been transplanted there, find his music extremely pleasing. A song beginning "O'Rourke's noble fare will ne'er be forgot," translated by Dean Swift, is of his composition; which, though

perhaps by this means the best known of his pieces, is yet by no
means the most deserving. (Goldsmith 1854, 271)

Goldsmith's reference to the peasantry as being a culturally significant source of literary materials reflected a growing conviction
among writers that would climax later in the century in the English
literary movement known as Romanticism. Such a view of the peasantry would also appeal to the democratic political principles of groups
like the United Irishmen. Significantly, Goldsmith's allusion in 1760
to Swift's connection with Carolan and traditional Irish music presumed that this connection was widely known.

The title of John Lee's *Favourite Collection of the So Much Admired Old Irish Tunes, the Original and Genuine Compositions of
Carolan the Celebrated Irish Bard. Set for the Harpsichord, Violin, and
German-Flute*, published in Dublin in 1780, reflected the popularity of Carolan in particular and Irish music in general among middle-
and upper-class Irish audiences. The interest in Irish music was
shared by the Catholic Irish, the Anglo-Irish Protestants, and the
Scots-Irish Presbyterians. Carolan's patrons included Catholics and
Protestant gentry.

Harp music, in particular that of Carolan, was central to the
eighteenth-century interest in Irish music. Harpers' tunes made up
the bulk of the first printed collection of Irish music, John and William
Neal's *Collection of the Most Celebrated Irish Tunes Proper for the Violin,
German Flute, or Hautboy*, published in Dublin in 1724. Although the
title, obviously directed at middle- and upper-class audiences, contained no reference to harps, half of the tunes in the collection were
attributed to Irish harpers in the explanatory notes about the tunes,
and most of the other tunes had been collected from harpers (Neal
1986, xxvii). The Neals were not familiar with the Irish language.
The title of Carolan's tune "Plearaca na Ruarcach" was given as "Plea
Rarkeh na Rourkough or ye Irish weding improved with diferent
divitions after ye Italian manner with A bass and chorus by Sigr.
Lorenzo Bocchi." There was clearly no concern for preserving ancient
musical traditions or for the music as revealing a significant cultural
achievement. That would come later in the century when the
connection between antiquarian research and traditional Irish music,
such as was suggested in Goldsmith's essay on Carolan, would be

demonstrated by people like Joseph Cooper Walker, Charlotte Brooke, and Edward Bunting.

In the meantime, the enormous popularity of John Gay's *Beggar's Opera* (1728), which included several traditional Irish tunes, encouraged the interest in traditional Irish music (Boydell 1986, 590). During the second quarter of the century, "Eileen Aroon" and other airs became popular at Dublin concerts, and music publishers printed small books containing "country dances" consisting of reels, jigs, hornpipes, and set dances, mostly to Irish tunes (Hogan 1966, 93).

A number of Irish airs, with new words, appeared in plays produced in Dublin in the 1770s and 1780s, such as John O'Keeffe's musical comedy *The Shamrock; or, St. Patrick's Day* (1777). Some of Carolan's tunes and other Irish airs, such as "Savourneen Deelish," were used by William Shield for songs in *The Poor Soldier* in 1784. The production of *The Shamrock* concluded with the following spectacle:

> A grand emblematical festive choral procession and pageant, consisting of kings of Leinster, Ulster, Munster, and Connaught; Strangbow [sic], earl of Pembroke; de Courcy, baron of Kingsale [sic]; Sitric, king of the Danes; Hibernia in a triumphal car; each attended with their respective arms, achievements, ensigns, and appendages, druids, bards, games, banshees, leporehauns [sic], Hibernians in their original and present state, Peace, Fame, Hospitality, Industry, etc. etc. To conclude with a song by Carrolan [sic], the ancient Irish bard, and grand chorus of all the character; Carrolan Mr. Owenson. (Boydell 1986, 597).

Such theatrical spectacle had some interesting similarities to the elaborate "Grand Procession, or sublime spectacle," as the *Belfast Newsletter* called it, that marked the Belfast celebration of the Harp Festival and the fall of the Bastille in July 1792. That procession, which included hundreds of Volunteers, United Irishmen, and other costumed celebrants, featured a six-foot by eight-foot standard, one side of which pictured a Volunteer presenting a figure of Liberty to Hibernia, mounted on a triumphal car (Joy 1817, 372–74). Public pageantry had been an important part of political life in Ulster. A contemporary account of a celebration at Ballymena for the election of a candidate in 1776 described "ten thousand men with blue cockades," "four hundred free-masons, attired in their jewels, armed with carabines for the purpose of saluting, and preceded by a large band of music," and five hundred "patriot virgins" (Joy 1817, 135).

The "patriot virgins" in that political pageant provide a context for the final lines in the poetic dedication by the "editors" of the 1795 *Paddy's Resource* that announced the purpose of the collection:

> . . . should but one Patriot more
> Be added to his Country's store;
> Should from the Virgin's heart one sigh
> Be breath'd to Heav'n for Liberty—
> We never, never shall complain,
> Nor think that we have toil'd in vain.

One account of the Battle of Ballinahinch in 1798 claimed that afterwards the bodies of two woman had been found, "fantastically dressed in green silk, who had carried the rebel standards. They had been known as the Goddess of Liberty and the Goddess of Reason, and were apparently the town prostitutes" (Pakenham 1972, 264).

Drama and spectacle, including symbolic insignia, would often be a part of United Irish movement. When William Drennan first proposed a secret society of reformers in 1784, he suggested it be organized along the lines of "the ceremonial attached to Free-masonry" and include symbolic rituals and insignia (Stewart 1976, 83–84). In a paper entitled "Idem Sentire, Dicere, Agere," circulated in Dublin in June 1791, Drennan suggested organizing a secret society to be called the "Irish Brotherhood" (a name eventually replaced by Wolfe Tone's suggestion of "Society of United Irishmen"), which he described as follows: "It is proposed that at this juncture a Society shall be instituted in the City, having much of the secrecy, and somewhat of the ceremonial attached to Free-Masonry—with so much secrecy as may communicate curiosity, uncertainty and expectation to the minds of surrounding men—with so much impressive and affecting ceremony in all its internal economy, as without impeding real business, may strike the soul through the senses, and addressing the whole Man, may animate his philosophy by the energy of his passions" (Drennan 1844, 155).

The Mr. Owenson who portrayed Carolan in the grand pageant that concluded *The Shamrock*, only a year after the Ballymena political pageant described above, was Robert Owenson, the father of Sydney Owenson, later Lady Morgan. A native Irish speaker from Mayo who had anglicized his surname MacEoghain to Owenson, Robert Owenson was a popular performer noted for his unique ability to sing both the original Irish and new English lyrics to old tunes. During the years following the start of the Volunteer movement, in the character of a simple country player named "Darby Mulroney or Phelim O'Flanagan" or "Phelim Ouffnocarrolocarney MacFrame," Owenson charmed town and country audiences with his large store of Irish "cries" and "lilts," and with his Irish and English renderings of the "planxties" of Carolan. His most famous composition in Irish was a prelude entitled "Pleaharca na Rourcough," set to Carolan's tune "Plearaca na Ruarcach" (Clark 1965, 290).

According to Lady Morgan's *Memoirs*, at her christening (c. 1776) her father sang "first in Irish and then in English Carolan's famous song of 'O'Rourke's Noble Feast' " (1862, 1:14). Her godfather was her father's friend Edward Lysaght, an eloquent barrister and noted wit, who was also known for his ability to sing in both Irish and English. Some of Lysaght's own songs would appear in the *Northern Star* and in *Paddy's Resource*. In 1783, the young Wolfe Tone acted in two amateur productions in Galway in a company made up of gentry and Volunteers that was directed by Robert Owenson.

The memoirs and surviving papers of many United Irishmen indicate their familiarity with eighteenth-century music and musical dramas. As Tom Dunne remarked, "if Tone read the major Enlightenment and Revolutionary writers, he made virtually no reference to them, even in his Journal or diaries, which instead have many references to and excerpts from ballads, plays and novels" (1982, 26). The Drennan Letters in the State Paper Office of Northern Ireland also attest to the strong interest in contemporary dramatic and musical productions among Belfast and Dublin United Irishmen. Notices about plays and musical events frequently appeared in the *Northern Star*.

The close connection between cultural and political nationalism was particularly apparent in the harp festivals celebrated in late eighteenth-century Ireland. Three harp festivals were held in Granard, County Longford, in 1781, 1782, and 1783. According to a letter that Richard Lovell Edgeworth wrote to Lady Morgan in 1806, Maria Edgeworth from nearby Edgeworthstown attended at least one of them and wrote an account of it, now lost, for a local newspaper (Morgan 1862, 2:293). The Granard festivals had been organized and the prizes subsidized by James Dungan, a native of Granard who became a wealthy merchant. Inspired by the annual meetings or competitions he had seen among pipers in the Scottish Highlands, Dungan wrote to a friend proposing they organize a competition of harpers: "The Welsh harp is increasing. The Scotch bagpipes are increasing, but poor Erin's harp is decreasing" (Fox 1911, 174). A ball for local gentry was held in conjunction with the harp festival in order to encourage attendance. Five hundred people attended the ball in 1781; more than a thousand attended the 1783 ball. Seven harpers performed in 1781; nine in 1782 and 1783 (Fox 1911, 174–87).

Several of the same harpers who had played at the Granard festivals performed at the Belfast Harp Festival, 10-13 July, 1792. The dates of that festival had clearly been planned to coincide with the celebration of the anniversary of the fall of the Bastille planned by the Volunteers and the newly formed United Irishmen for 14 July. As was mentioned earlier, one of the organizers of the festival, Robert Simms, was involved in the concurrent founding of the United Irishmen and a few months later became a part-owner of the *Northern Star*. The other three organizers, Henry Joy, Robert Bradshaw, and James McDonnell, had close ties with the United Irishmen; even if they did not share their political radicalism, they did share an interest in Irish music and culture.

The announcement of the harp festival that the organizing committee printed and circulated in Belfast in December 1791 deserves to be quoted in full:

> Some inhabitants of Belfast, feeling themselves interested in everything which relates to the honour, as well as the prosperity of their country, propose to open a subscription, which they intend to apply in attempting to revive and perpetuate the ancient Music and Poetry of Ireland. They are solicitous to preserve from oblivion the few fragments which have been permitted to remain, as monuments of the refined taste and genius of their ancestors.
>
> In order to carry this project into execution, it must appear obvious to those acquainted with the situation of this country that it will be necessary to assemble the Harpers, those descendants of our An-

cient Bards, who are at present almost exclusively possessed of all
that remains of the Music, Poetry and oral traditions of Ireland.

It is proposed that the Harpers should be induced to assemble at
Belfast (suppose on the 1st July next) by the distribution of such
prizes as may seem adequate to the subscribers; and that a person
well versed in the language and antiquities of this nation should
attend, with a skillful musician to transcribe and arrange the most
beautiful and interesting parts of their knowledge.

An undertaking of this kind will undoubtedly meet the approbation
of men of refinement and erudition in every country. And when it is
considered how intimately the spirit and character of a people are
connected with their national Poetry and Music, it is presumed that
the Irish patriot and politician will not deem it an object unworthy
his patronage and protection. (Fox 1911, 97–98)

The ancestral connection claimed at the end of the first para-
graph is interesting because, of the organizers, only James McDonnell
could claim some native Irish blood. McDonnell was a Protestant, but
his father was an Antrim Catholic who had hired the harper Arthur
O'Neill to teach his three sons to play the harp. McDonnell had
attended a hedge-school conducted in "one of the Red Bay caves by
Maurice Traynor, a Roman Catholic" (Benn 1877, 160). The other
organizers were Presbyterians of Scottish descent. Presumably, the recent vogue for things Celtic gave them a basis for their claim to a
connection with Irish harpers, whom they claimed were "descendants
of our Ancient Bards."

Their announcement referred to the popular view that the harpers possessed what remained of the poetic as well as the musical traditions of ancient Ireland. The announcement makes it clear that the
original intention had been to collect both the musical and poetic
remains by having both a musician and someone "well versed in the
language and antiquities of his nation" present. In fact, the only musician who was present the following July was Edward Bunting, who did
transcribe the harpers' music. Likewise, the original goal of attempt-
ing "to revive and perpetuate the ancient Music and Poetry of Ireland" in fact became largely an effort at preservation. Bunting's three
collections were the most important result of the festival in that regard:

A General Collection of the Ancient Irish Music (1796); A General Collection of the Ancient Music of Ireland (1809); and A Collection of the Ancient Music of Ireland (1840). At the urging of Thomas Russell, Bunting's first collection was subsidized by the Belfast Society for Promoting Knowledge, to which many United Irishmen belonged. The second collection and the folksong collecting expeditions that preceded it were largely funded by the McCracken family, with whom Bunting lived from 1784 until 1814.

Bunting's collections were well known to United Irishmen. For example, a note to a song entitled "Oh Union For Ever" that was printed in the United Irishmen's Dublin newspaper the Press on January 1798 said, "Such persons as are not in possession of the national musick [sic] may sing it to the tune of Logie of Buchan," a widely-known Scots tune. "The national musick" refers to Bunting's 1796 collection because that phrase was repeatedly used in the Northern Star's ads and editorials promoting Bunting's work. Thomas Russell and Thomas Addis Emmet had copies of Bunting's 1796 collection with them in prison. Russell sent tunes to Bunting while imprisoned from 1796 until 1802, and upon his release from prison wrote to a friend that he was taking his copy of Bunting with him to Europe where, he said, he would do everything possible to promote it (McNeill 1960, 211). William Drennan contributed song lyrics based on literal translations from the Irish to Bunting's 1809 collection.

The Belfast Harp Festival was announced in newspapers throughout Ireland, including the two United Irish newspapers being published at that time, the Northern Star in Belfast and the National Journal in Dublin. The Northern Star's announcement of the festival, which appeared on 25 April 1792, included the following statements: "The preservation of our national music must appear to be a matter of no small importance to every lover of the antiquities of Ireland. . . . When you think of the British commemoration of a single artist, with what ardour should it inspire us to revive and perpetuate the native music of Ireland." The harp festival offered an occasion when the religious, political, and social divisions that so polarized Ireland at the time could be transcended by a shared enthusiasm for Irish art and culture. One cannot imagine a less threatening cultural icon for Irish people of all social and religious backgrounds to rally behind. The motley assortment of ten impoverished harpers who assembled in Belfast that July certainly posed no serious threat to English power in Ireland. None of the ancient words had survived so, lacking lyrics, the music transcended sectarian and political rhetoric and conflicts, and offered a paradigm of the "Union" of all Irishmen that was the goal of the United Irishmen.

The harpers' bardic dimensions also paralleled the mission of the United Irishmen. On 18 July 1792, a *Northern Star* editorial about the harp festival claimed that the harpers who had performed were only "partial representatives of the ancient bards," who had been at once poet, musician, historian, and philosopher, because only music had survived among contemporary harpers. The United Irishmen were clearly ready to assume the missing roles of poet, historian, and philosopher, and to create words for the traditional melodies.

When the United Irishmen used the literary and political potential of Irish music in their songs, they used some of the harpers' tunes, such as Carolan's "Planxty Connor." It is somewhat difficult to tell by the titles of the tunes used by the United Irishmen what their origins were. For example, the name of the tune for the song "Swains Awake!" in the 1796 *Paddy's Resource* is "Shepherds I Have Lost My Love." However, according to Edward Bunting, that was the English name for the old Irish melody "Sin sios agus suas liom" ("down and up with me"), which he had obtained from the famous Belfast harper Dominic Mungan (1840, 98).

The majority of the tunes used by the United Irishmen came from a broad range of Irish and Scottish musical traditions. Songs had been an important part of many earlier Protestant and Catholic political movements. The importance of songs in the Volunteer movement has already been discussed. Secret agrarian societies such as "The Hearts of Oak" and "The Hearts of Steel" also had songs and marches. In Armagh in 1763, "The Hearts of Oak," a Protestant agrarian terrorist society, was described as follows: "[they] filled at least two miles of road and were formed into companies with each a standard or colours displayed . . . drums, horns, fiddles and bagpipes" (Fitzpatrick 1989, 171). Songs were also part of the rural Catholic Defender movement, as was the "tree of liberty," which was a common image in United Irish verse. Loyalist Protestant yeomanry corps also had songbooks with tunes such as "The Boyne Water." The tune and several lines of the United Irish song "Freedom Triumphant" were taken from that Protestant marching song.

Many United Irishmen belonged to Masonic societies, another example of the European dimensions of the movement. Masonic meetings were frequently announced in the *Northern Star*. Drennan's plans for a secret society proposed that its signs and ceremonies resemble those of the Masons. The Masons had songbooks, such as a chapbook published in 1777 entitled *A Collection of Songs to Be Sung by Freemasons* (Adams 1987, 185). A song entitled "The Free Mason's Song" had appeared in Allan Ramsay's *Tea-Table Miscellany* (1740, 362–63). Its refrain, "A free and an accepted mason," was the title of a tune used several times for United Irish songs. The United Irish meetings, often held at taverns, were marked by a conviviality similar to that described in "The Free Mason's Song":

> Come let us prepare,
> We Brethren that are
> Assembled on merry occasion:
> Let's drink, laugh and sing,
> Our wine has a spring;
> Here's a health to an accepted mason.
> (Ramsay 1740, 362)

The United Irish song entitled "A Council Called!" to the tune " Free and An accepted Mason" that appeared in the 1795 *Paddy's Resource* had clearly been modeled on "The Free Mason's Song" for it began as follows:

> Come let us prepare,
> We statesmen that are
> Assembl'd on this dread occasion;
> Let the engines of state,
> Before 'tis too late,
> Repel the impending invasion.

Stanzas like the following in "The Free Mason's Song" would have had added appeal after the United Irishmen became a secret society in 1795:

The world is in pain
Our secret to gain,
And still let them wonder and gaze on:
They ne'er can divine
The word or the sign,
Of a free and an accepted mason.
(Ramsay 1740, 363)

The French and American Revolutions also provided models and materials for United Irish songs. Popular revolutionary songs set to traditional tunes were an important force in the French Revolution, and the success of such songs in politicizing the French people was not lost upon the United Irishmen. The gay French song "Ça Ira" appeared in 1790 and was one of the most popular revolutionary songs in France for the next decade. The *Northern Star* published a translation of "Ça Ira" on 4 April 1792:

Thus it shall go, thus it shall go,
The people shall for e'er repeat,
Thus it shall go, thus it shall go,
In spite of mutinies we'll succeed.

A different translation of "Ça Ira," which appeared in the 1795 *Paddy's Resource*, was truer to the gaiety of the French original: "Come let us dance, let us dance, / Happy, happy days have appear'd at last."

In 1792 a Paris journal had printed this declaration: "May the songs of liberty echo in all places, and fill the tyrants of the earth with profound terror" (Darnton and Roche 1989, 12). During that same year, two of the most popular French revolutionary songs, "The Carmagnole" and "The Marseilles," appeared (Rogers 1949, 17). The 1795 *Paddy's Resource* contained a "translation" of "The Carmagnole," set to the Scottish tune "Dainty Davy." That first edition of *Paddy's Resource* contained a translation of "The Marseilles." With the typical United Irish flair for eclecticism, the 1795 *Paddy's Resource* also contained a song entitled "The New Viva La," which combined French phrases and references; an invocation to the muse in the English literary mode; the Scots tune "Willy Was a Wanton Wag"; rhetoric popularized by antiquarians, Volunteers, and Dublin dramatists about Hibernia being enslaved, and Freedom arising and singing accompanied by her harp; and "Gothic" language about "storms and tempests" and that "gothic structure," the Bastille.

The United Irishmen also drew upon songs from the American Revolutionary War. Two songs in the 1795 *Paddy's Resource*, "The Glorious Exertion of Man" by Samuel Neilson, which had been composed for the 1792 celebration of Bastille Day, and "The Star of Liberty," were to be sung to the tune "General Wolfe." That was the name of the tune popularized by Thomas Paine's song "The Death of General Wolfe," first published in a Pennsylvania magazine in 1775, and which was popular among English and American radicals. Likewise, Paine's song "The Liberty Tree" had provided an important motif to the Volunteers, Defenders, and United Irishmen (Paine 1925, 10:301–2, 312–13). Sonneck Upton's *Bibliography of Early Secular American Music* (1964) lists numerous eighteenth-century American tunes that are also found in the *Paddy's Resource* songbooks. The music of late eighteenth-century political songs traveled freely back and forth across the Atlantic, and tunes from popular songs of the day undoubtedly enhanced the effectiveness of political songs.

The United Irish song tradition influenced the patriotic song tradition in America. American editions of *Paddy's Resource* were published in Philadelphia in 1796 and in New York in 1798. In 1797, an American Society of United Irishmen was founded in Philadelphia, the destination of many United Irishmen, including Wolfe Tone, who had emigrated to America in 1796. John Daly Burk, a United Irishmen who emigrated to the United States in 1795, was instrumental in disseminating United Irish tunes there. His *History of the Late War in Ireland* (1799), an important but neglected contemporary account of the United Irish movement, quoted extensively from *Paddy's Resource*. An American songbook entitled *The American Republican Harmonist; or, a Collection of Songs and Odes Written in America* was published in Philadelphia in 1803 by William Duane, one of several Irish-born editors of Republican papers in America. Duane published an anthology of poetry and other materials from the Dublin United Irish newspaper *The Press* in 1802. His songbook included forty songs, not all of which were set to tunes. Despite the emphasis on "American" in his songbook's title, twelve of the songs were set to tunes already popularized by the United Irishmen, such as "Anacreon in Heaven" and "The Night Before Larry Was Stretched," each of which was used three times. The tune "Anacreon in Heaven," which had originated with a London philosophic society in the 1780s, was used for John Adams and Thomas Jefferson's presidential campaign songs (Ewen 1966, 368). In 1812, Francis Scott Key set "The Star Spangled Banner" to "Anacreon in Heaven."

Scottish tradition offered the United Irishmen, many of whom were of Scots-Irish descent, an especially rich source of tunes. Most of the songs in the first two editions of *Paddy's Resource*, printed in Belfast in 1795 and 1796, were of Ulster origin. John Hewitt has described the indigenous Scottish poetic tradition that flourished in Ulster in the late eighteenth century. Many of the general traits that Hewitt ascribes to these poets also could describe United Irishmen in Belfast: membership in Masonic societies and book clubs; liberal Presbyterianism; radical and democratic politics; the composition of verses to well-known airs; and a fondness for drinking songs and satire (Hewitt 1974, 67). According to Hewitt, singing secular songs was highly popular in rural Presbyterian communities (1974, 39). Many of the poets Hewitt labels "rhyming weavers" were also United Irishmen, such as James Orr and James "Jemmy" Hope, who contributed songs to the *Northern Star*.

Many of the tunes used in the 1795 and 1796 *Paddy's Resource* songbooks were of Scottish origin. Some had appeared in print much earlier in the century. For example, the popular tune known as "Lochaber," later used for several United Irish songs, had first appeared in Allan Ramsay's *Tea-Table Miscellany* (1724-37). In Ireland the tune was known as "Limerick's Lamentation," but United Irish songs always indicated the tune as "Lochaber." Several other traditional Scottish tunes published in the *Tea-Table Miscellany* were also used for United Irish songs: "Dainty Davie," "O'er the Hills and Far Away," "Willie Was a Wanton Wag," and "Gillikranky."

Allan Ramsay had anthologized several hundred traditional Scottish tunes in the four volumes of his very popular *Tea-Table Miscellany* between 1724 and 1737. About thirty editions of the *Miscellany* were published before the end of the century. Ramsay did not include the music for his songs, only the names of the tunes to which the songs were to be sung, a practice that presumed the tunes were well known. Nor would the United Irish songbooks print music; they too gave only the names of tunes. Most of Ramsay's songs were either in Scots dialect or in the English pastoral mode. By including materials from peasant tradition, urban street ballads, popular comic operas, and pastoral poetry, Ramsay's songbooks displayed a blending of literary modes such as would characterize the various editions of *Paddy's Resource* at the end of the century.

The idea that each country has a distinct "national music" had been well established by the end of the eighteenth century. David Herd articulated this idea in the preface to his influential collection entitled *Ancient and Modern Scottish Songs* (first published in 1776), which opened with his declaration that "the common popular songs and national music . . . exhibit natural and striking traits of the character, genius, taste and pursuits of the people" (1973, ix). The idea that music expressed a nation's character and identity encouraged the United Irishmen's interest in traditional and popular music. Herd's collection included seventeen tunes used in United Irish songs.

Robert Burns's publication of Scottish songs fostered the idea that a people's character is expressed in their songs. Burns's popularity in Ulster encouraged United Irishmen to set many songs to Scottish tunes. His famous collection of traditional Scottish tunes set to new or old lyrics, *Poems Chiefly in Scottish Dialect*, was published in Belfast in 1787, 1789, 1790, and 1793, and in Dublin in 1789 and 1790. Burns was also a major contributor to the early volumes of the *Scots Musical Museum*, a series of anthologies of traditional Scots tunes and songs, edited by James Johnson, which began to be published in 1787 and were very popular in Ulster. "Maggy Lauder," "Duncan Davison," "Dainty Davie," "Green Grow the Rushes," and "My Ain Kind Dearie" were among the many tunes popularized by Burns that were used for United Irish songs. Unlike Ramsay, Burns generally reprinted or imitated the colloquial dialect of Scottish folksongs rather than the artificiality of English odes and pastoral poetry. The enormous popularity of Burns's songs demonstrated the growing interest in authentic folksongs during the eighteenth century, as well as the adaptability of old tunes to new lyrics. Several United Irish songs used Scots dialect in the manner of Burns's songs and local Ulster poetry.

The literary, antiquarian, political, and musical dimensions of the United Irishmen's eighteenth-century backgrounds demonstrate the complex and eclectic origins of the political and literary traditions they founded. The pluralism inherent in their literary nationalism deserves to be better known because it offers an important antidote to the increasingly xenophobic and sectarian literary nationalism that developed in the course of the nineteenth century.

• 3 •

The Ulster and Dublin Backgrounds
of the United Irishmen

The United Irishmen's literary works owe much to the cultural mi-
lieus of Ulster and Dublin. J. R. R. Adams's invaluable study *The
Printed Word and the Common Man: Popular Culture in Ulster, 1700–
1900* surveys the diverse works available in Ulster, where the literacy rate was significantly higher than elsewhere in Ireland and
where the majority of the earliest United Irish songs were written.
Songs were an important part of popular culture in Ulster. According to Adams, songs and ballads, printed individually and in
songbooks, numbered in the thousands. They ranged from plaintive
love songs to obscene ballads and thus appealed to a broad range of
tastes. Many patriotic songs were published during the 1770s and
1780s (Adams 1987, 74–76). The language of late eighteenth-century songs and ballads was eclectic: literate, poetic, often archaic
English diction; vernacular Scots or Irish language and phrases; old
formulaic words in the oral style. All those styles, as well as the
"humour, wit and sarcasm" that Adams claims was the most common characteristic of popular songs in Ulster (1987, 34), would
surface in United Irish songs.

Adams's survey of printed works demonstrates that popular religion and drama were also important components of popular culture.
Consequently, popular religion and drama also provided an important
context for the literary works of the United Irishmen in the 1790s.
Religion and politics were closely connected in the minds of eighteenth-century Ulster Presbyterians, the group from which the earliest
United Irish societies in Ulster drew most of their members. Indeed,

65

A. T. Q. Stewart has argued that the United Irish movement was "a Presbyterian initiative" (1977, 102).

The connection between politics and religion had been articulated early in the eighteenth century by Francis Hutcheson, a native of County Down who became a professor at Glasgow University where his influence earned him the title "Father of the Scottish Enlightenment." His political writings were enormously influential in both Ulster and America. Hutcheson's idea that all power is vested in and consequently derived from the people was widely accepted by Ulster Presbyterians such as his friend Thomas Drennan, a Presbyterian minister and the father of William Drennan. Hutcheson's earlier influence in Ulster, especially among clergymen, explains why Thomas Paine's ideas found such fertile ground there in the 1790s. In Hutcheson's view, political rights encompassed moral duties, thus bringing one's duties as a citizen into the moral realm of religion. According to Hutcheson, tenants of greedy landlords and anyone oppressed by tyrants had a moral right to resist. As a consequence of Hutcheson's influence, political activism assumed moral and religious dimensions in the popular mind (Fitzpatrick 1989, 177–78).

The connection between religion and politics is also apparent in the popularity of prophecies in Ulster, where they were soon put to overt political use. The publication of prophecies increased dramatically in the last two decades of the century. By the 1790s, according to Adams, prophecies "flooded off the presses, and millenarianism, combined with a real feeling that God was working to change the social order, especially when events in France were considered, spread over the country" (1987, 89). As evidence, Adams lists the following publications that appeared in 1795: *An Examination of the Scripture Prophecies Respecting the Downfall of Antichrist . . . and the Late Revolution in France Shewn to Be Plainly Foretold* (Belfast); *Extracts from the Prophecies of Richard Brothers* (Belfast); *Prophetical Extracts Particularly Such as Relate to the Revolution in France* (Strabane); Robert Fleming's *Rise and Fall of Antichrist* (Belfast); and *The Shaking and Translation of Heaven and Earth* (Belfast and Monaghan editions) (1987, 89). The first title listed, commonly known as *Scripture Prophecies*, was advertised and promoted in the *Northern Star* throughout the summer of 1795.

Two years earlier, three of United Irishman William Steel Dickson's sermons had been published under the title *Scripture Politics*. Dickson, a Presbyterian minister in Portaferry, had taken the United Irish oath in December 1791 and was a contributor to the *Northern Star*, which published several ads for *Scripture Politics* in 1793. Dickson's sermons demonstrated the religious tenets that were behind the overt political and literary use of religious prophecies. Dickson cited passages from scripture which made "the following particulars appear plain and undeniable": "the controul of religion over governors, governments and nations," and "the necessity of sending extraordinary prophets, to reprove and correct political fraud, oppression, and violence, and thereby avert national ruin" (1812, 103). According to Dickson, Scripture "teaches us, that as it is the duty of teachers of religion to rebuke the partiality, unjustice, and oppression of governors, and expose the abuses of government, so it is the duty of the people to call for and enforce reform" (104). The prophetic tone of Dickson's sermons was a common feature of Presbyterian sermons both in Ulster and America, and of much United Irish verse.

The United Irishmen were also directly involved in the dissemination of prophecies. According to Samuel McSkimin's *Annals of Ulster, from 1790–1798*, the following resolutions were passed at a meeting of the United Irishmen at Rasharkin, County Antrim:

> Resolved: That we behold plainly the case of not everyone knowing the prophecies of Thomas the Rhymer, and the prophecies of Alexander Peden, all useful to the people in making our laws, and as many of our brethren cannot read them, and explain them, and tell about them;

> Resolved: That Donald O'Kennedy will read to the county of Derry, and that Archy Woods will read to the county of Antrim, and that they tell the French news to everybody, and dispute with all who dare to contradict them. (1849, 32)

Samuel McSkimin claimed the following political prophecy had been very popular in Ulster in 1798: "A wet winter, a dry spring, / A bloody summer, and no king" (1849, 66). A paper confiscated by the authorities (SPOI 620/48/46), and possibly in Thomas Russell's hand, labeled "Part of Collon Kills [sic] Prophecy in the Year 1412," includes a prophetic chronicle of 1790–1799, such as "1797 / Will appear Gog and Magog who will make war against the Inhabitants of the Earth"

(Miller 1987, 100). The references to "Gog and Magog" are interesting in that those were two nicknames that Tone used in his journal to refer to his associates John Keogh and Robert McCormick.

Thomas Russell's reputed success in recruiting Ulster Presbyterians to United Irish membership was undoubtedly due in part to his conviction that political activities had a religious, even messianic, dimension. In a letter written from prison to his friend John Templeton in Belfast, Russell declared that "men will see the only true basis of Liberty is Morality, and the only stable basis of Morality is Religion" (Trinity College, Dublin, Madden Papers, 873/638). Russell's journals demonstrate his deepening millenarial convictions. Like Dickson, Russell frequently found a Biblical precedent for his political arguments. Russell used a passage from Psalms, "It is a goodly thing, brethren, to dwell together in unity," as the epigraph for his pamphlet *A Letter to the People of Ireland on the Present Situation of the Country*, published in Belfast shortly before his arrest in 1796. The title page included his name and the declaration that he was "An United Irishmen." Such boldness was unusual, for most United Irish pamphlets, even the satires, were published anonymously. Russell's pamphlet, largely religious in its impetus, has a strong millenarial ring to it, as did many of his writings.

As John Gray perceptively observed of Russell: "He lies outside any attempt to impose a retrospective modernising and rationalist gloss on the revolutionary movement of the 1790s. His combining, however, of a populist political agenda with religious millenniarism rendered him particularly in tune with Ulster of the 1790's" (1989, 9). In 1803, Russell asked for a stay of execution of several days, which was denied, in order that he might complete a millenarian work based on the Revelations of St. John and Francis Dobbs's notorious predictions of a Second Coming. Dobbs, who was also a playwright, had published a four-volume work in 1784 entitled *Universal History, Commencing at the Creation and Ending at the Death of Christ* in which he attempted to prove that history was the fulfillment of messianic prophecies. Like Dobbs, Russell would use antiquarianism for literary purposes in some of the poetry he wrote in prison, and he too used political history to reveal religious prophecies and vice versa.

Both Dobbs and Russell were "minor" writers, but their writings embodied important currents in eighteenth-century popular culture. Prophecy and millenarianism have been important social and political forces in disparate cultures in nearly all parts of the world during many historical eras, and such beliefs were particularly important in connection with nationalism in eighteenth- and nineteenth-century Ireland (Donnelly 1983, 102–39; Murphy 1972, 19–22).

United Irish poems and songs frequently had a millenarian and messianic ring. For example, the fourth issue of the *Northern Star* on 11 January 1792 published "Ode for the New Year, 1792" in which the Muse, much in the manner of ancient bards, prophesied:

> This flame of freedom must precede
> Thy promised reign of peace:
> The age Millenial is decreed
> But war's alarms must cease.

Despite contemporary and subsequent charges that the United Irishmen were godless rationalists and radicals, much of the movement's literary propaganda had a distinct religious dimension. Moreover, the cult of martyrdom in which the United Irish poets placed executed United Irishmen had clear messianic overtones.

Popular culture also provided the United Irishmen with less somber literary contexts. United Irish writings owed a debt to popular drama as well as to the patriotic Dublin plays mentioned earlier. The three most popular plays in eighteenth-century Ulster provide insight into popular tastes that help us understand both the audiences the United Irishmen tried to reach and the literary works they produced to politicize these audiences. According to J. R. R. Adams, the following three plays were published so many times that they achieved mass popularity among all classes, even at the peasant level: Allan Ramsay's *Gentle Shepherd: A Pastoral Comedy* (1725); John Michelburne's *Ireland Preserved; or, the Seige of Londonderry* (1705); and Robert Ashton's *Battle of Aughrim; or, the fall of Monsieur St. Ruth: A Tragedy* (1756) (Adams 1987, 69–70). *The Gentle Shepherd* was primarily read and recited rather than performed, although the *Belfast Newsletter* reported a performance of the play in Belfast in 1795.

Allan Ramsay's Gentle Shepherd, a pastoral comedy set in a village a few miles from Edinburgh, combined the Scots vernacular, the English pastoral mode, and songs set to traditional tunes (Ramsay 1974, 42–104). Editions were published in Belfast in 1743, 1748, 1755, 1768, and 1792, in Newry in 1764, 1776, and 1793, and in Strabane in 1789, making it one of the most locally reproduced texts of the century (Adams 1987, 69–70). Ramsay had clearly been inspired by the success of the first volume of his Tea-Table Miscellany (1724), which was been published the year before he wrote the play. Both the songbook and the play gave prominence to Scots songs intended to be sung to traditional tunes. Ramsay's play demonstrated the literary potential of combining vernacular subjects and modes with more elite literary conventions.

Similarly, a song entitled "The Winter of Age" was published in Dundalk about 1797 with the note that it was "translated from the Irish in 1793" to the air "Kathleen Trail." The opening lines demonstrate the song's combination of the English pastoral and the Irish song tradition: "Come Clora, let's roam, while in soft wanton gales, / Blythe zephyrs disport upon Boyne's limpid stream" (E. R. Dix typescript, Royal Irish Academy). This popular dimension of the pastoral illuminates the United Irish use of the pastoral mode in some of their songs and poems. Thus, the United Irish song "Swains Awake!" to the tune "Shepherds I Have Lost My Love," published in Paddy's Resource in 1796 and 1803, which appears at first glance to have been an attempt to reach only a highly literate upper class audience, actually would have had broad popular appeal. The song begins:

> SWAINS! we've slept and lost our love,
>   FREEDOM! fair as ANNA,
> Fav'rite wish of all who rove
>   Within the Isle of GRANU.
> We for her our forks would wield,
>   Armour of our meadows;
> Bare our breasts and stand the shield
>   Of orphans and of widows.

Moreover, as noted earlier, the tune, despite its title, was actually the old Irish tune "Sin sios agus suas liom" (Bunting 1969c, 98). "Swains

Awake!" was thus typical of the combination of literary modes characteristic of United Irish verse, the model for which had been given to
them by street ballads and by popular writers such as Ramsay.

John Michelburne's *Ireland Preserved; or, the Siege of Londonderry*,
first published in 1705, was reprinted in Belfast in 1744, 1750, and
1759, in Newry in 1774, and in Strabane in 1787, (there were probably more reprints, now lost) (Adams 1987, 70). The play is a bombastic drama set in the times of the siege of Londonderry, where the
author was military governor during the events he describes
(Michelburne 1841, 235–58). It concludes with the English Lieutenant General Hamilton saying: "Farewell, stubborn and ungrateful town
of Derry, a nest of traitors and rebels." The anti-Jacobite prejudice to
which the play had originally appealed diminished during the course
of the century as the Jacobite threat all but disappeared. Therefore,
Hamilton's remark probably assumed more and more patriotic overtones for Irish audiences as friction between the Irish, both Anglo-
Irish and Presbyterian, and the English intensified during the 1770s
and 1780s.

Ireland Preserved portrayed the people of Londonderry upon their
deliverance singing songs to the tunes "The Boyne Water," "Erin Go
Bragh," "Auld Lang Syne," and "My Ain Kind Dearie." That combination of Protestant and Catholic, Scottish and Irish tunes illustrates
how the literary integration of disparate cultural traditions generally
precedes any political integration. Later in the century the United
Irishmen would use all four tunes in their *Paddy's Resource* songbooks.

The Ulster folk play "par excellence," according to J. R. R. Adams,
was Robert Ashton's *Battle of Aughrim*, (first published in 1756), of
which there were numerous local editions (Adams 1987, 70). Written
in heroic verse, battle scenes were described in couplets like these:

> Death in each quarter does the eye alarm,
> Here lies a leg and there a shattered arm,
> There heads appear which cloven by mighty bangs,
> And severed quite, on either shoulder hangs.
> (Adams 1987, 71)

The play appealed to Protestants and Catholics alike, for despite its
undeniably pro-English bias, Jacobite characters such as Patrick Sarsfield

were portrayed as gallant figures. Indeed, the play resembled Mason's
Caractacus in its portrayal of the Celt as a brave warrior with a long
tradition of tragic defeat.

The prologue celebrated both "glorious William" and how "bravely"
the Irish forces fought. Protestants and Catholics alike could respond
to the play's celebration of Ireland:

> Hail! Sweet Hibernia, hospitable isle,
> More rich than Egypt with her flowing Nile;
> Fair garden of the earth, thy fragrant plains
> Are seats of war; and thy sweet purling streams
> All run with blood, and vengeance seems to trace,
> The shining remnant of Hibernia's race.
>
> (Ashton 1826, 25)

The rhetoric of the opening speech by Patrick Sarsfield to St. Ruth
would reappear later in the century in the writings of the Volunteers
and United Irishmen: "By us the famed Hibernia shall be freed, / Our
Fleur de Lis and Harp we will display" (Ashton 1826, 1). That popular image of French and Irish in a fight for freedom against England
certainly lingered among both the Catholics and Protestants to whom
the play had appealed. It would assume new resonance when the
promise or threat, depending upon the point of view, of a French
invasion loomed during the 1790s.

The lurid, melodramatic elements in Ashton's play would also
have had broad popular appeal. Jemina, the daughter of the Irish
Colonel Talbot, is in love with Sir Charles Godfrey, a young English
gentleman of fortune whose sister is married to a colonel on the
English side and who has volunteered to serve on the Irish side after
falling in love with Jemina at first sight. In a song at the beginning of
the second act, Sir Charles suggests to Jemina that if he should die in
battle, she should take her own life. In the final act, after Sir Charles
has died in her arms, Jemina stabs herself with his sword and dies. The
United Irishmen would use lurid melodrama frequently in their verse
in the months before the 1798 uprising. Jemina was a prototype of the
tragic maidens who became a stock motif in many United Irish songs.

William Carleton's account of the popularity of *Ireland Preserved*
and *The Battle of Aughrim* deserves to be quoted in full for the insight

it provides into late eighteenth-century literary taste, especially the appeal that historical and political subjects could have when presented in literary modes that were popular and entertaining:

> A usual amusement at the time was to reproduce the "Battle of Aughrim," in some spacious barn, with a winnowing cloth for a curtain. This play, bound up with the "Siege of Londonderry," was one of the reading-books in the hedge schools of that day, and circulated largely among people of all religions; it had, indeed, an extraordinary influence among the lower classes. "The Battle of Aughrim," however, because it was written in heroic verse, became so popular that it was rehearsed at almost every Irish hearth, both catholic and protestant, in the north. The spirit it evoked was irresistible. The whole country became dramatic. To repeat it at the fireside in winter nights was nothing: the Orangemen should act it, and show the whole world how the field of Aughrim was so gloriously won. The consequence was that frequent rehearsals took place. The largest and most spacious barns and kilns were fitted up, the night of representation given out, and crowds, even to suffocation, as they say, assembled to witness the celebrated "Battle of Aughrim."
>
> At first, it was true, the Orangemen had it all to themselves. This, however, could not last. The catholics felt that they were as capable of patronising the drama as the victors of Aughrim. A strong historic spirit awoke among them. They requested of the Orangemen to be allowed the favour of representing the catholic warriors of the disastrous field, and, somewhat to their surprise, the request was immediately granted. The Orangemen felt that there was something awkward and not unlike political apostasy in acting the part of catholics in the play, under any circumstances, no matter how dramatic. (Quoted in Adams 1987, 71)

The dramatic mode was clearly highly popular in Ulster. Not surprisingly, many United Irish prose satires, such as James Porter's *Billy Bluff and the Squire* (1796) and William Sampson's *Trial of Hurdy Gurdy* (1794), would be written in dialogue form as minidramas. The *Harp of Erin*, the short-lived United Irish newspaper in Cork in the spring of 1798, even published an original drama satirizing the current crisis.

THE DUBLIN LITERARY SCENE IN THE 1790S

Although Ulster, especially Belfast, had been the origin of most
United Irish poetry and prose satire from 1792 through 1797, Dublin
became the center of United Irish literary activity from the founding
of the *Press* there in 1797 until the publication of the fourth and final
Paddy's Resource songbook sometime in 1803. Therefore, a brief survey of the Dublin literary scene in the 1790s is in order.

Two Dublin journals published in the 1790s provide valuable insight into that literary milieu and demonstrate how rich and eclectic
it was. The *Masonic, or Sentimental Magazine* was published from July
1792 through June 1795 and the *Anthologia Hibernica* was published
from January 1793 through December 1794. They were sold at book-
sellers in Dublin and in Belfast, where the *Northern Star* carried ads
for both.

The *Masonic, or Sentimental Magazine* included among its subscribers Napper Tandy and Thomas Moore, who was active in United
Irish circles at the time. It printed a variety of literary items and also
carried political news. It published a series of articles reporting the
trial of William Drennan and Archibald Hamilton Rowan for writing
and publishing seditious literature, and another article on the controversy surrounding the recall of Fitzwilliam as Lord Lieutenant in 1795,
an event that dashed United Irish hopes for political reform. On the
literary side, the magazine reprinted Thomas Gray's "Bard" in its first
volume, and thus set the tone for much of what followed. Typical
items included a reprinting of Gray's "Elegy Written in a Country
Churchyard"; a play entitled *The Rights of Man: A Farce*; original
poems on "Liberty"; a poem entitled "Translation of the Celebrated
Irish Song of the Coolun"; a poem eulogizing an ancient Irish king;
several poems idealizing the Irish peasantry; and a poem entitled "The
Triumph of Erin" in which the figure of a bard was central.

The *Anthologia Hibernica* contained an even wider range of materials because it included science as one of its subjects. Its full title,
*Anthologia Hibernica: A Monthly Collection of Science, Belles-Lettres,
and History*, paralleled the three avowed interests of the Royal Irish
Academy. Not surprisingly, three dozen members of the Royal Irish
Academy, which helped to subsidize the journal's publication, subscribed. Other subscribers included Francis Rawdon and his mother

the Countess of Moira, Joseph Cooper Walker, Thomas Moore, Sydney Owenson (later Lady Morgan), Charles O'Conor, and Sylvester O'Halloran. Subscribers among the United Irishmen were Wolfe Tone, Napper Tandy, William James MacNeven, Oliver Bond, Henry Sheares, and Robert Caldwell, who was a founder of the *Northern Star* (*Anthologia Hibernica* 3:v–xii).

Like the *Masonic, or Sentimental Magazine*, the *Anthologia Hibernica* represented a combination of English and Irish literary traditions. An engraving of "Grana Uile" being introduced to Queen Elizabeth at the beginning of the second volume had undeniably symbolic overtones. Although much of its contents had political significance, the *Anthologia Hibernica* was less avowedly political than The *Masonic, or Sentimental Magazine*. At the outset in January 1793, the *Anthologia Hibernia* announced that it would reflect no religious or political disputes, that it was the organ of no sect or party (3:iv). Its emphasis remained historical, not political; however, many of the "historical" articles it published about early Irish culture had an inevitable political subtext.

The *Anthologia Hibernica* printed a number of political, if not partisan, articles. For example, it frequently reported "Foreign News" from France, as in an article entitled "The Trial of the Late French Queen" (2:379)." It also reprinted the new French calendar and translations of French poems on political subjects such as "The Triumph of Republicanism" (2:126). The journal's own politics were contradictory enough to be rather neutral. Although the inclusion of the French materials and a poem on the evils of Irish absentee landlordism suggested a liberal, if not radical, political stance, a short review of a book entitled *Speculations on the State of Ireland shewing the fatal Causes of her Misery, the evil Influences under which she languishes* in December 1793 read in part as follows: "The publication seems well adapted to the intellects of that class called 'defenders,' whose object and schemes are as inexplicable as this rhapsody. . . . To represent our happy life as languishing in woe and misery, is as false as the suggestion is dangerous and inflammatory" (2:441). The Defenders, of course, were the Catholic peasant movement in Ulster that favored Catholic emancipation and became increasingly revolutionary in the course of the 1790s.

In general, however, the political views of the *Anthologia Hibernica* can best be described as patriotic. For example, the opening sentence of the lead essay for the November 1793 issue, entitled "An Account of Dungannon, with a beautiful and correct View of the Meeting-House in that celebrated Place," clearly celebrated the political principles of the famous Volunteer Convention that had been held in that meetinghouse: "While domestic legislation, freedom of commerce, and the emancipation of a great body of the people from penal laws and political incapacities, are objects dear to Irishmen, the name of Dungannon will be remembered and respected" (2:321). By 1793, those same Volunteer principles had become central to the platform of the United Irishmen.

Not everything in the *Anthologia Hibernica* was of an Irish nature. The contents also included such things as a continuing section featuring mathematical problems and solutions; an "Ode to a Poppy"; translations of Horace and Virgil; a "Paraphrase of Anacreon's Fifth Ode" and "Pastoral Ode" by Thomas Moore; and a "Hymn to Narayena," the Hindu spirit of God. Other items were Celtic, but not Irish. The issue for July 1793 contained Robert Burns's "Tam O'Shanter." A lengthy poem serialized in several issues, entitled "Songs of the Aboriginal Bards of Britain," by George Richards, Fellow of Oriel College, Oxford, had Mason's ancient Briton, the Celtic Caractacus, for its hero. In a note before the poem, Richards suggested that the poem "may bring to the reader's recollection the sublime Bard of Gray," which it certainly did (2:301). Likewise, a lengthy poem entitled "Stone-henge" depicted the druids and "raptur'd bards" of the Celtic Britons holding rituals there (3:220–23).

The majority of articles, however, clearly focused on Irish subjects. Examples include "Remarks on the Irish Language" (January 1793); "The Antient Arms of Ireland," by Sylvester O'Halloran (March 1793); "Ancient Nobility of Ireland" (January 1793); "History of the Rise and Progress of Architecture in Ireland" (July 1793); "Essay on the Ancient Name of Ireland" (January 1793); a "Sketch of the History of the County of Antrim" from the fifth through the fourteenth century that cited both Catholic and Protestant historians (April 1794); and "Biographical Notices" of Charles Vallancey (October 1793), Henry Brooke, and Charlotte Brooke, who was praised as the translator of "ancient and modern Irish bards" (March 1794). The *Anthologia Hibernica* also contained numerous poems in imitation of Macpherson's purported Ossianic translations.

Both ancient and modern Irish bards were a central subject in the pages of the *Anthologia Hibernica*, the contents of which demonstrated how Irish antiquities had become more a matter of literary than historical interest. For example, an essay entitled "Observations on the Romantic History of Ireland," written in October 1793 by Edward Ledwich, an outspoken critic of Vallancey's theory about the Phoenician origins of the Irish, declared the tales surviving from ancient times to be romantic fables rather than history (2:249). In many ways, criticism such as Ledwich's explains why Irish antiquarianism became more and more literary in its emphasis. What was not history was nevertheless wonderful literature.

Moreover, the fascination with early Ireland was becoming increasingly contemporary as well as literary. Joseph Cooper Walker's "Historical Essay on the Irish Stage" (December 1794) surveyed Irish drama from bardic times through contemporary folk plays. A poem entitled "The Irish Peasant" (November 1793) portrayed the survival of ancient Irish musical traditions in the person of a "pleas'd and contented" peasant: "A pair of jew's-harps skillfully he plays, / That vibrate Coolun's am'rous, plaintive lays" (2:382).

Relatively recent Irish songs like "The Coolun" interested *Anthologia Hibernica* readers. After the editors requested in December 1793 that someone "favour us with 'Grainne Weal' in Irish and English" because "it would gratify the wishes of many," an English version appeared in October 1794 entitled "Granuweal: An Old Song." The comic, patriotic mode of the song was in the convivial tradition of Volunteer songs. Here are the first three of its eight stanzas:

> A courtier call'd Dorset, from Parkgate did sail,
> In his majesty's Yacht, for to court Granuweal;
> With great entertainment he thought to prevail,
> And rifle the charms of Granuweal.

> CHORUS:
> Sing Budderoo, Didderoo, Granuweal,
> The Fox in the Trap we have caught by the tail,
> Come fill up your bowls and to drink never fail,
> Sing success to the sons of brave Granuweal.

> Says the courtier to Granu, if you will be true,
> I will bring you to London, and do for you too;

Where you shall have pleasure that never will fail,
I'll laurel your Shamrock, sweet Granuweal.

CHORUS

Says Granu to Dorset, if that I would do,
Bring my fortune to London, my children would rue;
We would be like Highlanders eating of keal,
And cursing the union, says Granuweal.

(4:300)

"Granuweal" would be a common motif in United Irish songs.

The *Anthologia Hibernica* also published songs in Irish with English translations. The editors used one such poem, published in December 1793 and entitled in English "Vision of McBrady," to demonstrate stylistic features of poetry in Irish. The poem, which recounted
an Irish peasant's mock-heroic travels throughout Ireland, was by
"Owen McIntire" who, according to the editors, was an "itinerant
poet, piper, and antiquarian" who knew little English (2:456). The
contributor of the original poem and the translation claimed that the
translation imitated the style as well as the content of the original:
"The structure of the verse is the same as in the original; the six last
lines are in imitation of a species of composition, call'd by our poets,
'Abhran,' the verses chiming or corresponding in the middle, as well
as rhiming at the end, as is the case with several kinds of Irish poetry,
and may serve to give the English reader an idea of the nature and
structure of Irish verse" (2:456).

Similarly, the Irish lyrics, the music, a literal prose translation,
and a version in English verse of a "celebrated old Irish fragment"
entitled in English "The Dove" were published in May 1793. The
poem was the "musings of an old Irish bard in Clare in the last
century" as he passed the "ruin of Leiminagh" (1:364–65), or Leamaneh,
the ruined residence of the famous Maire Rua whose history and
legendary exploits survive in Irish oral tradition today, as do the ruins
of her house (MacNeill 1990).

Other contributions to the *Anthologia Hibernica* demonstrated a
multitude of new interpretations for Irish materials. One contributor
who called himself "The Sgeald" sent in two prose tales as "a speci-
men of the composition of the ancient Irish sgealds or bards," suppos-

edly by one of his ancestors who had been "chief bard of the O'Nials in the fourteenth century." His version of the supposed bardic tale began: "Gentle swan-bosomed nymphs, with blue grey eyes of Ireland, listen and swell the soft sound with your notes, while I gently awake the living strings." He then told of how "Breasgeall, high bosomed maid of Tara" mistakenly loved a "death-giving" Viking invader and brought ruin on herself and her family when "Erin's arms" defeated her lover's forces. He concluded his tale with several paragraphs pointing out "the danger and impropriety of precipitate and instant love" and quoting Shakespeare's *Romeo and Juliet* (3:197–99).

Fortunately, such a moralistic use of bardic antiquities never developed very far, although the political implications of the bard and his lore would have a long future indeed in Irish literary nationalism. It is important to note, however, that at the outset the political use of the bard and the song tradition he supposedly founded was not parochial, sectarian, or revolutionary. The goal of the original patriotic and political use of the images fostered by Irish antiquarianism, even in United Irish verse, was not separation from England, but rather the recognition of Ireland's cultural identity and political rights.

The literature published in the *Anthologia Hibernica* represented an integration, however awkward, of English and Irish literary and cultural traditions such as had been symbolized in the *Anthologia Hibernica* engraving of "Grana Uile" being presented to Queen Elizabeth. United Irish literary works also integrated the various literary and cultural traditions within Ireland, providing a model for social, political, and religious unity within the island.

THE SYNTHESIZERS: JOSEPH COOPER WALKER AND CHARLOTTE BROOKE

The works of Joseph Cooper Walker (1761–1810) and Charlotte Brooke (1740–1793) brought together many of the literary, the scholarly, the popular, the Celtic, the antiquarian, the political, and the musical dimensions of eighteenth-century Irish culture discussed thus far. Walker's *Historical Memoirs of the Irish Bards* (1786) and Brooke's *Reliques of Irish Poetry* (1789) prefigured the synthesis of literary modes, cultural theories, and musical styles that would occur in the literary productions of the United Irishmen. Both works were in the library of the Belfast Society for Promoting Knowledge and were known to the United Irishmen, as they were to most educated persons in Ireland at the end of the eighteenth century.

In addition to synthesizing many eighteenth-century cultural, literary, and musical developments in their works, Walker and Brooke suggested a new dimension—a literary one—for antiquarian subjects and traditional Irish music. In that regard, both Walker and Brooke were influenced by Charles Henry Wilson's *Poems, Translated from the Irish Language into the English*, a collection of Irish poems published in London in 1782 that contained six translations. According to Seamus O Casaide, Wilson also published another collection of translations from the Irish sometime between 1780 and 1790, entitled *Select Irish Poems, Translated into English*, that included eighteen translations (O Casaide 1920, 59–70). The only translation common to both works, and identical in both, was a text and English translation (not Swift's, and evidently Wilson's own) for Carolan's "Plearaca na Ruarcach." Wilson's 1782 collection contained a dedication in English verse to Lord Francis Rawdon. The second poem in Wilson's other collection, an original poem rather than a translation from the Irish, was a poetical address entitled "To Colonel Vallancey," which also paid tribute to Francis Rawdon for his interest in the Irish language. In "To Colonel Vallancey" Wilson declared that "the historian's prose . . . shall aid the verse," and that "the heav'nly numbers" would be inspired by the historian's "generous labours" (Leerssen 1986, 421–22). Those lines proved prophetic, for Walker and Brooke, both inspired by Wilson's translations, soon demonstrated the literary significance of Irish antiquarianism.

The publication of Wilson's translations evidently attracted little attention. Neither the *National Union Catalogue* nor the *British Museum Catalogue* lists his collections. However, his translations were known to Walker and Brooke, both of whom refer to Wilson in their own books, and in the nineteenth century to Walter Scott, James Hardiman, and Nicholas O'Kearney. According to D. J. O'Donoghue, Wilson was the son of a County Cavan clergyman, studied at Trinity College Dublin, and became a parliamentary reporter in London (O'Donoghue 1892, 261–62). He was the anonymous author of *Brookiana* (1804), a collection of anecdotes about Henry Brooke's life and opinions, which suggests that he knew Henry and his daughter

Charlotte, who were also from County Cavan. In any event, Wilson's translations provided an important model for Charlotte Brooke and for her mentor, Walker.

Even an edited version of the title of Joseph Cooper Walker's influential work suggests its remarkable diversity and richness: *Historical Memoirs of the Irish Bards; interspersed with anecdotes of, and occasional observations on the Music of Ireland; also an historical and descriptive account of the Musical Instruments of ancient Ireland, with an appendix containing . . . the ancient Musical Memoirs of Cormac Common; the Life of Turlough O'Carolan; An Essay on the Origin of Romantic Fabling in Ireland; and Select Irish Melodies.* Needless to say, the extensive "appendix" is almost as long as the body of the work. Walker focused on both poetry and music, which according to the popular eighteenth-century view had been the two traditional pursuits of the Irish bards. He presented a historical outline of the progress of Irish poetry and music from the earliest times to the eighteenth century, and included translations of several Irish poems.

Walker was a wealthy Protestant and member of the Royal Irish Academy who spent his life pursuing various scholarly interests, including Italian art and Irish antiquities. His interest in poetry and in eighteenth-century vernacular survivals of the ancient bardic tradition suggested important new contemporary and literary dimensions for what had previously been antiquarian and scholarly pursuits. Although subjects from early Irish history and tunes from Irish tradition had been incorporated into eighteenth-century plays, previously there had been no interest in the Irish poetry that had originally celebrated those subjects or accompanied those tunes.

The authorities Walker cited covered the entire range of Irish and Anglo-Irish scholarship on Irish antiquities. He included excerpts from his correspondence with Charles O'Conor, Charles Vallancey, and Sylvester O'Halloran. He cited their works and those of Geoffrey Keating, Roderick O'Flaherty, Sir James Ware, Fernando Warner, and others. Walker even quoted literary works such as Mason's drama *Caractacus* and Macpherson's Ossianic translations. Walker carried on an extensive correspondence about Irish antiquities with Thomas Percy after Percy became Bishop of Dromore in 1782 (Nichols 1817–1858, 7:681–758). Percy's *Reliques of Ancient English Poetry*, which had emphasized the literary value of traditional poetry and contemporary survivals of ancient bardic traditions, had clearly influenced Walker.

Walker's appreciation of what he considered to be the contemporary survivals of the ancient Irish bardic tradition is apparent in his inclusion of an account of Cormac Common, a blind eighteenth-century poet from Mayo, and the Irish text and translation of one of Common's elegies, as well as a lengthy biographical notice of Carolan, together with translations of several of Carolan's songs. The relatively recent date of the Irish poems by Common and Carolan suggested a living literary tradition in Irish. The translations also offered a new subject matter and a potential new mode for poetry in English. A similar conjunction of ancient and modern is apparent in Walker's section entitled "Select Irish Melodies," in which he brought the bardic dimensions of this subject into the eighteenth century by including several tunes still current in Irish tradition. In that section Walker also printed Arthur Dawson's famous early eighteenth-century English lyrics for Carolan's "Bumper Squire Jones," and thus underscored the contemporary literary potential of the Irish song tradition.

Charlotte Brooke had provided Walker with the majority of his translations in *Historical Memoirs*. The translations in her own collection *Reliques of Irish Poetry* offered continued proof of the poetic possibilities that Irish poetry offered to English verse. Walker's note about Brooke and her translations in his collection praised her contact with the living tradition of Irish poetry on her father's estate, where she had heard poems recited in Irish in the fields and had seen manuscript versions as well. According to Walker, when his anonymous female translator had read Macpherson's Ossianic translations she recognized, beneath all the ornamentation, indigenous Irish materials already familiar to her. After he had persuaded her to contribute some of her translations to his work, Walker urged her to publish her own collection. In her preface to *Reliques* she thanked Walker for "every assistance which zeal, judgment, and extensive knowledge, could give" (Charlotte Brooke 1789, ix). She also acknowledged the assistance of her godfather, Sylvester O'Halloran.

But Charlotte Brooke owed her original inspiration to her father, Henry Brooke. Aaron Seymour's 1816 "Memoir of Charlotte Brooke's Life and Writings" aptly described Henry Brooke as embodying "patriotism to excess" (Symour 1970, xii). Brooke had always intended to learn Irish, but he never did. Likewise, although he had recognized the literary potential of the antiquarian materials of his friends O'Conor and O'Halloran, he never completed any of his proposed literary reworkings of those materials. According to Charles Henry Wilson in *Brookiana*, Henry Brooke studied the translation of Irish poems furnished him by a friend (Wilson 1804, 1:86–87). In 1743, he published the prospectus for a collection of "Ogygian Tales; or, a Curious Collection of Irish Fables, Allegories, and Histories"; however, the tales were never written (Snyder 1965, 114–15). Yet his interest did not wane. In addition to the poetic epilogue to Howard's *Siege of Tamor* in 1773, Brooke wrote a long fragmentary poem about an ancient Ulster hero, entitled "Conrade," that showed the influence of Macpherson.

Even Henry Brooke's proposed history of Ireland, for which he published a prospectus in 1744 but which he never completed, was to have had a decided literary focus. Although Charles Henry Wilson does not give details about Brooke's projected history of Ireland, the Dublin journal *Anthologia Hibernica* published a copy of Brooke's prospectus in September 1793. The title was to have been *The History of Ireland from the earliest Times; wherein are set forth the ancient and extraordinary Customs, Manners, Religion, Polities, Conquests and Revolutions of that once hospitable, polite, and martial Nation; interspersed and illustrated with traditionary Digressions, and the private and affecting Histories of the most celebrated of the Natives* (Henry Brooke 1793, 2:188–91).

Henry Brooke emphasized that the bards had been poets even more than historians and that their poetry inspired patriotic youth to arms. Such a view of poetry would become more and more appealing as the century progressed. Brooke claimed that the literary creations of the bards, even when they had no historical basis in fact, would be included in his history because of their literary merit. At the same time, he would omit "many things, which, though true in fact, are tedious" (Henry Brooke 1793, 191). His aim was clearly literary appeal rather than historical accuracy. Repeatedly referring to the ancient Irish as the ancestors of his potential subscribers, who would have been largely Anglo-Irish, Brooke concluded the prospectus as follows: "I shall shew to the most prejudiced and incredulous, that your ancestors were deep in learning, pious in their religion, wise in their institutions, just in their laws, and continued, for many ages, the most generous and valiant people that lived upon the face of the earth" (1793, 191).

Fortunately, Charlotte Brooke shared her father's enthusiasm for the literary possibilities of Irish antiquarian materials, but not his habit of abandoning proposed projects. She learned Irish as a young girl and began translating Irish poetry, much of which had originated in the seventeenth century and was still current in Irish tradition. In 1789, she published *Reliques of Irish Poetry: Consisting of Heroic Poems, Odes, Elegies, and Songs, Translated into English Verse: with Notes Explanatory and Historical; and the Originals in Irish Character; to which is subjoined an Irish Tale*. The collection demonstrated that Irish poetry was a living as well as an ancient tradition that offered hitherto unexplored riches to English verse. Charlotte Brooke incorporated ancient and contemporary traditions, for she included both translations of poems about ancient heroes and eighteenth-century songs. She brought together elements of English literature, Celticism and antiquarianism, traditional music and popular culture, all of which were infused with a patriotic ardor that had distinct political overtones in 1789.

The title page included an epigraph in Irish script, the translation of which would be: "O, Ossian we are charmed by your stories." The tone, atmosphere, and diction of Brooke's translations exhibited the influence of Macpherson's supposed translations. However, her inclusion of the original Irish poems and songs, none of which was earlier than the sixteenth century, at the end of her collection, was an obvious refutation of Macpherson, who had not supported his claim for the Scottish origin of his Ossianic materials by including any original texts. Unlike Walker, Brooke never cited Macpherson in her text. In her preface she did praise O'Conor, O'Halloran, and Vallancey, and she cited them as authorities in the introduction and notes for each of her four main sections: "Heroic Poems," "Odes," "Elegies," and "Songs" (Charlotte Brooke 1789, iii).

Robert Welch's evaluation of Charlotte Brooke's translations in *A History of Verse Translations from the Irish, 1789–1897* cites their vapid rhetoric, stiffness, and monotony, as well as their tendency to inflated paraphrase, ornament, and poetic clichés. He attributes those traits to the view of Irish poetry that Brooke had inherited from what Welch called "the haze of late eighteenth-century Celticism, derived from Gray, Mason, and MacPherson." Despite these flaws, Welch concludes, "the importance of the *Reliques* in the development of Anglo-Irish literature can hardly be over-estimated" (1988, 38–43).

Brooke's *Reliques* attracted widespread interest and favorable reviews in Ireland and England. Her materials had both literary and political appeal. The Countess of Moira was among those she thanked for materials to translate (1789, ix). The subscribers to her *Reliques* included several future United Irishmen: John Philpot Curran, Edward Hudson, William James MacNeven, and Whitley Stokes, as well as Samuel Whyte, the poet and influential teacher of Thomas Moore and others, and John Corry, who contributed verse to the *Northern Star* in 1796 (Charlotte Brooke 1789, xi-xxiii).

Brooke's work contained many references to "our Irish bards," and thus exemplified the deepening Anglo-Irish identification with Irish culture. Brooke even declared that the Gaelic blood "from our heroic ancestors" flowing through Anglo-Irish veins was "ennobling" (1789, viii). According to Brooke, "the productions of our Irish Bards exhibit a glow of cultivated genius,—a spirit of elevated heroism,—sentiments of pure honor,—instances of disinterested patriotism,—and manners of a degree of refinement, totally astonishing, at a period when the rest of Europe was nearly sunk in barbarism" (1789, vii). She emphasized the contemporary dimensions of the ancient bardic tradition by using "extant" poetical remains as the basis of many of her translations. Many of her sources were manuscripts, but she included oral sources as well.

Charlotte Brooke's "Heroic Poems" and "Odes" were largely translations of Fenian and Red Branch tales, including some dialogues between Oisin and St. Patrick and the legendary "Cucullen's" slaying of his son. The final "ode," however, was a translation of a sixteenth-century poem written by a Mr. Fitzgerald about his voyage to Spain. Several of her "Elegies" had been either recently collected from oral informants or written down in manuscripts only a few decades earlier. Two of her "Songs" were by Carolan; another was by Patrick Linden, an early eighteenth-century Irish poet in County Armagh. The allusion in her final song to the ancient legends of Deirdre and Blanaide demonstrated how eighteenth-century Irish songs were a link to very ancient traditions indeed.

The last stanza of her final song translation, "The Maid of the Valley," exemplifies Brooke's concept of the bard:

My muse her harp shall at thy bidding bring,
And roll th' heroic tide of verse along;
And Finian Chiefs, and arms shall wake the string,
And Love and War divide the lofty song!
(1789, 261)

The bard's twofold function included singing of wars and heroes and thus gave a political context to his poetry. The following passage from Walker's *Historical Memoirs*, which Brooke quoted in her "Thoughts on Irish Song," demonstrates the political subtext that lurked in their conception of bards and their poetry, both ancient and modern:

> We see that music maintained its ground in this country, even after the invasion of the English but its style suffered a change; for the sprightly Phrygian gave place to the grave Doric, or soft Lydian measure. Such was the nice sensibility of the Bards, such was their tender affection for their country, that the subjection to which the kingdom was reduced, affected them with heaviest sadness. Sinking beneath this weight of sympathetic sorrow, they became prey to melancholy: hence the plaintive sadness of their music
>
> (1789, 234).

Brooke also quoted Walker's argument that when "the sword of oppression" banished the bards and their patrons to "gloomy forests," the new setting "considerably increased their melancholy" (234).

The political dimensions of the ancient bard's or modern Irish poet's songs are central to Charlotte Brooke's original poem, "Maon: An Irish Tale," which concludes the collection. Rather than a specific earlier Irish poem, this time her source was "the ancient history of Ireland" as "related by Keating, O'Halloran, Warner, etc." (323). Brooke's poetic introduction to "Maon" declared that she had been inspired by the "Muse of ancient days," the ancient Irish bards:

Who train'd of old, our sires to fame,
And led them to the field;
Taught them to glow with Freedom's flame,
And Freedom's arms to wield.
With the wild War-Song fir'd the soul,
And sped the daring blow!—

> Or, bow'd to Pity's soft controul,
>   Wept o'er a dying foe.
>   (325)

While Gray's "Bard" had been Welsh, Mason's Caractacus an ancient Briton, and Macpherson's Ossian had supposedly been Scottish, Brooke's bard was Irish and named "Craftine." He appeared in her mind's eye and urged her to write a poem in English about Maon. His exhortation to her included the following lines:

> Long, her neglected harp unstrung,
>   With glooms encircl'd round;
> Long o'er its silent form she hung
>   Nor gave her soul to sound.
> Rous'd from her trance, again to reign,
>   And re-assert her fame,
> She comes, and deigns thy humble strain
>   The herald of her claim.
>   (328)

Brooke's references to bards calling warriors to fight for freedom, to harps unstrung, to Ireland rousing from her trance, all echoed images popularized earlier by Volunteer verse, and prefigured the poetry of the United Irishmen and of their literary heir, Thomas Moore.

Charlotte Brooke died in Dublin in 1793. During the early 1790s she was a close friend of Jane Hamilton, the mother of United Irishman Archibald Hamilton Rowan, and of the Countess of Moira (Seymour 1816, lxix, cxxiii). Two years after her death, the United Irishmen incorporated parts of her *Reliques* into their Gaelic magazine entitled *Bolg an tSolair*. Given her frequent presence in Dublin in the early 1790s, it is probable that some of the United Irishmen who also visited Moira House had met her there or elsewhere. They certainly knew her work, in which she provided an important model for their own synthesis of numerous Irish cultural and literary traditions.

• 4 •

United Irish Newspapers

Newspapers, songbooks, and prose satires were central to the United Irish movement. When the United Irishmen wrote verse to inspire and then to celebrate the political and eventually the rebellious deeds of their movement, the popular eighteenth-century image of the bard provided a model. The United Irishmen thus sought to reconstruct the symbolic relationship between literature and politics that supposedly had once existed in early Ireland: song and story could both inspire and celebrate patriots and their deeds. But because United Irish poems and satires integrated a variety of literary and cultural traditions, theirs was not a parochial literary nationalism. The United Irishmen envisioned and created a literary prototype for social, political, and religious unity in Ireland.

Within three months of the United Irish Society's founding, the United Irishmen in Belfast established the *Northern Star* newspaper to propagate the society's message. According to the anonymous *Sketch of the Life of Samuel Neilson*, published in 1804, forty-two hundred copies of each issue of the paper were regularly sold (8). Newspapers were frequently read aloud to groups of people, so the *Northern Star* achieved a significant circulation. The editor and principal proprietor of the *Northern Star* was Samuel Neilson, a Belfast merchant and the son of a Presbyterian minister.[1] The other original shareholders were all Belfast Presbyterians, mostly merchants, some of whom had second thoughts about their earlier radicalism and withdrew their support within a few years. Neilson, however, remained a central force in both the political and literary activities of the United Irish Society.

The editorial address "To the People" on the first page of the *Northern Star*'s first issue (2 January 1792) argued that "Parliamentary reform" and the "union of all Irishmen" of all religious persuasions were essential to "the prosperity of Ireland." That somewhat practical mercantile emphasis on economic and social well-being remained a central concern of the Northern Star, which was filled with business news, advertisements, obituaries, and social news. Songs and poems, the appeal of which went beyond the rational arguments about reform and politics in editorials and essays elsewhere in the paper, were included in every issue. The significant amount of space devoted to everyday human and business concerns and to literary works qualifies the stereotype of the United Irishmen as merely radical political theorists and violent rebels.

The first page of every issue of the Northern Star depicted the title surrounded by a device representing two women in classical costume, one holding a sword and one a harp, supporting between them a shield bearing a sun with a harp at its center. At first the shield was surmounted by a crown, but the crown was eventually replaced by a star. Such iconography was appropriate for a newspaper that considered one of its functions to be inspiring patriotic deeds through the power of music and song so that the light of liberty would shine in Ireland and reduce the power of the English crown.

The songs and poems that appeared regularly in the Northern Star were from a variety of sources and represented a wide range of subjects and literary styles, from formal odes in stilted language to songs in colloquial dialect. Although most Northern Star poetry was political, other poems, such as "Verses on Presenting a Withered Rose to a Lady" (28 January 1792) and "Hymn to Health, Imitated from the Greeks" (1 February 1792), had no political message whatsoever. The anonymous writers who contributed poems and songs were ministers, weavers, solicitors, and former soldiers, thus representing the union of all social classes that was fundamental to the United Irishmen's political creed. The tunes to which the songs were published were of diverse musical origin: Irish, Scots-Irish, English, and even American and French. Despite the fact that the Northern Star covered a broad range of topics, an increasingly distinctive "Irish" note was apparent.

News and verse about slavery frequently appeared in the Northern Star, because the antislavery movement had clear relevance to the Irish situation. The 1780s and 1790s produced a flood of poems, dramas, and narratives about slaves as the African joined the American

Indian as an embodiment of the "noble savage." Antislavery polemicists whose works were popular in eighteenth-century Ireland included Robert Burns, Thomas Paine, and John Wesley (McCullough 1962, 75). Today, William Blake's "Little Black Boy" from his *Songs of Innocence* (1789) is probably the best known of such works.

The first issue of the *Northern Star* contained a seven-stanza poem, with no author or tune indicated, entitled "The Negroe's Complaint." The piece was later reprinted, minus two stanzas, in *Paddy's Resource* in 1795 and 1803 to the tune "How Imperfect is Expression." Although R. R. Madden attributed it to Thomas Russell (Madden 1860, 2:159), the poem was by the English poet William Cowper, one of the most important of the antislavery poets. Written in 1788, the poem was widely published in periodicals and broadsides between 1789 and 1791 to the tune "Hosier's Ghost," which had appeared in Percy's *Reliques of Ancient English Poetry*. The slave's plea, "Deem our nation brutes no longer," and his rebuke to his masters echoed similar rhetoric in United Irish verse and prose:

> Slaves of gold, whose sordid dealings
> Tarnish all your boasted pow'rs,
> Prove that you have human feelings,
> Ere you proudly question ours!
> (*Northern Star*, 2 January 1792)

On 14 January 1792, the *Northern Star* published a "Song" entitled "The Dying Negro," to the tune "The Son of Alenomack," that Madden also mistakenly attributed to Thomas Russell, though Russell was probably responsible for its inclusion in the *Northern Star*. The song was later reprinted in the 1795 *Paddy's Resource* to the Scottish tune "Lochaber." The song's actual origin suggests the larger context of English and American radical poetry in which United Irish verse must be viewed. Although the English poet Thomas Day wrote a celebrated poem of this title in 1773, the poem printed in the *Northern Star* was by Dr. Frank Sayers, an English physician. Sayers's song, entitled "The Dying African," was to the tune "Son of Alknomoack." The tune's title suggests Sayers's debt to a poem entitled "Death Song of a Cherokee Indian," which used the refrain "For the son of Alkomock can never complain." That song has been credited both to the American poet Philip Freneau (Freneau 1963, 2:313–14) and to the English poet Mrs. Anne Hunter. The song also appeared in Royall Tyler's *Contrast*, first performed in 1787 and first printed in 1790 (Fairchild 1961, 461–67).

Madden's ascription of these two slave poems to Russell is further evidence of his untrustworthiness as an editor, of the eclectic literary tastes of the United Irishmen, and of how elite and popular literary traditions intermingled in the eighteenth century. In his journal for 5 November 1794, Russell referred to having transcribed and "altered" a poem that had been published in London in the *Gentleman's Magazine* in August 1793 as "The African's Complaint on Board a Slave Ship," by "J. C.," with a nine-line Latin epigraph (Woods 1991, 174). The text of a song entitled "The Negro's Lament," one of four songs in a songbook published in Belfast in 1793 that Russell had in his possession when he was arrested in 1796 (SPOI 620/201), is almost identical to the poem in the *Gentleman's Magazine*. The Belfast version is anonymous, however, and the Latin epigraph has been deleted. Both 1793 texts were in dialect, as their last stanza indicates:

> De bad traders stole and sold me,
> Den was put in iron band,
> When I'm ded, dey cannot hold me
> Soon I'll be in Black-men land.
> (SPOI 620/201)

Russell's alteration of "The Negroe's Complaint" thus was not a revision of one of his own poems, as Madden presumed, but of one of these 1793 texts, probably that in the Belfast songbook. Russell's revision consisted of removing the dialect, as can be seen in his version of the last stanza:

> The cruel traders stole and sold me;
> Confin'd me with this iron band:
> When I'm dead, they cannot hold me;
> Soon I'll flee to black man's land.
> (Madden 1860, 2:162–63)

Much of the formal political verse published in the *Northern Star* had a prophetic, almost religious tone, which was not surprising since many regular contributors were Presbyterian ministers such as Sinclare Kelburn, James Porter, and William Steel Dickson. According to Belfast tradition, Kelburn once delivered a sermon dressed in his full Volunteer regalia, including his sword. A prophetic strain was apparent as early as the fourth issue of the *Northern Star*, which included a poem by "Pindaricus" entitled "Ode for the New Year, 1792" in which "The Muse for once shall all her powers to prophecy expand" (11 January 1792). This ode, in tune with both the international content of the news published in the paper and the international dimensions of the United Irishmen's political principles, envisions a millennial violence in which "millions rise thro' many a realm," including Poland and Africa, "against the Pride of high-stall'd Priests, / Who, Divis like, maintain'd their feasts, / and left the Poor forlorn!" With an ambiguity about violence that was to become a hallmark of Irish nationalism, the poet invokes the "Prince of Peace" to establish a peace to follow the violence prophesied by the Muse:

> This flame of Freedom must precede
> Thy promised reign of grace:
> The age Millennial is decreed,
> But War's alarm must cease.

A frequent contributor of political verse in such a serious and prophetic vein was named "Rev. James Glass, A.M.," whose poem" The Irish Bard" was discussed in chapter 1. The *Northern Star* poems by "Rev. James Glass," which evidence suggests may have been a pseudonym for James Porter, deserve special attention because they span the paper's entire existence and were the first United Irish poems to use what became common motifs in United Irish verse. The first poem by "Glass" to appear in the *Northern Star* was "Address to Mr. Paine, Author of the Rights of Man" (15 February 1792). The poem was an address by a "Bard" who, inspired by Paine, would tune "Ierne's harp" and sing "with bolder notes, with patriotic joy" rather than the "plaintive lays" in which she previously had "mourn'd her dearest rights, her freedom lost." The self-proclaimed bard declared that "The light of freedom" would "o'er the wretched Slave its Glory shed" as "Kings, whose thrones are stain'd with guiltless gore" would be replaced by the people's "supreme command." Given the poem's revolutionary message, it is not surprising that the poet used a pseudonym.

Several weeks later another poem by James Glass entitled "Address to the Patriot's of Belfast" (10 March 1792) reiterated poetry's crucial role in inspiring patriotic deeds. The poet, recalling how "France the torch of liberty displays" in "glorious deeds" that were immortalized in verse by French "Bards," asked the patriots of Belfast, "Shall not Belfast, which glows with all her [France's] fire, / To equal honors to the Muse inspire?"

These two poems display the same optimistic enthusiasm and bardic motifs that Glass would use in "The Irish Bard" (16 May 1792), in which he railed against invaders from Albion rather than the Vikings, who traditionally had been the invaders in earlier eighteenth-century verse. Although specifically "bardic" images waned somewhat in the *Northern Star* after 1792, they never completely disappeared. The final issues (8 May 1797) contained an anonymous "bardic" poem in imitation of Ossian sent in by the young Thomas Moore. James Glass's message and images exemplify the new bolder note that the United Irishmen introduced into patriotic verse. After the tragic outcomes of the 1798 and 1803 United Irish rebellions, Thomas Moore, who learned to write poetry during the 1790s by imitating the "bardic" verse of the United Irishmen, would "re-string the harp" yet again to a more plaintive elegiac tune. During the 1840s, the Young Ireland poets, in reaction to Thomas Moore, would once again strike a bolder note as the United Irishmen had.

The *Northern Star* promoted the Irish language. Occasionally it published poetry supposedly translated from the Irish, such as "Ma Vurneen Delish Val Macbree" (8 July 1796), a love poem with the note "N.B. The above verses are translated from the original Irish." The *Northern Star* even published the Irish etymology of the name Belfast on St. Patrick's Day, 1796. In September 1795, the Northern Star Office launched *Bolg an tSolair: or, Gaelic Magazine*, the first magazine ever devoted to the study of the Irish language, edited by Patrick Lynch. The title page bore the insignia of a harp and declared that this first issue had been printed at the Northern Star Office, Belfast. The United Irishmen evidently planned to continue the magazine for the preface concluded: "In order to render the work more useful to the public, it shall be continued in numbers, at a low price, and as this first is partly taken up with Grammar, in all future numbers, historical comments, and a greater variety of poems, songs, etc.

shall be given" (*Bolg an tSolair* 1795, x). Prose and verse contributions were to be sent to the "compilers" of the magazine at the Northern Star Office. If any further issues were printed, none have survived.

A *Northern Star* editorial (20 April 1795), probably written by Lynch's student Thomas Russell, praised "Mr. Lynch's attempt to revive the Grammatical and Critical Knowledge of the Irish Language in this town," and claimed that a knowledge of Irish had scholarly and practical applications. Irish was a "help to students of Irish and Eastern Antiquities, especially with regard to Druidical Theology and Worship," and was an important means of communication with the people for merchants. Clearly the implications for using Irish in their propaganda to communicate "sentiments and instruction" was of great interest to the United Irishmen as well. Russell's noted popularity among the Ulster peasantry was no doubt partly due to his knowledge of Irish.

Numerous ads for *Bolg an tSolair* appeared in the *Northern Star* from August to October 1795. An editorial on 3 September 1795 entitled "Irish Language" praised Lynch's efforts "to revive and preserve a knowledge and taste of the beauties of the Irish Language, by his publication of the Gaelic Magazine." The editorial, quoting from the preface to *Bolg an tSolair*, declared the magazine's attempt "to recommend the Irish language to the notice of Irishmen" was necessary because "many tongues and pens have been employed to cry it down, and to persuade the ignorant that it was a harsh and barbarous jargon, and that their ancestors, from whom they derived it, were an ignorant, uncultivated people."

Lynch's preface defended both the language and the culture from which it emanated: "never was any language fitter to express the feelings of the heart" and "abounding in terms of art, and words to express every thought of the mind." Ireland "was the seat of the muses, from the times of remotest antiquity" and "no nation ever encouraged poets and musicians more than the ancient Irish." Calling Irish "the mother tongue of all the languages in the West," Lynch cited the noted Welsh linguist Edward Lhuyd's preference for Irish over Welsh. According to Lynch, foreign scholars praised the "purity and perfection" of Irish and its usefulness to the study of the antiquities in the British Isles as a whole. Indeed, "the old Irish were the possessors of Great Britain, before these Britons who were the ancestors of the

Welch." Lynch also had great praise for contemporary translations
from the Irish, especially Charlotte Brooke's, "with what becoming
dignity the ancient bard appears in modern dress." Irish music enthusiasts were also a potential audience for *Bolg an tSolair*: "Those who
delight in Irish music (which seems greatly to prevail at present) shall
also be entertained with the choicest of airs" (iii–x).

That first issue of *Bolg an tSolair* contained 120 pages and included
an abridged Irish grammar (fourteen pages); a vocabulary of English
and Irish (eighteen pages); "Travelling Dialogues"; "Sentences from
Scripture," the Lord's Prayer and the Creed; and, from Charlotte
Brooke's *Reliques of Irish Poetry*, a lengthy excerpt from a Fenian poem
entitled "The Chase" and six songs, in Irish and in English. The songs
were all of eighteenth-century origin, thus emphasizing the contemporary as well as the ancient riches of Irish language and culture.

"The Chase" was a significant selection because it presents a very
heroic picture of the early Irish Fenian warriors and a moral about the
value of people *uniting* in order to achieve victory against a common
enemy. Chasing a doe, Finn comes upon a beautiful weeping maiden
who claims to have lost her ring in a lake. While he searches for her
ring, the maiden, who is actually a fairy and an enemy of the Fenians,
puts Finn under a spell that prematurely ages him. After squabbling
among themselves, the Fenian warriors join together, defeat the treach-
erous fairies, and force them to release Finn from the spell.

Much of the verse published in the *Northern Star* glorified Irish
history and culture. A poem entitled "Tara" (18 April 1796) exemplifies how United Irish verse combined a formal invigorating tone re-
sembling the exhortation of a sermon with a bardic emphasis on
patriotic deeds. Irish history became a call to battle rather than a
source of plaintive elegiac despair in lines that celebrated "Glorious
Tara" as the "seat of ancient heroes" whose "mighty deeds" included
using "arms to overthrow" the "invading foe." Tara's "patriots" were
inspired by bards who "mid sacred groves, / Tun'd the harp in sublime
strains."

"Tara" typifies the eclectic way in which United Irish verse appropriated diverse elements of eighteenth-century literature and culture.
In the language and style of eighteenth-century English poetry, the
poet uses Irish history, recently popularized in antiquarian writing as a
symbol of Ireland's ancient greatness, to create a call to political ac-

tion that echoes Volunteer verse and Presbyterian sermons. The bard who "tuned the harp in sublime strains" in "sacred groves" embodies the literary doctrine of the sublime as well as the religious fervor of the clergyman, which makes his patriotic verse a call to action rather than the lament of despair voiced in earlier poetry such as Thomas Gray's "Bard." Although such a romanticized use of Irish history as a call to political action has been generally credited to Thomas Davis and the Young Irelanders in the 1840s, their acknowledgement of a debt to United Irish poetry clearly has substance, despite the fact that it has been ignored by political and literary historians to date.

The Newry poet John Corry, whom R. B. McDowell in one of his rare references to United Irish poetry mistakenly calls John Boyd (1979, 371), contributed at least seven poems to the *Northern Star* between 1 June 1796 and 3 March 1797. Corry wrote formal political verse in the manner of "James Glass," as well as more informal lyrical poetry that embodied the popular style of other United Irish verse. A collection of Corry's poetry, entitled *Odes and Elegies Descriptive and Sentimental; with The Patriot, A Poem* and published in Newry in 1797, was dedicated to "The People of Ireland . . . a great Nation," with the epigraph "Delightful Love! My Soul inspire / Teach me to tune Ierne's Lyre / To Social Amity." The iconography of the picture that preceded the poems (a harp and book in a sylvan setting), and the poems themselves, were in the same mode as the verse about love and politics that appeared in the *Northern Star*. Not surprisingly, the list of subscribers to Corry's *Odes and Elegies* is also a list of prominent Ulster United Irishmen: John Haslett, Alexander Lowry, William McCabe, Henry Joy McCracken, Mrs. Samuel Neilson, James Porter, Thomas Russell, Thomas Stott, Thomas Storey, John Hughes, Charles Hamilton Teeling (later Charles Gavan Duffy's literary and political mentor), Luke Teeling, Bartholomew Teeling, as well as Dubliners William Drennan and Oliver Bond.

One of the first poems in *Odes and Elegies*, Corry's "Ireland, An Ode," which had appeared in the *Northern Star* on 22 August 1796, traced Ireland's history from its creation to the present. Corry's view of Irish history is worth noting because it prefigures the view of Irish history found in later nationalist verse. The poem opens with a portrait of Ireland at once beautiful and free, and celebrates the Irish victory over the Danes:

> SUBLIME above the circling sea
>   IERNE's picturesque mountains rise;
> The God of Nature made her free,
>   And bless'd her clime with genial skies.
> Here Liberty's inspiring voice
> Made her courageous sons rejoice;
> . . . .
> How glow'd our Bards with patriot fire,
>   Whilst heav'nly Freedom's praise they sung;
> Their eager fingers swept the lyre,
>   To sounds of martial glory strung.
>
> (*Northern Star*, 22 August 1796)

The poem then describes an idyllic, romanticized, post-Clontarf Ireland, and how such Irish innocence and peace did not last because "petty chieftains" and "Proud Tyranny" trampled "the Rights of Man." Corry's depiction of how Irish disunity in the past had tragic consequences reinforced the United Irish call for unity among Irishmen of all classes and creeds:

> By treachery invited o'er,
>   A foreign nation hither came,
> Then Liberty forsook our shore,
>   And Ireland lost her ancient fame;
>   Yet Patriotism oft assail'd
>   The proud Oppressor who prevail'd,
> And kept a slipp'ry footing here,
>   Whilst vile Disunion's baleful night,
>   Shut out the rays of Freedom's light,
> And foster'd slavish fear.

The concluding stanza calls upon the Lord to assist the United Irish efforts to achieve "Christian unity." Such religious language, typical of much United Irish verse, belies the charges that the United Irishmen were godless radicals.

Corry's patriotic verse, like that of many United Irishmen, envisioned violent battles as a prelude to any peace and Christian unity, and used history to preach the United Irish message. The central poem in Corry's *Odes and Elegies*, "The Patriot," opens with a romanticized picture of an idyllic Ireland disrupted and enslaved by the invading Danes. The Irish, inspired by their bard Connal's "ode," defeat the Danes and "liberty" is "secur'd by native might." The lesson of history is clear: if the Irish, inspired by patriotic verse, had once forcibly expelled invaders, they could do so again. Cormac, Ireland's greatest hero, dies in the battle, although his heroism lives on in Connal's songs. The image of the patriot who died for his country and then is celebrated in song became a standard motif in United Irish verse once their members began to die on the scaffold or on the battlefield. Corry wove a sentimental love story into "The Patriot" in which Cormac's beloved, Ellen, dies of grief as she mourns him. The adoring and often grieving female was a stock motif in United Irish verse.

Although "The Patriot" couched the call to action in terms of Irish history, other poems by Corry offered a more international perspective. For example, "The Tears of Liberty! An Ode" (31 October 1796), which appeared in the *Northern Star* within weeks after Samuel Neilson, Thomas Russell, and other Belfast United Irishmen had been arrested and sent to prisons in Dublin, compares their imprisonment to that of Lafayette and Kościuszko. However, although that poem's style and its central image of Liberty weeping for her imprisoned sons have no overtly Irish overtones, there is an obvious parallel between the figure of Liberty and the popular image of Ireland weeping for her imprisoned sons that was used in many United Irish poems. Likewise, the poet's vision of Liberty as a figure descending from "Heav'nly light" who speaks to him predicting Ireland's coming liberation from slavery has interesting parallels with the native Irish aisling in which Ireland appeared to poets in a vision as a woman.

Other poems that Corry contributed to the *Northern Star* in 1796–1797 were in the much more popular and colloquial vein that came to characterize United Irish verse once the movement began to seek a more broadly based lower-class audience about 1795. Corry's "Union and Truth, A Song" (5 August 1796), which was also published in the second *Paddy's Resource* songbook in 1796, is an example of the United Irishmen's attempt to write popular songs. Using a common "Derry Down" refrain, Corry's song appealed to the popular antitithe sentiment by prophesying that "tyranny," in the form of a "tythe-loving prelacy," would "expire at the feet of bless'd union and truth."

Although Corry's language may appear stilted and somewhat abstract to us, such language often flavored popular ballads of the day.

"Popular" materials in J. R. R. Adams's *Printed Word and the Common Man: Popular Culture in Ulster, 1700–1900* and Georges-Denis Zimmermann's *Songs of Irish Rebellion: Political Street Ballads and Rebel Songs, 1780–1900* frequently contain a surprisingly "elevated" literary diction. Leslie Shepard has explained the historical development of the "popular" and "literary" dimensions of the broadside ballad:

> With the decline of folk memory and the oral tradition, the broadside ballad grew out of the remains of traditional balladry, flourishing between the sixteenth and nineteenth centuries and absorbing popular poetry and song. In the eighteenth century, cultured literary interest in broadside and traditional balladry resulted in the injection of a robust and romantic strain into a poetry and literature that had become anaemic. The period of the printed broadside ballad marks a curious exchange between two social strata. While the ballad brought romance and folk imagery into stilted literary forms, the broadside ballad soon took over the worst affectations of polite poetry. (1962, 34)

Other songs in the more popular style, which became increasingly common in the *Northern Star* in 1796, often celebrated contemporary events, such as popular efforts at harvesting the fields of imprisoned United Irishmen in which many hundreds of people often participated. "The United Shearers" (10 October 1796), to a tune called "Dusky Night" that is known today as "A Hunting We Will Go," combined elements of popular work songs with abstract political dogma:

> The yellow harvest o'er the plain
>   Was ripe both corn and wheat,
> When Patriots assembled were
>   The abundant crops to reap.
>
>   Then a shearing we will go,
>   Then a shearing we will go,
>   To cut the grain of each brave man,
>   Who to jail for truth did go.
>
> Now o'er each hill and through each vale,
>   Let National Union sound,

'Till Bigotry and all its train
Lie prostrate on the ground.
Then a shearing we will go, . . .

The fact that the popular song "A Hunting We Will Go" began with the words "The Dusky night rides down the sky" explains the United Irish reference to the tune "Dusky Night." Such naming practices make it difficult to trace some of the tunes used in United Irish songs.

The best example of the new popular and lyrical poems in the *Northern Star* is the song "The Exiled Irishman's Lamentation" (27 July 1796), which was set to the popular traditional Irish melody "Savourna Deilish" (*sic*). The song was originally known as "Eileen Oge" and also called "Erin go Bragh," which had already been used in Dublin operas such as *The Poor Soldier* in 1783 and *The Surrender of Calais* in 1791. It appeared anonymously, but was subsequently ascribed to George Nugent Reynolds. The song had evidently achieved popularity even before it appeared in the *Northern Star* on 27 July 1796, where it was prefaced by this note: "ERIN GO BRAGH! The following popular song we present to our readers as in some degree expressive of the situation of an Armagh exile." A letter from Mary Ann McCracken to Henry Joy McCracken in Kilmainham, dated 16 March 1797, also attests to the song's popularity: "There were six prisoners brought to town this evening, for refusing to swear allegiance, and came in undismayed singing Erin go Brath" (Fitzhenry 1936, 89).

Noteworthy for both its Irish refrain and its lyricism, "The Exiled Irishman's Lamentation" is quoted in full in appendix B because of its popularity within the United Irish movement and because it became one of the most popular nationalist songs of the nineteenth century. "The Exiled Irishman's Lamentation" appeared as the last song in the 1796 *Paddy's Resource* and as the third song in both the 1798 and 1803 *Paddy's Resource* songbooks. The song's Irish air and refrains, the immediacy and poignancy of its first-person narrative voice, and its focus on practical concerns like taxes, loss of land, and emigration explain its popularity.[2]

Significant variations in wording occurred in later versions of "The Exiled Irishman's Lamentation" published by the United Irishmen. The different versions of the song, the result of the dynamic changes of living oral tradition, illustrate its popularity. Moreover, the changes in wording are an index of important changes in the United Irishmen's political agenda as violent revolution replaced reform. For example, although the exiled Irishman in the version that appeared in the *Northern Star* in 1796 hears the sound of "Friendship advancing— delusion retreating," the speaker in the version published in the 1803 *Paddy's Resource* songbook hears "Frenchmen advancing—tyrants re- treating." That change also reflected stylistic changes in United Irish verse, which over time became less abstract and more concrete and contemporary in reference. A more lurid and sensational note also became apparent. For example, the 1803 version of "The Exiled Irishman's Lamentation" contained the line: "With what grief I be- held my COT burn'd to the ground, O!"

Some songs in a popular and colloquial vein had appeared in the *Northern Star* from the beginning. Poems in Scots dialect, obviously inspired by the verse of Robert Burns, were published in the paper as early as April 1792. A contributor who identified himself as "L. M. of Craigarogan," probably Jemmy Hope's brother-in-law Luke Mullan, who lived at Craigarogan and was a known contributor of verse to the *Northern Star*, sent in a poem entitled "Epistle to Jamie Fleck" in Scots dialect with the note that it was occasioned by seeing the poetry of Robert Burns (14 April 1792). In the following issue, Samuel Thomson of Carngranny contributed an "Epistle to Robert Burns" in Scots dialect (18 April 1792). However, John Hewitt has argued per- suasively in *Rhyming Weavers and Other Country Poets of Antrim and Down* that such dialectical Scots poetry also represented an important indigenous Ulster poetic tradition (1974, 1–5).

Other songs in the *Northern Star* used the style of popular Irish folk songs to address the Catholic peasantry. "A New Song by Phelimy Freebairn for the Use of His Countrymen" (17 November 1792) was set to the popular jig tune "Larry Grogan," which a ploughman in Porter's *Billy Bluff and the Squire* had been punished for humming:

> Arrah Paddy my joy,
> What makes you so shy,
> To take up with your Protestant Brother, your Brother;
> Sure you never can thrive,
> If you both do not strive
> To live on good terms with each other.

The use of short lines in the song bears an interesting resemblance to the mid-line rhyme common to popular Gaelic verse, but once again literary styles transcended social distinctions. John Philpot Curran, the prominent barrister who defended many United Irishmen, used the style in his songs. Moreover, R. R. Madden claimed that "Advice to Paddy," the title under which the Phelimy Freebairn song was printed in the 1795 *Paddy's Resource* songbook, was one of the "numerous admirable songs" that Edward Lysaght had "written for the United Irishmen, and which he was wont to sing in their social circles" (Madden 1887, 82). An eloquent barrister and noted wit, Lysaght was known for his ability to sing in both Irish and English. He had been a Volunteer and had close ties with several United Irishmen. In 1800, he strongly opposed the Act of Union. Tradition credits Lysaght as the author of several popular Irish songs, including "The Rakes of Mallow" and "Kitty of Coleraine," which was sometimes printed to a tune called "Paddy's Resource" (De Charms 1966, 197).

Many songs in the *Northern Star* ranged well beyond Irish tradition for their tunes and subjects. Some were based on popular sailors' songs. An untitled song, that appeared on 6 April 1793 to the tune "Vicar of Bray" is based on a British seaman's song against the evils of "impressing" sailors against their wills:

> Thus while the flatterers of a court
> Who prate of Freedom's blessing,
> Yet ev'ry Hell-born war support,
> And vindicate impressing;
> Thus while these *things*, miscall'd the *Great*
> Are fattening on the nation,
> Your Tars are dragged to serve the state,
> To wounds and mutilation.
>   (6 April 1793)

The versions of the song that appeared in the *Northern Star* (11 June 1795) and in *Paddy's Resource* in 1795 under the title "The Tender's Hold" conclude more defiantly and ominously by predicting the demise of "pension'd" oppressors. The 1795 versions also replaced the word "British" with "Irish" wherever it appeared. All three versions, in the sentimental and melodramatic cast of much United Irish verse, portray the "sun-burnt seaman" returning to land and clinging to his wife and children as once again "the impressing fiends appear, / And all their joys are blighted."

When the earliest United Irish version of "The Tender's Hold" had been published in the *Northern Star* in 1793, a note indicated it was "by the author of 'The Origin of Kings'," a formal, philosophic poem that had appeared the previous summer. Clearly the United Irish writers could write in either the formal or the colloquial vein at will.

Other songs in the *Northern Star* exhibited wide-ranging origins and blended formal and informal styles. A "Song, Addressed to the Irish Volunteers" appeared on 1 December 1792, the words of which make clear that it was to be sung to the tune "God Save the King," which is indeed the tune to which it is set in the 1795 *Paddy's Resource* songbook. The first stanza is identical to an "Ode" by the American poet Philip Freneau, the first record of which is its performance at the 1791 November Festival of the London Revolution Society (Freneau 1963 2:99–101). Evidently, Freneau's "Ode" quickly became a popular radical song, for it was sung in Philadelphia in 1793 and was published in "R. Thompson's" *Tribute to the Swinish Multitude*, the 1795 songbook published by an English radical society. The verses in the *Northern Star* version of 1792, which do not correspond with the version published in the 1795 edition of Freneau's poems, suggest Freneau's song generated stanzas that became a part of the repertoire of songs sung by radicals in America, Ireland, and England at their political meetings and convivial occasions, which were often one and the same.

The informal and convivial tone of some United Irish verse in the *Northern Star* is apparent in the song entitled "The Bunglers: or, British Bacchanals," to the tune "Green Grow the Rushes," to which Robert Burns set several of his songs (12 September 1796). The song also demonstrates the satirical tone that characterized a great deal of the literary materials in the paper. The last stanza illustrates the song's satiric portrait of drunken British revelers who underestimate their radical French and Irish opponents:

> If Grunters henceforth dare to brag
> Of LIBERTY or REASON, O,
> We'll then apply our new state gag—
> And tuck 'em up for *treason* O.

Then let us all carouse and drink;
    For, till affairs grow riper O,
Folks must not *say*, tho' they may think—
    That JOHNNY pays the piper O!
        Push about the Glasses, O
        Push about the Glasses, O
    For, what care we how things go on,
        While blushing Nectar passes, O!

The song appeared, set to the same tune, in the 1796 and 1803 *Paddy's Resource* songbooks. However, as time passed and the United Irishmen were actively recruiting Catholics to their ranks, they deleted the anti-Catholic implications of references to the French Revolution as having knocked "Popish Temples" down. The 1803 version replaced "Popish Temples" with "cursed Bastiles." Other changes in that 1803 version indicate that the song had attained oral currency because "they're" became "their," a common transposition when printed songs had entered living oral tradition.

United Irish satiric verse in the *Northern Star* even used the comic stage figure of Paddy and his "Irish blunders," but with an ironic twist that credits him with a common sense and shrewdness that turns the laugh on the English. An untitled song published on 21 March 1796 to the old Irish tune "Shelagh Negirah [*sic*]" used comic Irish dialect to celebrate Ireland and an Irish peasant who rightly prefers Ireland to England. "Pat" emigrates to England only to confront its poverty and other social evils, and joyously returns to "sweet Ireland":

The English may talk of our bulls if they will,
But the bulls in *ould* Ireland are far better still
Than any I've seen since I left Londonderry;
Our bulls, faith and troth, are all fat and merry.

The increasingly popular and colloquial dimensions of the literary materials in the *Northern Star* are also apparent in prose satires that the newspaper began to publish in late 1793. The most important examples are the *Review of the Lion of Old England; or, Democracy Confounded, A Faithful Report of the Trial of Hurdy Gurdy,* and *Billy Bluff and the Squire.* Each satire first appeared in serial form in the *Northern Star* and the United Irishmen considered these works important enough to publish them in their entirety in separate editions. William Sampson's *Trial of Hurdy Gurdy* and James Porter's *Billy Bluff and the Squire* were discussed in chapter 1 because they provide important contemporary testimony of the significant role that songs and popular literature played within the United Irish movement.

William Sampson and Thomas Russell's *Review of the Lion of Old England* appeared anonymously in serial form in the *Northern Star* in 1793 and was published in two editions in 1794. The poem purported to be a review of an epic poem about the adventures of a good-hearted but too-easily-flattered Lion of Old England. The preface to the second edition in 1794 declared that the "chief motive" of the "editor" was "bringing to confusion the arrogant presumption of Democracy" (v). To that end, the "reviewers" celebrated the Lion for declarations such as "Scorn the vile traders, who to peace incline, / War, raging war, is glorious and divine," and "These bloody Frenchmen all to Hell must go!" (71).

Most of the "review" satirized both English politics and literary conventions. For example, this description of the "review" preceded Canto I: "As this sublime effort of the Imagination, contains all the treasures of genuine Poetry and bold Fiction, we scruple not to announce it to the world, as a beautiful specimen of the Epic Art: equally calculated to delight the Fancy, inform the Judgment, and amend the Heart" (5). Although such literary parody appealed to a more elite audience, the more colloquial style of *Hurdy Gurdy* (1794) and *Billy Bluff* (1796) exemplifies the increasingly less elite nature of United Irish literary productions. Significantly, *Review of the Lion of Old England* was never as "popular" as the other United Irish prose satires.

Analysis of the literary works in United Irish newspapers has so far focused on the *Northern Star*. The three other United Irish newspapers, none of which lasted nearly as long as the *Northern Star*, also included songs and satires and also illustrate the increasingly "popular" nature of United Irish literature. When the first United Irish Societies were founded in Belfast and Dublin in late 1791, the original plan was to have the movement publish newspapers in both cities. But the Dublin paper, the *National Journal*, never achieved the popularity or the longevity of the *Northern Star*.

Two thousand copies of the "Prospectus" for the *National Journal*, written by Wolfe Tone, were published in Dublin on 5 October 1791 and declared that publication of the paper would begin on the first Tuesday in January 1792. However, the first surviving issue is number four and is dated Monday, 2 April 1792, which indicates that publication did not actually begin until the last week in March 1792. Very few issues of this paper have survived. The last surviving issue is number nineteen and is dated 7 May 1792. One explanation for the paper's quick demise is that it had twenty shareholders who, according to William Drennan, disagreed about how the paper should be run (Drennan 1931, 60–63, 71, 89).

The literary and popular dimensions of the paper were clear from the beginning. Tone's "Prospectus" declared that, although the primary mission of the paper would be political, the "lower departments" of poetry and drama, in which Tone himself was avidly interested, would also be important subjects because, "though of less consequence" than political reform, poetry and drama "are not without their use, as affecting the manners, the taste, and even the amusements of the people." Tone predicted that in the *National Journal* "the real voice of the People may find a pure and constant channel of promulgation." He defined the "People" in the broadest possible sense: "But it is not merely to the politician, or the man of letters, that this Paper shall be open, the Artisan, the Mechanic, and the Husbandman, are called upon to communicate through the *National Journal* for the public good, such useful discoveries and improvements as may occur in their respective occupations" (Public Record Office, London, Home Office 100/34/9).

Like the banner of the *Northern Star*, that of the *National Journal* contained a symbolic design that combined violent, revolutionary symbols with musical and literary devices. A lady seated next to a harp, with a spear resting against her body and holding a shield bearing the United Irish emblem of clasped hands and the motto Unite and Be Free, held a pen with which she had inscribed these words on a pillar: Let the Will of the People Be the Law of the Land, and Love One Another. The spear and the harp of the *National Journal* emblem, like the sword and the lyre of the *Northern Star* emblem, suggest that from the beginning the possibility of violence coexisted with the propagandistic power of the literary and musical arts at the heart of the United Irish movement.

The several issues of the *National Journal* that have survived contain little of the poetry envisioned by Tone, who evidently did not

have much to do with the publication of the paper other than suggesting, unsuccessfully, at one point that his friend Thomas Russell be
named editor (Drennan 1931, 60–61). The *National Journal*, a much
duller paper than the *Northern Star*, contained little local news and
relatively few ads and editorials. For example, the issue for 4 April
1792 contained no poetry or other literary pieces.

The issue for 2 April 1792 included a clever parody of an ad for a
play, which read *"The Cat Let Out of the Bag; or, A Play Without a
Plot; Being a Tragical, Farcical, Operatical, Pantomical, Serious, Satirical,
Nonsensical Pasticcio*, acted the Devil knows where, By a Company of
the Devil knows who, and written by Sir Drawcansir Slashtem, Bart."
The ad claimed the play contained "notes critical, philosophical, philo-
logical, polemical and political" by an odd assortment of persons, such
as noted United Irishmen (Napper Tandy and Simon Butler), antiquarians (Colonel Vallancey), Irish figures both legendary and historical ("Paddy Whack" and Arthur O'Leary), and contemporary political
figures (Edmund Burke, Henry Grattan, and Thomas Paine). The *National Journal* for 7 May 1792 contained a short mediocre poem prais-
ing Napper Tandy. Although the *Northern Star* flourished for over five
years, the *National Journal* ceased after a few weeks.

Four months after the popular and influential *Northern Star* was
suppressed in May 1797 by government order in Belfast, the Dublin
United Irishmen began publishing a newspaper, the *Press*, that was
much more interesting and popular than the *National Journal* had
been. Arthur O'Connor and Thomas Addis Emmet were the main
forces behind the *Press*. O'Connor had been imprisoned in February
1797 for several inflammatory addresses he had published in the *Northern Star*. After his close friends Thomas Addis Emmet and Edward
Fitzgerald furnished his bail in August, O'Connor set about founding
the *Press* with their help.

O'Connor's "Prospectus," published in the first issue of the *Press*
on 28 September 1797, declared the paper a successor to the *Northern
Star* and its purposes as follows: "To extinguish all party animosities,
and introduce a cordial Union of ALL THE PEOPLE, on the basis of
toleration and equal government, as it is a primary duty, so it shall be
the especial care of THE PRESS; to call into action all that is noble
and generous in the minds of IRISHMEN individually, as a sure means
of rendering them collectively a great and happy nation; to cultivate

the seeds of virtue, heroism and industry, which are inherent in their minds, shall be of chief objects of its unceasing vigilance." Like the *Northern Star* and the *National Journal*, the *Press* was to include literary as well as political items. In addition to the "earliest intelligence" of contemporary events, "to diversify scenes so dismal, we shall glean whatever may be most instructive or amusing in the *Belles Lettres*."

Although satire had become a regular literary feature in the *Northern Star*, the prose published in the *Press* was mainly in the form of earnest rather than satiric discourse, and the verse was predominantly romantic rather than satiric in its political stance. A noteworthy new feature of poetry published in the *Press* was its emphasis on contemporary events, most notably the trial and execution of United Irishman William Orr in October 1797. In addition, the *Press* added the motifs of martyrdom and blood sacrifice and a lurid and sensational element to the evolving tradition of Irish political poetry.

Playful, clever satire such as Porter's *Billy Bluff* is relatively rare in the pages of the *Press*. As government prosecution intensified and as trials and executions increased, United Irish literary propaganda became more serious in tone. One of the few examples of satire to appear in the *Press* was a poem entitled "The Goose Pye" on 8 February 1798, by "A PADDY." In it, a Lord, who "damns Hibernia for a Bitch" because of the "dangerous things" that people "unite and cry," presents the situation in a suitably musical frame of reference:

> The Irish Harp, with notes divine,
> Attunes her fav'rite airs and thine,
> . . . .
> . . . therefore districts are all burn'd,
> The Widow and the Orphan spurn'd
> Lest from our places *we* be turn'd,
> Or be obliged to trip, or prance
> To curs'd *Ça Ira*—tune of France.

Some of Mrs. Henrietta Battier's satires appeared anonymously in the *Press*, most notably several cantos of "The Bitter Orange, An Heroic Poem," which satirically portrays the machinations of English rule in Ireland by quoting dialogues from within Dublin Castle. The first canto, published on 23 January 1798, depicts the Castle's "plan" to send "spies, pimps, informers, harbingers of death" with the instruction "to excite the treason first, and then inform." The second canto, published on 27 January 1798, describes how the Castle sent spies to the Liberties like "a swarm of wasps from a putrid hive." Battier's heavy-handed satires impressed the young Thomas Moore, who re-called her fondly in his *Memoirs* as "my poetical friend" and described her popularity as a satirist in the 1790s (1853, 40–45). Like Moore, Battier contributed to the *Anthologia Hibernica* as well as to United Irish publications.

Two other satires to appear in the *Press* were a poem entitled "How to Be a Great Lord" on 25 January 1798 and an announcement on 14 December 1797 of a new play "A New Pantomine, called THE IRISH MAROONS, or a Trip to the Land of Potatoes," which was "now in rehearsal for the political theatre in College-green" and "beau-tified with many delightful and enchanting scenes, particularly a hunt after the *wild Irish* by a party of *Ancient Britons*, several charming *conflagrations, rapes,* and *murders,* by groups of Orangemen; with some diverting incidents in *hanging, shouting,* and *torturing,* by the loyal Wicklow Militia." That sensational tone was common in the "news" and verse published in the *Press*.

Verse published in the *Press* was more frequently romantic or sensational than satiric. The first poem to appear was William Drennan's "Erin," published anonymously on 5 October 1797 with the note "To Its Own Tune" and the notice that it had first appeared in a London paper. Although it is likely that this notice was accurate, because Irish and English radical societies and publications regularly shared songs and published each other's materials, no English publica-tion of "Erin" has been traced. When Drennan published "Erin" as the first poem in his *Fugitive Pieces, in Verse and Prose* in 1815, he described it as "a party song, written without the rancour of party, in the year 1795" and proudly pointed out that in it he had created the popular epithet "Emerald Isle" (1815, 4). "Erin" was the opening song in the *Paddy's Resource* songbooks of 1798 and 1803, a fact that sug-gests Drennan may have been involved in the preparation of both songbooks.

"Erin" is quoted in full in appendix B because of its poetic merit and its prominence in United Irish publications. Drennan's "Erin" incorporated many motifs central to United Irish literary works and to later Irish literary nationalism: the feminine persona of Erin, at once "proudly insular" and defiant, tearfully catalogues the glories of ancient Ireland and her subsequent woes, and calls the "men" of Ireland to her cause to the accompaniment of her harp. The poem's message, a call to unity and forgiveness rather than to violent revolution, underscores Drennan's growing disaffection with the United Irish movement as armed revolution supplanted literary propaganda as their means to political reform in 1797 and 1798.

The six months of the *Press*'s existence marked the United Irish movement's acceptance of armed rebellion. Drennan steadfastly refused to replace the moral force of reasoned and poetic argument with the violence of physical force. Even in his poem "Glendalloch," written in 1802, in which he lamented the recent Union with Britain, he rejected armed rebellion. Drennan's vision of Irish history in "Glendalloch" and in several other poems presented early Ireland as a free, cultured, and happy land until invaded by the barbaric English. Drennan's "Juvenal's 8th Satire, Imitated" (the *Press*, 7 October 1797) included these lines about Irish history:

> Thrice blest in fate, had Strongbow never bore,
> His band of robbers to green ERIN's shore!
> In savage times, the seat of learning known,
> In times refin'd, itself the savage grown . . .

Although Drennan disassociated himself from the armed violence of 1798 and 1803, he maintained a personal allegiance to individual United Irishmen and to the movement's larger goals. In 1803, castle spies reported that Drennan followed Thomas Russell into a Dublin house (TCD, Sirr Papers, 869/7). In Belfast in the early 1790s, Russell had been a favorite of Drennan's sister, Martha, wife of United Irishman Samuel McTier. Mary Ann McCracken gave R. R. Madden the following unpublished poem by Drennan about Robert Emmet's trial in 1803, which he reprinted in *Literary Remains of the United Irishmen*:

> Prostrate, unarmed, no more alive,
> Had ceased Kilwarden's breath,
> The savage strife was then to give
> A death wound after death.

When Emmet, self-convicted stood,
    In fate already hung,
Longed to taste the blood
    And piked him with his tongue.

Now which of these barbarians say,
    Waged the most bloody war,
The savage of the bloody fray,
    Or the savage of the Bar?
                        (Madden 1887, 49)

Drennan's literary activities as poet and as editor of the *Belfast Magazine* (1808–1814) continued the original United Irish program of educating the people, as he phrased it in "Glendalloch," "harp . . . in . . . hand." His son William was associated with the Young Ireland movement in the 1840s and wrote poetry for the *Nation*.

The usual style of Drennan's United Irish verse was different from what became the most common mode of United Irish verse—songs to popular tunes. Drennan's only song, "Erin," was "to its own tune," and his poetry was generally in a formal vein. His two other known contributions to the *Press* were elegies on the death of William Orr, whose trial and execution in October 1797 was the subject of numerous songs, editorials, and letters in the *Press*. Orr, though defended by counselors John Philpot Curran and William Sampson, was convicted of administering the United Irish oath on the basis of perjured testimony and, according to later accounts, intimidation of a jury, several members of which were deliberately made drunk as they deliberated Orr's fate.

Drennan's "William, An Elegy" was published in the *Press* on 31 October 1797, by "The Minstrel," with no tune indicated. Drennan's evocation of Orr's final moments with his wife typifies the poem's sentimentality:

Then, William, how pale was they cheek
    Where beauty so peerless did dwell;
As the breast of they love thou didst seek,
    To bid her a dismal farewell.

Ah, clay cold was her breast with despair,
    And closed were her eyes from thy view,

While sense had abandoned her ear,
As abhorring to hear thy adieu.

Such melodramatic scenes became more and more frequent in verse published in the *Press*. The vehemence of Drennan's final stanza was also representative of the tone of much that was published in the newspaper:

Then be wither'd the barbarous hand
Did execute such a decree!
And the heart that did give the command,
A stranger to rest may it be.

Drennan's vengeance was typically a curse rather than a call to arms. Evidently, Drennan afterwards rejected the sentimentality of this elegy because he did not include it with his other United Irish verse in *Fugitive Pieces* in 1815. It was reprinted, however, in the 1798 and 1803 *Paddy's Resource* songbooks, where it was to be sung to a tune entitled "Hark, 'Tis a Voice from the Tomb," which probably referred to a hymn by Issac Watts, first published in 1707, that began "Hark, from the tombs a doleful warning sound" (Upton 1964, 178).

Drennan's second elegy on Orr, "The Wake of William Orr," published in the *Press* on 13 January 1798 and reprinted in appendix B, is a more restrained and effective elegy and a finer poem. Although its formal style made Drennan's elegy distinct from the more songlike United Irish verse, it used many motifs common to United Irish verse: six centuries of ceaseless battle for freedom from England; the hysterical woman mourning her fallen lover, who had died for Ireland; the dawning day as an image of coming Irish freedom; and the Christ-like martyrdom of the virtuous patriot laid low by treachery.

The martyred patriot and blood-sacrifice motifs were present in the *Press* from the beginning. The "Prospectus" in the first issue had declared: "It is a saying, that the blood of the Martyrs was the seed of the church. The propagation of politics bears a close affinity to that of religion" (28 September 1797). On 30 December 1797, the *Press* published a letter "To the Irish Nation," signed by Arthur O'Connor, about recent government legal action against the paper for libel, that concluded: "They may make us martyrs, and Liberty's roots will be fertilized by the blood of the murdered."

William Orr's execution gave the United Irishmen their first martyr. On 4 November 1797, a letter by "Bolingbroke" on Orr's execution compared Irish heroism to that of Sparta and declared: "The
peasant who is to be shot, or the ploughman who is hanged, may feel
and sustain his fate with fortitude, and leave behind him an example
not to deter but rather to inspirit others; his memory will be revered,
and his name handed down to posterity, in the village or hamlet
where he resided, and he suffered, as a political martyr."

Another important elegy on Orr, published in the *Press* on 23
November 1797, was "Elegiac Ode to the Honored Memory of William Orr." The elegy was "By the Author of *Hibernia, Man of Age* etc.,"
who would thus have been easily identified as William Hamilton
Drummond. Drummond had contributed poetry to the *Northern Star*,
and his *Hibernia* and *Man of Age* had been published by the Northern
Star Office in 1797. *The Man of Age* anticipated the lurid journalism
of the *Press*. In it, Drummond described a landlord as a ruthless tyrant
who had ruined and betrayed a tenant's daughter and implied that a
revolution might remedy such injustices.

Drummond's elegy on Orr used the standard United Irish poetic
motifs of harps, slaves, martyrs, weeping widows, and orphans.
Drummond even used Drennan's "Emerald Isle" epithet, but went
beyond the curse and the vision of the rising sun of freedom that had
concluded Drennan's elegies on Orr. Drummond called for "vengeance"
and "retribution" to combat the "maniac rage" of "phrenzy'd despo-
tism." Because he also celebrated "the love of Liberty and Truth,"
however, Drummond's elegy embodied the tension between reason
and violence, between moral force and physical force, that characterized United Irish verse as well as the literary nationalism of future
generations.

A noteworthy example of the voice of reason and moral righteousness in the *Press* was the series of "Letters from the Mountains"
that Thomas Addis Emmet wrote under the pseudonym "Montanus,"
a wise old man offering instruction on political philosophy and contemporary events. Taking a philosophical high road and placing his
confidence in the power of moral rather than physical force, Montanus
attributed recent political developments in Ireland to "the genius of
rational inquiry" that had recently made such "giant strides" around
the world (3 October 1797). Typical of Montanus's position of calm

objectivity was his unromanticized description of the Irish peasantry as "an indolent, much-enduring race, submissive to their superiors, even to an excess of servility" (14 October 1797). Yet he went on to warn that extreme oppression and misery could rouse them to insurrection. Montanus therefore argued for "temperate concessions" from the government that would "satisfy the major part of the reformers and detach them effectually and immediately from their more violent associates" (31 October 1797). He defended the United Irishmen as seeking "only parliamentary reform by peaceable and constitutional means" (9 November 1797).

Yet even Montanus eventually used the lurid and sentimental mode that became more and more typical of the *Press*. On 28 November 1797, his letter to "Satanides" described his crimes in Ireland thus: "the youth, the stay, and comfort of their drooping age, was torn from his infirm and decrepid parents; the affectionate husband was torn from his shrieking and disconsolate wife; the laborious and protecting father, from his famishing and helpless infants." Montanus declared to Satanides, "The blood of slaughtered thousands rises against you. . . . The day comes, when justice shall prevail; when Ireland shall raise her head from the dust, and perform a solemn sacrifice to the constitution"; when Satanides would "meet the ignominious death of a traitor."

By March, even Montanus was clearly losing patience with reason and justice as the means for achieving reform. On 1 March 1798, he warned the "Aristocracy of Ireland" that they were "living on a volcano," and urged them to "awake" and join "the agitated element, which now rises and swells, to dash and bear away the corruptions of the state." In his final letter, on 3 March 1798, Montanus retreated from threats of violence back to rational arguments about how freedom and reform would enable people to be "ennobled and purified with the constitution," thus providing a chance for all to advance to "happy times." But such proponents of moral force would soon be overruled by advocates of physical force like Arthur O'Connor.

The prose pieces in the *Press* were generally more powerful and entertaining than anything that had appeared in the *National Journal*. A letter published on 14 October 1797 addressed the "Rulers, Magistrates, and Men of Power in Ireland" as follows: "Go prate you big-bellied corps of gluttons, extol the protestant ascendancy, get drunk with claret, and belch God save the King, damn all reformers, and curse the weaver who humbly begs relief—thus will ye support the Constitution in Church and State."

The *Press*'s hyberbolic rhetoric and its news became increasingly lurid and inflammatory. On 17 October 1797, the paper published what it claimed was the Orangeman's Oath: "I, A.B., do hereby swear, that I will be true to the King and Government, and that I will exterminate, as far as I am able, the Catholics of Ireland." The news on 19 October included an account of how "the chastity of an innocent virgin of a respectable family was forcibly violated in the presence of her bound, gagged and agonized brother" by a Scotish regiment which had taken them prisoner on the false or pretended charge of sedition. On 7 November, a letter "To the People" recounted various Orange atrocities and urged them to "assert your rights" and "if necessary, in defence of Liberty, die in the last ditch." An "Ode," published on 5 December 1797 and reprinted in the 1798 *Paddy's Resource* songbook, urged Erin's heroes to emulate Brian Boru and march with cannons to the battlefield where "tyrants' blood in streams shall flow." A letter to the government on 26 December declared that every man hung, kidnapped, or shot "adds at least ten to the union," and warned the government to pray "to Heaven that the People may have mercy enough to let you get whole to the scaffold."

Lurid melodrama eventually replaced reasoned arguments about moral righteousness. An "Ode" by "Sarsfield" on 6 January 1798 began "Hark! heard ye not those dreadful screams?" It described how a "naked aged corpse stained with gore" hung on a tree outside a peasant cottage, and predicted how "With hasty pace, lo! vengeance comes, / Indignant ERIN breaks her chains." The 11 January issue reprinted a "want ad" that had supposedly appeared in the *Strabane Journal* on 20 April 1795: "Wanted: twelve beautiful girls" between fourteen and eighteen of "virtue pure and unsullied . . . for the service of the Officers who compose the mess of his Majesty's Wicklow Regiment of Militia." The same issue included graphic accounts of hangings and burnings by the same militia in County Carlow.

On 1 February 1797, the *Press* printed a letter addressed to the "Fair Country Women" of Ireland, asking their support and recounting Ireland's oppression in lurid terms: "Think of the infant tossed from the point of the bayonet into the flames. Think of the wretched mother, shut up with her little children in her once happy dwelling, and there roasted, that the music of their shrieks may entertain the ear of the savage murderer. . . . Think of your sex dishonoured by the impious and lawless bandits, that should have been the defenders of their country. Think of the despairing mother sitting by the road-side, tearing her hair, while her children wither famished at her feet, or butchered, or burned, or deflowered!" The 3 March 1798 issue described how fathers and sons had their heads roasted on their own fires to extort confessions of concealed arms.

Some of the most strident rhetoric in prose and verse in the *Press* came from the pen of young Thomas Moore, who at the time was a student at Trinity College and, by his own later account, an avid reader of the *Press* and a contributor to it, as well as a close associate of Robert Emmet and other United Irishmen. Moore's "Letter to the Students of Trinity College" appeared anonymously on 2 December 1797. Referring to the Trinity professors who had outlawed the United Irish Society within the university as "the drivelling despots of our monastery" and to his fellow students as the heroes who would bring about the "resurrection of Ireland" and "raise her to that rank in the climax of nations from which she is fallen so many, many degrees!" Moore declared: "Let us march against the tyrant; let us conquer or die!"

Moore's letter was largely composed of rhetorical questions such as the following:

> Can you see poor Ireland, degraded, tortured, without
> burning to be revenged on her damned tormentors? . . .
> Can you behold without indignation, that horde of foreign
> depredators, who murder the happiness of our country,
> and gorge on the life-blood of Ireland? . . .
> What is trial by jury? a mere show—a farce—where the
> jury is acted by drunkards, a villain personates the
> accuser—and the doom of the victim is hiccuped out by a
> Bacchanalian, or pronounced with true stage-effect,
> amidst the tears of a dramatic judge!

Moore concluded his letter: "Let us show these ministerial minions . . . that Ireland has sons untutored in the school of corruption, who love her Liberties, and, in the crisis, will die for them."

Moore's poetic contribution to the *Press* was "Extract from a Poem in Imitation of Ossian," a prose fragment in the poetic style of Macpherson's Fenian bard Ossian (19 October 1797). Moore's Ossianic prose-poem is quoted in full in appendix C because this aspect of his early career is so little known and because an excerpt cannot do justice to the full effect of Moore's effusion. The poem demonstrates how familiar he was with the Ossianic mode and the standard motifs that the United Irishmen had appropriated from that tradition.

Although Moore acknowledged in his *Memoirs* that his Ossianic fragment had been published in the *Press*, he neglected to mention that it had appeared five months earlier in the final issue of the *Northern Star* on 12 May 1797. Either Moore never saw a copy of that last issue, or he deliberately chose to downplay his ties with the United Irishmen by mentioning only his publications in the *Press*. I discovered Moore's contribution during my reading of the *Northern Star* when I noticed it was identical to his contribution to the *Press*, except for this prefatory note to the editor of the *Northern Star* from the author who signed himself "PITY": "Sir—Your letting the following extract from a Poem, in the manner of Ossian, have a place in your patriotic paper, will oblige yours truly."

On 20 February 1798, the *Press* published another poem in the Ossianic mode in which the spirit of William Orr leans down from a cloud and weeps over the figure of slumbering Erin before he "touches the lyre of song, the Heavenly harp of Union—and the orisons of freedom tremble over the chords—'twas a strain he loved, for he died singing it." This Ossianic or bardic note, though usually not as extreme as Moore's contribution or the example of Orr as a heavenly bard, was an important element in the *Press*, wherein bards were the model for the paper's attempt to inspire and celebrate Irish patriots.

A poem entitled "The Contrast, or Antient Valour and Modern Prudence, A Fragment" on 2 November 1797 by "Z.," the pseudonym of a frequent contributor to the *Press*, gave the bardic motif a modern twist. The poem celebrated the ancient Welsh bard "Taliesin" whose lyre and "well-strung harp" had "told of noble deeds." The poem stressed the relationship between singing and fighting, declaring that when the bard's harp became silent, "courage became a useless thing" and "few would fight, when none would sing." Warning that "Modern Prudence," who was "Celestial wisdom's sober child," could be "mild" or "fume" depending on "circumstance," the poem declared that even Prudence could become an amazon:

> With true Amazonian swagger,
> Her ladyship becomes a bragger,
> Like any termagant will tear,
> Will damn and sink and curse and swear,
> And if you are not instant dumb,
> Will twist your neck, and kick your bum.

The poem's stately bardic motifs and its colloquial threats epitomize the two stylistic extremes of verse in the *Press*.

Although the *Press* continued the bardic mode of the *Northern Star*, the Irish language was not as dominant a feature in the *Press* as it had been in the *Northern Star*, perhaps because cultural matters took second place as events moved to their violent climax in the spring and summer of 1798. Only one supposed "translation" from the Irish was published in the *Press*: an anonymous poem entitled "The Fatal Battle of Aughrim," which appeared on 4 November 1797 with the note that it was "translated from the Irish."

The poem, by Thomas Russell, was actually an imitation of Tobias Smollett's famous 1746 poem "The Tears of Scotland," an account of the tragic consequences of the Jacobite Rebellion set to a traditional Scots tune. R. R. Madden acquired a letter of Thomas Russell's in which he enclosed lines that he said he had written in imitation of Smollett's poem (Madden 1846, 160–62). Russell's poem corresponds to the poem published in the *Press* that had supposedly been "translated from the Irish." Two explanations are possible: either the editors of the *Press* deliberately lied about the origin of the poem in order to promote the Irish language or to associate the United Irish message more closely with "the people," or else, knowing of Russell's interest in the Irish language and aware that he did translate poetry from the Irish, they presumed his lines were an actual translation of an Irish original. Someone involved in the publication of the *Press* evidently noticed the similarity between Russell's poem and Smollett's. Five days after it published "The Fatal Battle of Aughrim," the *Press* published "The Tears of Scotland" and mentioned that "Dr. Smollett" was the author (9 November 1797).

The style and the message of Russell's "Fatal Battle of Aughrim" certainly typified the United Irish verse in the *Press*, despite its being based on a Scottish original. Russell's lines parallel those of Smollett's quite closely, as a comparison of the opening lines suggests. Smollett's "Tears of Scotland" began:

> Mourn, hapless Caledonia, mourn
> Thy banished peace, thy laurels torn!
> Thy sons, for valour long renowned,
> Lie slaughtered on their native ground;
> (9 November 1797)

Russell's began:

> Mourn, lost Hibernia! ever mourn,
> Thy freedom lost, thy laurels torn
> Thy warriors sunk on Aughrim's plains,
> And Britain loading thee with chains.
> (4 November 1797)

In both poems, of course, Britain is the oppressor. Like Smollett, Russell focused on the lurid and melodramatic aspects of the situation:

> And violation stalks around,
> Murder and lust pollute the ground.
> They mock the trembling mother's pain,
> The tears of beauty plead in vain!
> The rocks resound with widows' cries,
> The suffering air with orphan'd sighs!

Russell, however, added several standard United Irish motifs: slavery, the green flag, and the harp. Russell's presentation of Aughrim also resembled the plot of Robert Ashton's popular Ulster folk play *The Battle of Aughrim*, for which Russell's poem reads like a poetic gloss.

The image of the harp that was so dominant in United Irish verse was the basis for the title of the fourth United Irish newspaper, the *Harp of Erin*. The newspaper's forthcoming publication in Cork was repeatedly announced in the *Press* in January and February of 1798. Such fanfare was not prophetic of success, however, for the govern-

ment suppressed the new paper less than two weeks after it first appeared. The *Harp of Erin's* short history is sketchy, but Roger O'Connor,
Arthur O'Connor's brother, and John and Henry Sheares were connected with it. The paper's motto was the United Irish slogan *It is
Newly Strung and Will be Heard.*

According to advertisements in the *Press*, the *Harp of Erin* would
"record the afflictions of our fellow countrymen . . . praise their vir-
tues and deplore their suffering" (27 January 1798). The musical
motifs of the paper's title and motto were echoed in ads that declared the *Harp of Erin* "with simple Minstrelsy will attune itself to
the dirge of the departed; or in louder strains, will call upon the
living patriot to assert the rights of his country." As so much United
Irish writing had done, the paper would thus follow the bardic model
of inspiring and celebrating Irish patriots. When the Stamp Office
delayed authorizing the publication of the new paper, the *Press* observed: "The Commissioners of Stamps we are sorry to say, do not
appear to be amongst the admirers of *Irish Music.* But the Harp is
new strung and will be heard" (15 February 1798). The new harp
was not heard for long, however. The first issue appeared on 7 March
1798, the last on 17 March 1798.

One of the *Harp of Erin's* declared goals was to tell of "the acts of
violence, robbery, and inhumanity committed upon our miserable fellow countrymen" (10 March 1798). It is difficult to imagine how such
discordant "news," or the paper's celebration of patriotic blood-sacrifice as a Christ-like triumph, would contribute to the paper's other
avowed goal of a "United Ireland" wherein "a fraternal love shall
animate the People, and Peace and Commerce shall diffuse plenty
and happiness over the whole face of the Country; and we will all join
in the Song of Peace and Liberty, and the HARP OF ERIN shall
resound in the full symphony of Joy" (10 March 1798). No amount of
musical imagery could disguise the great gap between the miserable
present and the joyous future.

A similar contradiction and tension are also apparent in the poems
that the *Harp of Erin* reprinted from the *Press*. The first issue reprinted
Drennan's "Wake of William Orr" and his "Erin." The third issue, on
14 March 1798, reprinted the "Ode" by "Sarsfield" that had so luridly
catalogued atrocities. Drennan's call for Irish unity and mercy to its
oppressors is difficult to reconcile with "Sarsfield's" call for violent

retribution. Such a tension between moral and physical force, so evident in the verse of the United Irishmen, would remain at the heart
of Irish nationalism for many generations.

The *Harp of Erin* reprinted some prose articles from the *Press*, but
it also published some interesting original materials, especially satire.
The first item on 14 March 1798 purported to be an extract from a
forthcoming "Tragi-Comedy, call ERIN." Characters included the anti-
Irish conspirator Satanides (who had also figured in Thomas Addis
Emmet's "Letters from the Mountains") and "Judges, Lawyers, Attor-
neys, Bailiffs, Gaolers, Executioners, Ghosts, Witches and Hobgob-
lins." The "extract," the first scene in the second act, took place in a
lawyer's study and featured a lawyer and several peasants.

The first peasant complained to the lawyer of how forty men had
invaded his house one night, pillaged and threatened to burn it, then
arrested him and jailed him for five months without lodging any complaint against him. The lawyer responded, "The thief is indemnified."
The next peasant recounted how soldiers burned his cottage and raped
his daughter. The lawyer responded, "Whilst things cannot be cured,
they must be endured; my heart bleeds for you." The next peasant
told how soldiers shot his son, then murdered his pregnant wife and
other children. The lawyer responded, "The best advice I can give you
would be to shoot, hang, or drown yourself, but no, when things are at
the worst they must mend, times will soon alter; the only counsel I
can give you all is to learn humanity." The Munster United Irishmen
were clearly losing patience with legal means of redress. One suspects
this satire was aimed as much at the more cautious of the United
Irishmen, such as Thomas Addis Emmet, as at English atrocities and
the callousness of the courts.

The government had certainly lost patience with United Irish
newspapers. The week before the government suppressed the *Harp of
Erin* in Cork, a squad of militia had been dispatched to the office of
the *Press* in Dublin where they found the 13 March 1798 edition
partially printed. They reportedly seized the copies, broke up the presses
and types with sledgehammers, and entirely destroyed the printing
equipment (Inglis 1954, 103–4). But the United Irishmen evidently
managed to keep some copies because, when *Extracts from The Press*,
an anthology of materials from the paper, was published in Philadelphia in 1802, it included the last two issues, which had supposedly

been suppressed. After the suppression of these newspapers, the Dublin United Irishmen focused their efforts at literary propaganda on songbooks such as those the Belfast United Irishmen had published. Like the four United Irish newspapers, the four *Paddy's Resource* songbooks illuminate developments within the United Irish movement and represent an important phase in the evolution of Irish literary nationalism.

· 5 ·

United Irish Songs and Songbooks

The *Press* and the *Harp of Erin* published fewer political songs to popular tunes than the *Northern Star* had, probably because, beginning in 1795, the United Irishmen regularly published such songs in their several songbooks entitled *Paddy's Resource*. Even before they published the first *Paddy's Resource* songbook in 1795, they had published a collection of songs in July 1792 entitled *Songs on the French Revolution that took place at Paris, 14 July 1789. Sung at the Celebration thereof at Belfast, on Saturday, 14 July 1792.* This songbook contained six anonymous songs, some of which were subsequently published in the *Northern Star* or in the first *Paddy's Resource* songbook. Two of these songs also appeared side by side on a Belfast broadside in 1792 on which they were ascribed to Samuel Neilson and Thomas Stott (SPOI 620/19/87). Presumably, many other United Irish songs were published in that ephemeral manner, guaranteeing their popular circulation if not their survival for later scholarly analysis.

A brief survey of the six songs included in the July 1792 collection provides insight into the United Irishmen's earliest political views:

1. "A New Song on the French Revolution," by Samuel Neilson. This song had appeared in the *Northern Star* in June 1792 and would also be reprinted in the 1795 *Paddy's Resource* as "The Glorious Exertion of Man." No tune was given in the 1792 songbook; in 1795 it was to be sung to the tune "General Wolfe," a tune popularized by Thomas Paine's song "The Death of General Wolfe" (1775). The last two lines of Neilson's song demonstrate how the United Irishmen placed their quest for political liberty in an international context: "May its [Liberty's] radiance the whole Human Family cheer / And may tyrants be banish'd the world." The poem's motifs of light, of

125

slavery, and of the quest for liberty as a religious duty would all become common in later United Irish songs. The third stanza presents
the United Irishmen's vision of the importance of "educating" the
people, which Neilson was implementing as editor of the *Northern
Star* and, very probably, as editor of this songbook.

2. "A New Song Addressed to Englishmen," by Samuel Neilson.
This song also appeared in the *Northern Star* in June 1792. As in the
first song, Neilson, a Presbyterian, presented the struggle for freedom
in a religious context: "When kings become tyrants—submission is
sin! / A Being all just—EQUAL RIGHTS must have giv'n; / And who
robs me of these must offend the All-wise." Neilson also upheld the
violence of the Glorious Revolution as a potential model for the
present. Indeed, the United Irishmen's early verse contradicts their
claims that violent revolution had not been part of their program at
the beginning. The necessity of revolutionary violence is a common
motif in their early verse.

3. "Song on the French Revolution," by Thomas Stott, to the tune
"Poor Jack," which was also used for several later United Irish songs. The
song's references to Sparta, the "Star of America," "Washington's wisdom," and "Mirabeau's Fire" disappeared when it was printed in the
Northern Star in July 1792, and in the 1795 *Paddy's Resource*. The song
celebrates the necessity of being "United" in order to obtain freedom, and
uses the motif of martyred patriot-poets who had "fought" and "bled" for
"Freedom" and adorned "lofty Poetry's lays." Thus from the outset United
Irish verse presented both poetry and violence as options.

4. "An New Song Addressed to Irishmen," by Wolfe Tone. The
lyrics are reprinted in appendix B. No tune was indicated; the song
was reprinted in the 1795 *Paddy's Resource* to the tune and refrain of
"Ballinamoney." A *Northern Star* article about the dinner celebrating
the conclusion of the harp festival and the United Irishmen's celebration of the fall of the Bastille on 14 July 1792 reported that the song
had been sung at the dinner, so it clearly had originated as a song.

5. "Paddy's Bull's Expedition." Not surprisingly, given its apoliti-
cal nature, this mock-heroic account of a comic Irishman's trip to
London was not reprinted in any United Irish newspaper or songbook.
No tune was given, but the refrain suggests it was to be sung to the
Scottish tune "Langolee," popular in Ireland and America in the late
eighteenth century.

6. "The Wand'ring Sailor." This sailor's song about longing for home, with no particular political message or Irish references, was never reprinted in later United Irish publications.

The international, especially the American and French, references of these songs would continue in the *Paddy's Resource* songbooks, but in a much less dominant way. A more emphatic "Irish" dimension would dominate all the songs in the *Paddy's Resource* songbooks, as it had Tone's song in this collection. Indeed, more than any other of these six songs in the first United Irish songbook, Tone's song typifies the coming United Irish song tradition in its successful blend of popular lyricism and political propaganda.

One suspects that the last two apolitical songs were added to inject a popular note lacking in the first three songs, which were little more than poorly versified political ideology. Recent history had shown the United Irishmen the power of popular political songs. Song had been central to Irish political events in the Volunteer movement and in the sectarian strife between Protestants and Catholics in rural Armagh and Down. A 1788 eye-witness account of religious dissension in County Armagh explained that an attack by a group of Catholics upon a troop of Volunteers was motivated by the Volunteers having played "tunes which were an insult to Catholics" such as "The Protestant Boys" and "The Boyne Water" (Miller 1990, 71).

Such bitter sectarian feuds, which continued into the 1790s and culminated in 1795 in the famous Battle of the Diamond in County Armagh and the founding of the Orange Order, were another factor in the sudden escalation of United Irish song publication in 1795. Religious dissension was antithetical to the United Irish goal of "uniting" Irish people of all classes and religions. A contemporary account of the ongoing battles in the mid-1790s between the Catholic "Defenders" and the Protestant "Peep O' Day Boys," who in 1795 became known as the Orange Order, described the United Irish attempt to quell these sectarian battles as follows: "In this state of things, a new party appeared styling themselves 'Liberty Men,' but better known by the name United Irishmen. They emerged from their committee in Belfast early in 1796, and disseminated their doctrines with industry and ability. . . . They dispersed liberty-songs composed for an Irish climate" (Miller 1990, 137).

Although many of these "liberty songs" appeared in United Irish newspapers and the *Paddy's Resource* songbooks, many others appeared

in the form of broadsides which were distributed throughout the coun-
tryside. Contemporary accounts and surviving confiscated materials in
the Public Record Offices in Belfast and Dublin attest to the large
number of liberty songs. Many such songs specifically aimed at restor-
ing peace and unity between the "Scotch" (the popular name for
Protestants) and the "Irish" (the popular name for Catholics) in these
sectarian battles.

   One such song was "The Social Thistle and Shamrock," to the old
Jacobite tune "Charley Is My Darling." According to Mary Ann
McCracken, the song was composed by her brother Henry Joy McCracken
and another United Irishman (Madden 1887, 167–68). Henry Joy
McCracken, one of the United Irish liasons with the Defenders, had
close contact with the working class at his family's cotton factory and in
his business travels throughout Ulster. A Presbyterian, Henry Joy
McCracken, like his good friend Thomas Russell, was especially close to
the lower classes and very much of a social activist on their behalf
(Fitzhenry 1936, 47, 65). The thistle in the title of McCracken's song was
the traditional symbol for Scotland, just as the shamrock was for Ireland.
His song (reprinted in appendix B), which began in the popular "Come
all ye" style of the broadside, was one of the more successful United Irish
attempts to achieve a popular note. The chorus contains Scots and Irish
words and suggests the song was used as a drinking song.

   As was the practice of the time, the United Irishmen wrote songs
about current events. R. R. Madden reprinted several United Irish
songs on the celebrated Blaris-Moor incident in 1797 in which four
members of the Monaghan Militia were court-martialed and shot for
being United Irishmen. According to Madden, "these songs, which
were published by the United Irishmen, in ballad form, Charles Teeling
informs us, were written, to his certain knowledge, by Counsellor
Sampson" (1887, 177). William Sampson, more generally known for
his legal defense of United Irishmen at trials, was also the author of
several United Irish prose satires. Neither McCracken's song nor
Sampson's Blaris-Moor songs ever appeared in a United Irish newspaper or in a Paddy's Resource songbook, and thus were part of a larger
United Irish song tradition that included broadside ballads and song
sheets as well as songbooks.

   By 1795, when the United Irishmen published their first Paddy's
Resource songbook, they had clearly come to appreciate the role that

song could play in propagating their movement and its goals. The final phrase in the title declared the practical function for which the songbook had been published: *Paddy's Resource: Being a Select Collection of Original and Modern Patriotic Songs, Toasts, and Sentiments, Compiled for the Use of the People of Ireland.* Georges-Denis Zimmermann, the only scholar to date to discuss *Paddy's Resource,* included three songs from the first two *Paddy's Resource* collections in his *Songs of Irish Rebellion: Political Street Ballads and Rebel Songs,* 1780–1900 (1967).

The phrase "Paddy's Resource" deserves comment. According to Zimmermann, "Paddy's Resource" was the title of a cartoon printed in 1780 showing an Irish Volunteer ready to use his weapons to obtain free trade, with a caption reading: "Ireland long tuned her harp in vain, / The Cannon seconds now the strain" (1967, 38). The word "resource" was especially rich in meaning. The various definitions of "resource" in the *Oxford English Dictionary* show how suggestive the word was:

> *resource*—means of supplying some want our deficiency; a stock or
> reserve upon which once can draw when necessary.
> —collective means possessed by any country for
> its own support or defense.
> —an action or procedure to which one may have
> recourse in a difficulty or emergency.
> —a means of relaxation or amusement. (1989, 13:731)

The United Irish use of the word encompassed all those meanings. Suggesting innocent "amusement" as well as militaristic defense, "resource" possessed an ambivalence that foreshadowed the ambivalent rhetoric about violence that would become a hallmark of Irish nationalism in the nineteenth century. The songs in the *Paddy's Resource* collections maintained an ambiguous attitude about violence by celebrating both the undeniably violent French Revolution and universal brotherhood and peace. Likewise, the woodcut facing the 1795 title page, which depicted a woman embracing a spear in one arm and a harp in the other, represented both physical and moral force as means of attaining freedom. The slogans above and below the picture, however, emphasized the nonviolent resources of music and

song: Tun'd to Freedom, and Irishmen Unite—Tear Off Your Chains
and Let Millions Be Free.

Perhaps, too, by using the phrase "resource" the United Irishmen,
who delighted in ridiculing Edmund Burke by using his famous phrase
"the swinish multitude" to describe themselves, were deliberately echoing his use of "resource" in *Reflections on the Revolution in France* (first
published in 1790) in which he declared: "A revolution will be the very
last resource of the thinking and good" (1965, 35). "Paddy's Resource"
was also very likely the name of a traditional tune. In the third number
of his *Irish Melodies*, Thomas Moore indicated the "air" for the song "Ill
Omens" to be "Kitty of Coleraine; or, Paddy's Resource." Edward Lysaght,
who wrote several United Irish songs in the 1790s, was often credited
with writing "Kitty of Coleraine." Moreover, a soldier's tune entitled
"Paddy's Resource" is included in Lewis Winstock's *Songs and Music of
the Redcoats: A History of the War Music of the British Army, 1642–1902*
(1970). Although, according to Winstock, that tune was supposedly
not composed until 1855, the composer was a thirty-five-year-old
Irishman from Galway (1970, 158–61) who could have drawn the title
and perhaps even some of the melody from a traditional Irish tune, if
not from a United Irish songbook.

The poetic preface to the first *Paddy's Resource* made the purpose
of the songbook clear:

> To fan the Patriotic flame,
> To cherish the desire of fame,
> To bid the Irish Youth aspire,
> To emulate the noble fire
> Which dissipates the tyrant's bands,
> And Freedom gives to injur'd lands;
> To teach the blooming Maid to bless
> Him only with her tenderness
> Whose ardent mind, and nervous hand,
> Shall vindicate his native land,
> Or dares the stroke of death defy,
> For Virtue and for Liberty.
> Dear Countrymen, these are our aims—
> For this our Book some merit claims;
> Think us not vain, ours is the toil,
> From abler Authors to compile.

From this, should but one Patriot more
Be added to his Country's store;
Should from the Virgin's heart one sigh
Be breath'd to Heav'n for Liberty—
We never, never shall complain,
Nor think that we have toil'd in vain.

This preface, signed "The Editors," implies that the editors did not write the songs. The United Irishmen were deliberately vague about who wrote, collected, and published the songs. No authors were given for any of the songs, a practice that would hold true for all the later *Paddy's Resource* songbooks as well. The numerous and ongoing government prosecutions for libel and sedition against the editors of the *Northern Star*, and against individual United Irishmen such as Archibald Hamilton Rowan and William Drennan for publishing proclamations for the Dublin Society of United Irishmen, had no doubt made the United Irishmen wary. Separation of authorship of materials from their publication was a cornerstone in several United Irish defenses against government charges of libel.

Little subsequent evidence has come to light about what person or persons were responsible for the various *Paddy's Resource* songbooks. Recently, the 1795 and 1796 *Paddy's Resource* have been attributed to James Porter, but no firm evidence exists.[1] It is not even certain that *Paddy's Resource* was published at the Northern Star Office, though it is likely that it was. Another possible source of publication was the nearby Public Printing Office, owned and operated by United Irishman Thomas Storey, which regularly published United Irish materials.

The other mystery surrounding *Paddy's Resource* is that none of the four songbooks was ever advertised in any United Irish newspaper, although other potentially seditious publications such as *Billy Bluff* and *Hurdy Gurdy* were. However, because both of those works had been originally published in the *Northern Star*, it would have been impossible to avoid responsibility for them. One possible explanation for the lack of ads for *Paddy's Resource* is that, given the prosecutions they were already facing, the United Irishmen were simply being cautious. Another explanation is that there was no need to advertise, either because there was a great demand for the songbooks or because they were distributed free, as so many United Irish publications, especially songs and broadsides, were.

The circumstances behind the publication of the first *Paddy's Resource* songbook are easier to determine. The date of publication, 1795, coincides with the transformation of the society into a secret organization when their methods became more covert. Government suppression led to a more revolutionary and radical, rather than reformist, agenda for the United Irishmen, who reorganized into secret societies and increased their efforts at propaganda among the lower classes in 1795. United Irishman Charles Hamilton Teeling's *History of the Irish Rebellion of 1798: A Personal Narrative* (1828) describes how the rise and progress of the United Irish Societies involved music and song:

> As the vigilance of the government increased and the system of union became more pregnant with danger, for the insurrection act had now attached to it the penalty of death, the exertions of the people were redoubled. Music, to which the Irish are so peculiarly attached, and which, if I may use the expression, speaks the native language of their soul, was most successfully resorted to on this occasion; and the popular songs of the day, suited to the temper of the times, were admirably calculated to rouse the national spirit, and elevate the mind to contempt of danger and the most enthusiastic feeling which love of liberty and of country could inspire (1876, 11).

Although the *Northern Star* published poems aimed at the middle and upper classes as well as a few songs with a broader popular appeal, the much larger number of songs in the 1795 *Paddy's Resource* clearly addressed a more popular and diverse audience. The lyrics included political songs, formal odes, peasant dialogues, drinking songs, and military marches. Every piece had the title of the tune to which it was to be sung printed under the title of the song, the common format for the thousands of popular broadsides published in Ireland in the eighteenth century. Only ten of the sixty songs had appeared in the *Northern Star*, so the songbook represented a major escalation of the United Irishmen's effort to "educate" through song.

The language in the songs ranged from formal to colloquial, and included a smattering of Irish and French. The tunes were drawn from Irish, Scottish, English, American, and French tradition. Many of the tunes had previously been used by earlier political movements, by sailors and Masons, and in popular operas or broadside ballads. Such diverse materials are further evidence of how elite and popular culture were closely intertwined in eighteenth-century Ireland and among the United Irishmen. Significantly, the 1795 *Paddy's Resource*, like all the later songbooks, embodies the unity of sects, classes, and cultures the United Irishmen were seeking.

I will discuss each of the four *Paddy's Resource* songbooks separately, in chronological order, and will focus on songs not already considered in my survey of the United Irishmen's eighteenth-century backgrounds and their newspapers. Space does not permit a discussion of each of the sixty songs in the first *Paddy's Resource*. Therefore, I will discuss the first dozen or so songs, because they represent significant aspects of the entire collection. Then I will consider additional songs in the collection that embody other important aspects of the first *Paddy's Resource* songbook.

The first song in the 1795 songbook was "Liberty and Equality; or, Dermot's Delight," which was to be sung to the tune "Patrick's Day in the Morning," one of the most popular eighteenth-century Irish tunes that had been performed at the Belfast Harp Festival in 1792. The song, which was subsequently ascribed to Thomas Stott, consists of a dialogue (including some phrases in Irish) between two peasants, Teague and Dermot, who are digging potatoes. Dermot tells Teague, "Sure a wonderful hubbub has happen'd in France, boy" where "all ranks to the tune of EQUALITY dance, boy! / Round Liberty's Tree night and morning!" Dermot concludes the song with these lines:

> May poor Ireland, (I hope, Teague, the wish is no treason)
> Whose shamrocks her foes have so long trodden down,
> Spring up to the rank of POLITICAL REASON,
> Before the Potatoe be blossm'd next season.

In 1796, an Antrim blacksmith "was found guilty of posting up and publishing, on the door of his shop at Bushmills, a seditious libel entitled 'Liberty and Equality,' calling upon the people to plant the tree of liberty instead of the crown of tyranny" (McSkimin 1906, 36). According to McSkimin, popular feeling was so much in the blacksmith's favor that his sentence was more a triumph than a punishment. Despite the down-to-earth and "Irish" dimensions of the opening song, the collection as a whole is the most abstract and least Irish of the four *Paddy's Resource* songbooks.

The second song, "Liberty's Call" was set to the tune "Hearts of Oak" from an English sailors' song. "Liberty's Call" illustrates the international political context in which the United Irish movement first placed itself, and the complex cultural backgrounds of its songs. The song is an adaptation of the first American patriotic song, "The Liberty Song," the lyrics of which are usually credited to John Dickinson. The United Irishmen probably adapted it from a version that had appeared in the English radical songbook *A Tribute to The Swinish Multitude* (edited by R. Thompson in 1795), the likely source of nine of the sixty songs in the first *Paddy's Resource*. The variations between the song in the two collections suggest that the United Irishmen attempted to make it less vague and less English, and more specifically Irish. The lyrics of "Liberty's Call" represent an interesting combination of abstract political philosophy—Paine's "Rights of Man," "Freedom," "Liberty," "Truth," "Justice"—and practical grievances—taxes, tithes, and rents. The song's command "To die or be free" suggests the violence implicit in the United Irishmen's songs from the beginning.

The lyrics of the third song, "The Gay Dawn of Freedom," to the tune "The Washer Woman" (presumably the lively tune known today as "The Irish Washerwoman"), deliberately reject the plaintive note sounded in many earlier Irish political songs:

> Come rouse Sons of Free'om! no more let us mourn,
> Nor bedew with our tears hallow'd Liberty's urn,
> As if her blest influence no more would return,
> For in spite of All Tyrants we'll sing Ça Ira.

Thus evoking the "new light" from France, "the gay dawn of Freedom" that had "spread throughout Europe," the song envisions an Irish village "all happy and free" in which the people are rejoicing by singing the French revolutionary song "Ça Ira."

The "Bright Star of Reason" was celebrated in the fourth song, "Unite and Be Free," to the tune "The Green Cockade," a popular symbol of the United Irish movement. "Unite and Be Free" also introduced an anticlerical and anti-Catholic note that was apparent several times in this first *Paddy's Resource*. After the opening lines invited all "lovers of Union, of every degree, / No matter what Trade or Religion ye be" to join the movement, the song goes on to criticize "the creatures of kings, and the dupes of a priest" who "bow down to a bauble, or worship a beast."

The next song, "Church and State; or, The Rector's Creed," to the tune "Black Joke," continued the anticlerical vein. The song was a satire in which a Protestant rector declared he believed "the only two comforts of life / Are counting my stipend, and kissing my wife" and that "the people were born to be slaves, / To be pilfer'd and plunder'd by us artful knaves."

The next song, "The Rights of Man," to the tune "God Save the King," illustrates the American and English literary and musical backgrounds of the United Irish movement. The song was a version of the American poet Philip Freneau's popular political ode of the same title. Echoing Thomas Paine's famous pamphlet *The Rights of Man*, which had influenced so many United Irishmen, the song celebrated the power of "Reason and Truth" to bring about a "new era . . . enlightening all darken'd minds." Although it may seem strange to us that such a song was set to a tune which embodied all that the United Irishmen opposed, this reversal of a tune's original meaning was typical of eighteenth-century political songs. The tune to which the Orange song "The Boyne Water" was set had originally been a Jacobite tune. Likewise, "Yankee Doodle," a celebration of American individualism, originated in a British soldiers' song mocking the stereotypical Yankee. The United Irishmen delighted in taking traditional British tunes and turning them inside out. For example, a later song in the collection, "The Star of Freedom," was set to the tune of "Rule Britannia."

The next song, "The Race of Kings," declared that a new order was about to "rout" both kings and "mouldy parchments." Indeed, if any one idea characterizes this first *Paddy's Resource*, it is the confidence in the power of reason and unity to bring peaceful reform and revolution. The exhuberant tune "A Huntin' We Will Go" energizes the somewhat vague and turgid lyrics of the next song, "Demanding Freedom":

> No longer in the shades of night,
> Where late in chains we lay;
> The sun arises, and his light
> Dispels our gloom away.

Another stanza in "Demanding Freedom" portrays a spirited anti-clericalism towards Anglican and Catholic prelates equal to the energy of the lively tune:

> The mitred Villain as he rolls,
> In luxury and lust,
> He blinds and robs the silly fools,
> Committed to his trust.

The luxury of "Kings and Priests" was also the target of the next song, "See Your Country Righted," to the Scottish tune "Maggy Lawder," which was well known in Ulster, both in oral tradition and in print.

It would be a mistake, however, to considered such tunes as Scottish in a narrow sense. The common "Gaelic" culture that linked the Scottish and Irish peasantry and the recent controversy concerning Macpherson's appropriation of Irish materials added an undeniably "Irish" dimension to Scottish folk tunes. The writings of John Daly Burk, a United Irishman who emigrated to America in 1795, suggest the broad context in which many United Irishmen must have placed supposedly "Scots" melodies. In an essay entitled "An Historical Essay on the Character and Antiquity of Irish Songs," Burk argued that Macpherson's appropriation of Irish materials was part of a larger cultural conspiracy. Rejecting Robert Burns's compromise position that Ireland and Scotland, as Gaelic cultures, shared many melodies, Burk cited the "original Gaelic songs to which these airs were and are at this day sung in every part of Ireland" as evidence of the Irish origin of many so-called Scottish songs (1808, 1–2).

Another factor, according to Burk, was that when Scots-*Gaelic* tunes, such as "Lochaber," "Moll Roe," "Maggie Lauder," "Green Grow the Rushes," and "Nanny O" (all of which were used by the United Irishmen in the several *Paddy's Resource* songbooks), were set to Scots-English words, they were fair game for people like Thomas Percy who preferred to see them as English or Scottish rather than as Gaelic. Burk's familiarity with the Belfast Harp Festival in 1792 and with Bunting's collection of traditional Irish music, his many references to United Irish songs in the course of his *History of the Late War in Ireland* (1799), and the many American political songs he wrote to tunes used in the *Paddy's Resource* songbooks, place him in the mainstream of United Irish songwriting and suggest his essay voiced a commonly held assumption about the larger "Gaelic" nature of so-called Scottish tunes. Indeed, Henry Joy McCracken's song "The Social Thistle and the Shamrock" discussed earlier in this chapter, referred to historians and poets claiming a joint origin for the Scots and the Irish. Burk's arguments were especially appropriate in the case of "Lochaber" because Bunting and subsequent music scholars have claimed that an identical tune was known in Ireland as "Limerick's Lamentation." Nevertheless, given that the first *Paddy's Resource* was published in Belfast, its use of the Scottish tune title was appropriate.

The tenth song, "The Tree of Liberty," was also set to a "Scots" tune, "Roslin Castle," popular in oral tradition and in print, having appeared in Burns and in Johnson's *Scots Musical Museum*. Indeed, such tunes were so popular within Ulster that, if one did not accept Burk's arguments, one could argue that they had become "Irish" by a process of assimilation. The song's lyrics represent an amalgamation of political, philosophical, and religious motifs. The Liberty Tree, of course, was a powerful political symbol adapted from the American and French Revolutions. In the context of the song the tree represented a "great Reformation," thus adapting the religious significance of the earlier Protestant Reformation to the new battle for liberty. Religious truth had prevailed in the earlier Reformation; "truth and reason" would now triumph thanks to the "sacred" deeds of patriots who rooted out the "trees of corruption" and did away with "the splendour and pomp of a court." In addition to liberating Ireland, the patriots would "please the ALL-WISE."

The title of the next song was "Truth and Reason," but its tune, "My Ain Kind Deary," a seventeenth-century Scottish tune found in many eighteenth-century collections, added a colloquial dimension, as did the lines, "Let us now a bumper fill, / To patriots who led the way." Contemporary accounts indicate that United Irish meetings were frequently held at Belfast taverns where drinking and political discussion went on apace. Thus it is not surprising that a song would begin in a heroic vein with a prophetic vision of "bright Liberty descending" upon Ireland and conclude with lines common in drinking songs. The song's vagueness about exactly *how* liberty would be achieved was typical of these early United Irish songs. All bloodshed was attributed to the subjection of Ireland, none to its eventual emancipation when "No more wild discord rages, / 'TRUTH and REASON bear the sway'."

The opening stanza of the next song, "The Jovial Friends," makes clear that it too was a drinking song:

> My jovial friends with social glee,
>   The flowing can we'll quickly pass;
> Each breast will warm to Liberty,
>   While whiskey crowns each sparkling glass.

The song is set to a tune entitled "When Bidden to the Wake or Fair," which evidently referred to the old Scots tune "Nancy O" that William Shield had used for a song which began, "When bidden to the wake or fair," in his comic opera *Rosina* in 1782 (Simpson 1966, 505–7). The popular tune no doubt made the political rhetoric of the later stanzas more palatable. The same tune was used for the popular United Irish ballad "Edward," which lamented the death of Lord Edward Fitzgerald in 1798. It was published in the fourth *Paddy's Resource* songbook and as a broadside.

The next song, "The Star of Liberty," presents another example of how eighteenth-century songs encompassed the tavern, the military, the theater, and politics. Its tune, "General Wolfe," had been used by Philip Freneau for an American political song, but the tune originated in the soldiers' drinking song "Why, Soldiers, Why?" This drinking song is of particular interest because it was evidently one of the many traditional soldiers' songs that Thomas Russell, a former British soldier, shared with his good friend Wolfe Tone. Tone attributed the phrase " 'Tis but in vain for soldiers to complain," which echoes throughout his journal, to his friend Russell (1826, 2:22). The lyrics of "Why, Soldiers, Why?" indicate where Russell had found the phrase:

> 'Tis but in vain,
> (I mean not to upbraid you, boys),
> For soldiers to complain.
> Should the next campaign
> Send us to Him who made us, boys,
> We're free from pain.
> But should we remain,
> A bottle and kind landlady
> Cures all again.
>   (Winstock 1970, 58–61)

Although lyrics of "The Star of Liberty" bear little trace of the devil-may-care bravado of the soldiers' song, the tune itself served many important purposes for the United Irishmen. English soldiers were one of their prime recruiting targets and a tune already popular among them had obvious advantages. Moreover, the tune no doubt added some needed life to the lyrics. The antithetical imagery of "The Star of Liberty's" lyrics, which focused on black and white, night and day, dark and light, was also derived from popular song tradition. The song's vision of "deserts of darkness and dungeons of night" giving way to the "blaze" of the "Star of Liberty" is more powerful than the vague political rhetoric that dominated most of the songs in the collection, as are the vivid images of Edmund Burke "like a Bat" forced to "retire" from the "splendour" of Liberty's star and of the "pedants" he had "intrapt [sic] in his cobwebs like flies."

The songs discussed thus far typify the songs in the first *Paddy's Resource* songbook. Vague political rhetoric about Liberty, Reason, and Truth and numerous references to the French, and to a lesser extent the American, Revolutions dominated most of the songs. Significantly, however, the popular Irish tradition of depicting Ireland as a woman clearly exerted a strong influence on the *Paddy's Resource* songs. Images of Ireland as a woman, whether Hibernia or "Granuweal," outnumber the images of the female figure of Liberty in the French tradition. Even a song with the French-inspired title of "The New Viva La" combined the French figure of Liberty and the Irish figure of Hibernia. When Liberty appears in the poem, she does so in the way the female persona of Ireland appeared in the native Irish aisling: "glorious as the morning star" and shedding "beams of heavenly splendour."

The song "Hibernia's Harp Strung to Liberty," to the sailors' tune "Lash'd to the Helm," foreshadowed the more Irish and militant note that would be sounded in future *Paddy's Resource* songbooks:

> Hibernia's Harp indignant lay,
> And curs'd with ev'ry string the day,
> And mourn's her dearest birth-right lost,
> When Despots landed on her coast.
>   Her Harp shall be
>   By Liberty

> Soon tun'd to Freedom's sound;
> Her sons agree
> They will be Free,
> And put their tyrants down.
> . . . .
> To crush that pow'r
> That galls each hour
> And drive it from the land;
> Be this our aim,
> And highest fame,
> 'Till all join hand in hand.

Significantly, now that Hibernia's harp was "strung by Liberty," the harp not only "mourn'd" but also was "indignant" and offered curses as well as tears.

Two other songs issued more explicit calls to violent action and, not surprisingly, were both reprinted in the 1798 and 1803 *Paddy's Resource* songbooks. "Man is Free by Nature," which may have been written by Thomas Russell and was set to the tune "Gilly Crankey," began:[2]

> Why vainly do we waste our time,
> Repeating our oppressions?
> Come haste to arms, for now's the time
> To punish past transgressions.

"The Fatal Blow," to the tune "O'er the Hills and Far Away," also issued a call to arms:

> Come, come my Countrymen advance,
> Charge your musket, point your lance,
> . . . .
> Then haste to strike the fatal blow,
> And punish each tyrannic foe.

The majority of songs, however, emphasized the moral righteousness and the happy outcome of the struggle rather than any bloodshed that might be involved in it. According to the song "Truth's Bright Ray," the muse would "now take her flight, / And sing old Granu

Free." The song "The Triumph of Reason" offered an equally sanguine prospect of a future when the rising of "the sons of Granu" would "banish all our sorrow." The triumph of "Truth," "Liberty," and "Freedom" was to have tangible practical consequences, as described in the song "The Olive Branch":

> Commerce will raise her drooping head,
>   Dame fortune's hand-maid cheer the while,
> And honest Tradesman will get bread—
>   Then will the Sons of Granu smile.

No doubt the optimism of such early *Paddy's Resource* songs did much to influence the popular opinion, attested to by many contemporary accounts of the 1798 Rising, that a glorious new age of prosperity for the common man would be the outcome of any successful revolution.

The common people who would benefit from this new prosperity were variously portrayed. Songs such as "Injured Freedom," which portrayed a peasantry in the languid, pastoral tradition of Ramsay's popular *Tea-Table Miscellany,* and described how "Chearful [sic] Shepherds o'er the glade / Gently wake the plaintive flute" and how "beneath the budding thorn / Collin tunes his rustic air," clearly belonged to the more lugubrious eighteenth-century pastoral tradition. Given the literary, archaic, and passive nature of this song, it is not surprising that it was never reprinted in later *Paddy's Resource* collections.

A handful of songs in this first *Paddy's Resource* songbook portrayed the sufferings of a contemporary peasantry in lurid, sentimental terms, and thus foreshadowed what became a major motif in later United Irish verse. For example, "Adversity's Cot," which was reprinted in the 1803 *Paddy's Resource,* depicted several representative types of the peasantry: a "poor lab'rer, enfeebled and old" whose "children are hungry and poor" and whose "only abode" is now the workhouse; a "matron" who tearfully mourns "with accents all frantic and wild" for her son; and the son who had been "inveigled away" to Flanders as an English soldier where he met the following fate:

> There the poor victim lies on the blood moisten'd clay,
> And vultures and kites scream aloud for their prey;
> Whilst his poor mangled limbs the dire banquet invite,
> And no tear wets his corpse, but the dews of the night.

The song's final prototype of the common man was a sailor who returns "maim'd and wounded" from service in the English navy to become a wandering beggar.

An Irish peasant speaks for himself in the song "The Union of Parties" to the eighteenth-century jig tune, "The Cudgel." A Connaught peasant named Thady, having been driven off his land by his landlord, vigorously defends his right to "Catholic Emancipation" and predicts the day when "the tythers and the taxers of mankind / Will shrink with horror and fear." Although the line in the refrain of the original, "O the cudgel for me," becomes "A Union of Parties for Me" in the United Irish song, the threat of using a weapon in the original lyrics remains unspoken but suggested by the tune. Significantly, although the more abstract and philosophical of the 1795 songs were not reprinted in the later songbooks, "The Union of Parties" was.

The United Irishmen eventually realized that such examples of grievances and a more popular style were more effective propaganda than the formal celebration of abstractions like Unity and Freedom that predominated in the majority of these early songs. Even in this first collection, however, a handful of songs echoed the traditional internal rhymes and the dialect of popular songs in Irish and in English. For example, in the song "Billy's Undone by the War," to the popular tune "O! Dear What Can the Matter Be?", a clever Irish soldier serving abroad expresses his discontent with King "Billy" to a fellow Irishman in these words:

> Pat, can you tell what the Devil he's driving at?
> What is't we're fighting for, what is't he's striving at?
> A foul bit of work the damn'd Tory's conniving at!
> Billy's undone by the war.
> . . . .
> Then your Cabinet calls this a war of existence now,
> That's in *plain Irish* to die at a distance now, . . .

A colloquial note was also sounded by the popular tunes to which many of the songs were to be sung, especially in the tunes associated with drinking songs. For example, the rather dry lyrics of a song entitled "Republican Glee" were to be sung to a tune entitled "Drunk at Night, and Dry in the Morning." Some of the eighteenth-century tunes used for these first *Paddy's Resource* songs are still popular today: "O'er the Hills and Far Away," which had been used for Jacobite ballads, in numerous songs and operas, and by Robert Burns; "Cruiskeen Lan," which remains one of the most popular of all Irish drinking songs; "For He's a Jolly Good Fellow" (called "Mallbrouk" in *Paddy's Resource*); and "The Girl I Left Behind Me," a tune popular among soldiers, Dubliners, and country people in the eighteenth century. As part of their avowed intention to make their movement and their songbooks speak both "for the people" and "to the people," the United Irishmen clearly used the old songs of people of all classes and religions to craft new songs.

The last song in this first *Paddy' Resource* songbook was, appropriately, Tone's "Ierne United," which is reprinted in appendix B. Tone's song epitomizes the popular tone and lyricism at which the best United Irish songs aimed, and demonstrates that political verse can indeed both teach and delight. The placement of Tone's song in such a prominent position perhaps had something to do with his celebrated farewell visit to Belfast and departure for America from Belfast harbor in the summer of 1795.

The songbook concluded with a "Political Creed" in prose and sixty-two "Toasts and Sentiments." The creed began, "I believe that God is the impartial Father of the whole human race; that the rights of all men therefore must be equal; and that he who tamely resigns those rights, wrongs his posterity, degrades himself, and ought to be ashamed to live." The paragraphs that followed praised "frequent elections" and "universal suffrage," condemned "self-created legislators," hereditary monarchy, "national churches," tithes, and unjust taxes.

The "Toasts and Sentiments," many of which were reprinted in United Irish newspapers at various times and reported as having been used at United Irish meetings, included the following:

The Irish Harp tun'd to Freedom.

The men who write, and the men who fight for Freedom.

The literary characters who have vindicated the Rights of Man; and may genius ever be employed in the cause of Freedom.

The Proprietors of the Northern Star, and a just reward for their
useful labours in the cause of Freedom.

The industrious Poor; confusion and disgrace to their enemies.

Success to the labours of the Plow and the Loom.

The final toast was "peace on earth, and good will to man." The
publication of such toasts was a common eighteenth-century practice.
Earlier in the century a collection of forty-eight Irish political toasts
published by a society who styled themselves "the Independent Freeholders of the Province of Munster" and "Sons of Liberty" had included the toast "May all mitred Enemies of Ireland die of a conscious
Gangrene, for betraying their country" (*An Address* 1754, 46).

The second songbook, entitled *Paddy's Resource: Being a Select
Collection of Original Patriotic Songs, for the Use of the People of Ireland*,
was published in 1796. Several songs in it refer to patriots languishing
in prison, which suggests that it was published after the arrests of
Samuel Neilson, Thomas Russell, and other United Irishmen in September 1796. No place or publisher is given, though it was certainly
published in Belfast, probably at the Northern Star Office or at the
Public Printing House owned by United Irishman Thomas Storey.

The page opposite the title page contained a harp and this poem,
noteworthy for the high literary style in which it casts its "popular"
message:

> O! Liberty! thou goddess, heav'nly bright,
> Profuse of bliss, and pregnant with delight,
> Eternal pleasures in thy presence reign,
> And smiling Plenty leads thy wanton train;
> Eas'd of her load, subjection grows more light,
> And poverty looks cheerful in thy sight;
> Thou mak'st the gloomy face of Nature gay—
> Gives beauty to the sun, and pleasure to the day.

The poetic preface was in a somewhat less ornate style. Like the
preface to the first *Paddy's Resource*, it declared that the collection's
purpose was to recruit new patriots to the cause, but it added new
motifs that had not been present in the 1795 preface: patriots lan-

guishing in chains, Hibernia's past freedom, and the grievances of the poor.

> To animate the soul of Man;
> To imitate that glorious plan
> Of Truth and Virtue—Nature's laws—
> The Justice of his Country's cause;
> To know the wants, and feel the pains
> Of Patriots languishing in chains;
> To bid Saint Patrick's Irish band,
> UNITED firm, their Rights demand;
> To PERSEVERE—and view once more
> FREEDOM approach Hibernia's shore
> To Bless the Maid, whose lovely charms
> Inspires the Patriot Youth to arms
> His Country's Rights for to defend.
> The Poor and Virtuous to befriend;
> To teach, on Earth, Peace and good will,
> And every breast with joy to fill:—
> For this we toil, with fervent zeal,
> To add new Patriots to the common weal.

This collection contained forty-three new songs, three of which had already appeared in the *Northern Star*. These new songs contained fewer references to the French Revolution and to abstractions like Freedom and Reason. The florid declarations of abstract rights gave way to concrete complaints of injustice and to more explicitly Irish references and motifs, especially shamrocks. Nor were there any songs from the English radical songbook *A Tribute to The Swinish Multitude* or from American or French political song tradition.

The opening song, "Teague and Pat," is something of a continuation of the song "Liberty and Equality; or, Dermot's Delight," which had opened the 1795 collection. Both songs are dialogues between two peasants who are digging potatoes and are set to the tune "Patrick's Day in the Morning." Teague, who had been informed by Dermot of the good news of the French Revolution and the prospect that Ireland too would "spring up to the rank of Political Reason, / Before the Potatoe be blossom'd next season," in the 1795 song, now shares the news with a peasant named Pat as they are digging potatoes. References to European and French leaders and to the "Tree of French Liberty" in the 1795 song are replaced by Irish grievances in the 1796 song:

> Dear Pat give attention to what I now mention,
>> The times they are alter'd, now listen I pray,
> With sedition and treason, and every such nonsense,
>> Arrah! Pat, sure they tell us we are all gone astray;
> But hark you, dear Pat, these words have their meaning,
>> To humble poor Paddy, and to keep him down,
> But if ever we wish for to be a FREE NATION,
>> UNION, for sure Pat, is our only salvation—
>> On Patrick's Day in the Morning.
>
> Such tythes and such taxes, with laws to oppress us,
>> In any wise nation, sure never was known;
> Under placemen, with pensions, and their vile intentions,
>> The poor man and widow reluctant doth groan,
> In bastiles and chains the true Patriot complains,
>> Their innocent lives they wish to betray;
> Providence will attend them, mankind will befriend them,
>> The virtuous and brave will ever commend them,
>> On Patrick's Day in the Morning.

The use of dialect and the mid-line rhymes echoed popular songs. The final lines embodied the same joyous optimism that had characterized the 1795 collection:

> In transports of joy, they shook hands and did cry,
>> The time is approaching we yet WILL BE FREE,
> When Peace and Good Will every bosom will fill;
>> Then PADDY's RESOURCE shall have its free course—
>> On Patrick's Day in the Morning.

"Teague and Pat's" colloquialisms and recitation of Irish grievances continued in many of the songs that followed. The song "War, Cruel War and Starvation," to the tune "Ballinamoney," begins "I'll tell you, dear Pat," details the Irish woes of war and starvation, and includes one chorus that wished the devil would send all lords to Botany Bay. "Unity's School," to the tune "Mary Queen of Scots'

Lamentation," which Robert Burns had used for one of his songs, laments the fate of Hibernia's "sons" who "are into dark prisons now hurl'd," where they are accused by "a villainous perjured crew, / Who worship no God."

Some songs celebrated the tonic of drink, such as "The True Sons of Paddy," to the tune "Larry Grogan"[3]; "The Shamrock," to the tune "Cuckoo's Nest"; and "The British Bacchanals," to the tune "Green Grows the Rushes, O," which declared:

> Push about the Glasses, O—
> Push about the Glasses, O
> For, what care we how things go on,
> While blushing Nectar passes, O

Such drinking songs epitomize the more lyrical and popular dimensions of the 1796 *Paddy's Resource*.

Similarly, the lyrics of "The Triumph of Truth," the title of which suggests a formal ode in the tradition of most of the songs in 1795, actually resemble a popular song:

> Arrah Paddy, dear boy, my heart and my joy,
>   Tune up your Harp in the cause of your Country;
> With Republican glee still let us agree,
>   And gallantly plant the Tree of Liberty.'
> The people, you see, do now all agree,
>   In spite of the tribe that long divided them;
> We'll throw off the yoke—huzza for the stroke,
>   Sure gramachre, Paddy, we'll have day about with them.
>   Tol, lol, &c.

> Was Ireland Free, how snug I would be,
>   Myself and my neighbours would live so happily,
> No tax would we pay, but what would defray
>   The expence of the nation laid out honestly;
> Till that time shall come, let dissensions be mum;
>   What signifies quarrelling—we are Irishmen;
> All religious disputes hereafter be mute,
>   And Unite to oppose the men first raised them.
>   Tol, lol, &c.

Another representative song in the 1796 songbook was "Saint Patrick's Delight" to the tune "Moll Roe."

> Oh! if you have a mind to gain Freedom,
>   Go travel the globe all around,
> But the like of the old Irish nation,
>   In a corner is scarce to be found:
> Oh there you'll find true hospitality,
>   Whiskey and friendship galore;
> With ERIN GO BRAGH, on Green Ribbons,
>   The Ladies so much do adore.
>   Musha whack, &c.[4]

In contrast to the optimism and light-hearted gaiety of "The Triumph of Truth" and "Saint Patrick's Delight," other songs contained a darker, more violent note. Moreover, the somewhat muted militancy of the 1795 *Paddy's Resource* was much more pronounced in 1796. The song "The Charter of Brotherhood," to the tune "Viva la," declared that the "branch of Freedom" would only thrive in Ireland when its roots had been nourished by "Tyrants blood." Similarly, the song "Honest Pat," to the tune "The Girl I Left Behind Me," called upon Hibernia's Sons to "To crush those knaves that us enslaves / Our guns shall roar like thunder." To the now traditional images of "Old Granu" in "chains" who "groans, laments, and moans," were added a contemporary, if rudely versified, dimension:

> A bill of woe, by the junto,
>   Has passed through the House quick,
> For to defile Hibernia's Isle,
>   And bind down honest Patrick.

Other songs celebrated death. The song "The Virtuous Warriors," to the tune "Roslin Castle," asked, "Will you stand by old Ireland and die for her sake?" and declared, "What a glory it is for a warrior to fall, / By the thrust of a pike, or the force of a ball." Such a death was presented as part of the Creator's plan for "without His command not a sparrow can die." The song "Glorious Death," to the tune "Rights of Man," included the following stanza:

Glorious it is to die
In an attempt so high
   Glorious applause:
Leave Sweethearts, Friends and Wives,
Gallantly risque our lives,
Fame he will gain, who strives
   In such a cause.

Another song, "Granu's Call," to the tune "The Vicar and Moses" from a comic popular eighteenth-century song of that title (Simpson 1966, 735), called for military action to replace passive suffering:

With SHAMROCK and HARP,
  And UNION—but mark!
The willow too long we have worn it.
  With staff, pike and gun,
  Old Granu says come—
My Sons shall no longer endure it.

Even a song "By a Lady" was much more militant than a song she had published in the 1795 *Paddy's Resource*. Her 1795 song "Brethren Unite" to the tune "God Save the Rights of Man" called upon Hibernia to "Teach with a radiant smile" and "bid our sons Unite." In her 1796 song "The Imprisoned Patriot," such metaphors were accompanied by images of "dungeons of darkness" and an angry call to "gallant heroes" to "fight for thy Freedom" and "headlong hurl her enemies to the grave they dug for you."

The most important song, and probably the best, in the 1796 *Paddy's Resource* was the last one, "The Exiled Irishman's Lamentation" to the tune "Savourna Deelish [sic]," reprinted in appendix B and discussed in chapter 3 in connection with its original publication in the *Northern Star* in July 1796. It was reprinted in the 1798 and 1803 *Paddy's Resource* songbooks and throughout the nineteenth century.

The next two *Paddy's Resource* songbooks were published in Dublin, one in 1798 and the other probably in 1803. The 1798 songbook was clearly meant to be a continuation of the two earlier songbooks published in Belfast in 1795 and 1796. The poetic prefaces from each of those songbooks were reprinted after the title page, and the 1798 collection included twenty-seven songs from the earlier songbooks.

The printing of the title of the 1798 songbook, however, reflected a new emphasis: *Paddy's Resource; OR, THE HARP OF ERIN, AT-TUNED TO FREEDOM. BEING A COLLECTION OF PATRI-OTIC SONGS SELECTED FOR PADDY'S AMUSEMENT.* The emphasis on the "Harp of Erin" in the title is not surprising, as that had been a major motif in United Irish verse from the beginning. The phrase also recalled the recently suppressed United Irish newspaper of that title published for a few weeks in March 1798, and perhaps was a deliberate attempt to taunt the government. The government's suppression of both the *Harp of Erin* and the *Press* in March 1798 had made the publication of songbooks an even more important and safer means of propaganda.

Song was an important element in the Dublin political scene in the 1790s. R. R. Madden's numerous informants described a milieu as much literary as political:

> There are persons still surviving of 1798, who remember the time when Drennan's songs, and Lysaght's lyrical productions, and Curran's sallies of brilliant wit and humour, and all the un-premeditated jests, and black letter drollery, and erudite recre-ative scholastic humour . . . were in vogue in Dublin, and made to promote, if not the feast of reason, the flow of soul, at all convivial meetings; and they speak of them still as reminiscences of enjoyment of by-gone days, in which (pregnant with political strife as they were) the pleasures of social life were blended with literary tastes, and shared by persons of higher talents, of all politics, without distinction of creed or party, than are found to mingle in any social intercourse of the present day in Ireland. (Madden 1858b, 2: 268)

The 1798 songbook, which includes a dozen songs from the *Press*, was probably published in the early spring because none of its songs refers to the military events that occurred in the late spring and summer of 1798. The songbook might well have been printed by John Chambers, a printer and prominent Dublin United Irishman, who published many United Irish publications and was referred to in gov-ernment reports of the day as printing "political song books" (Pollard 1964, 12). Samuel Neilson, who was released from prison on 22 Feb-ruary 1798 and not arrested again until late May, may have had a hand in preparing the songbook. He almost certainly was involved in the publication of the 1795 *Paddy's Resource*.

The epigraph under the 1798 title provides insight into the Dublin political and literary milieu in which the songbook originated:

> Whilst Tyrants reign, in guilty state,
> And strive base slav'ry to prolong;
> My heart, with FREEDOM'S hopes elate,
> Shall join in Liberty's sweet Song.

A Dublin songbook entitled *The Political Harmonist; or, Songs and Poetical Effusions, Sacred to the Cause of Liberty*, by "A Cosmopolite," had used the same four lines as an epigraph. A copy in the Haliday Collection in the Royal Irish Academy is the "4th edition," printed in Dublin in 1797 by "William Porter." R. B. McDowell's list of "The Personnel of the Dublin Society of United Irishmen, 1791–94" includes a William Porter who was a printer and bookseller in Skinners' Alley and who was a member of the society at least as early as 8 February 1793, when he proposed a new member (McDowell 1940, 45). The fourth edition of *The Political Harmonist* contains a song concerning a trial in November 1794.

The preface to *The Political Harmonist* illuminates the attitudes about the political significance of songs among Dublin radicals in the 1790s:

> In those countries where Liberty predominates, Harmony is cherished with the utmost freedom, and their popular airs are chaunted with a degree of enthusiasm by people of every description. The Americans obtained their liberty by the heart-chearing [sic] sound of *yankee doodle*, and the French by the more exhilarating ones of *ça ira* and the Marseillois [sic] Hymn; such charming and inspiriting Harmony is sufficient in itself to inspire men with a love of Liberty, particularly when under such musical influence they have achieved the salvation of their country" (v).

Although the preface to *The Political Harmonist* declared that "songs encouraging riot and debauch among the lower orders should be discouraged" (vi), the titles of the tunes used for the political songs that followed suggest that the use of melodies from popular songs was common practice: "Ballinamona," "Alley Croker," "Poll and Partner Fox," "Dear Sir This Brown Jug," and "Bow Wow Wow." The titles of some songs suggest the more formal and philosophic nature of the lyrics: "Song to Liberty" and "Lines in Appeal to the Reasoning Part of Mankind."

A French emphasis is apparent in several songs, such as "Stanzas on the Prosperity of France." Another piece, entitled "Song Addressed to Simon Butler and Oliver Bond," celebrated two prominent Dublin United Irishmen. A "Song on the French Invasion," to the tune "Ballinamona," presents dialogue in dialect between two peasants in which "Patrick" talks "Phelim" into welcoming a French invasion to liberate Ireland. This piece resembles the opening songs in the first two *Paddy's Resource* songbooks, which were also peasant dialogues extolling the French, if not a French invasion. Thus the contents of the fourth edition of *The Political Harmonist* are similar enough to the *Paddy's Resource* songbooks to suggest that the United Irishmen may have played a part in its publication. In any event, the origins of the 1798 *Paddy's Resource* were broader than just the two previous *Paddy's Resource* songbooks published by the Belfast United Irishmen.

The frontispiece for the new *Paddy's Resource* songbook depicted several important United Irish symbols and mottos. A Phrygian cap irradiating like a sun portrayed the light imagery common in United Irish verse. Two clasped hands, symbolizing unity and adapted from the Volunteers' insignia, were similar to those often used on United Irish membership certificates. The ever-present harp was the third item on the frontispiece. Above these three symbolic devices was a banner inscribed in Irish script Erin go bragh (Ireland forever), and below them was a banner with the words Irishmen Unite.

Like the earlier songbooks, the songs in the 1798 *Paddy's Resource* represent a wide range of literary styles and political philosophies, thus symbolizing the unity of classes and parties that the United Irishmen sought. But literary and symbolic considerations aside, the various editions of *Paddy's Resource* also illustrate the significant tensions and complexities in the ideological development of the United Irish movement. The most apparent changes in emphasis in the 1798 *Paddy's Resource* were a much angrier and more militant tone and a more lurid and sensational depiction of injustices. In that sense, the collection resembled the *Press* more than the Belfast editions of *Paddy's Resource*.

The 1798 *Paddy's Resource* contained sixty-four songs, twenty-seven of which are from the 1795 and 1796 songbooks, plus thirty-seven new songs, twelve of which had appeared in the *Press*. The songs reprinted from the two earlier songbooks were generally the most militant in those collections. The first several songs in the new collection are representative of the whole. The opening song was William Drennan's "Erin," the first song to have been published in the *Press*, and suggests Drennan might have had some connection with the preparation of the songbook. Drennan's Erin calls her sons to unite "like the leaves of their shamrock," rather than fight. She associates violence with the oppressors "who would die [*sic*] her grass red from their hatred to green," and urges her sons to "be gentle as brave" and not to let "vengeance presume to defile, / the cause, or the men, of the Emerald Isle."

A much angrier tone is apparent in the second song, "The Shoot of Liberty," a new song to the tune "Mulberry Tree." It attacked "despots who long have been the scourge of our race," "vice-regal tyrants," "absentee landlords," "aristocrat harpies," and the "titl'd and pension'd." The third song was the sentimental "Exiled Irishman's Lamentation," discussed earlier and reprinted in appendix B, which avoided an explicit call to arms. The fourth song was a new one which declared that, although in the past "Erin's genius sung with woe," now was the time to "Rise Hibernians, regain your native land, / While patriot legions round you stand" and "drive the tyrants from your land."

The militant song "The Fatal Blow," from the 1795 *Paddy's Resource*, came next with its call for "vengeance": "Come, come, my countrymen, advance, / Charge your musket, point your lance." A new song, "Paddy's Complaint," then issued a call for "Death or Liberty" because Britain "with savage impious rage, / Laws of GOD and nature broke, / Against opinions War did wage." Next, "The Rights of Man," from the 1795 *Paddy's Resource*, extolled death in freedom's cause: "Death in so just a cause, / Crowns us with loud applause."

The militant tone shifted back to romantic sentimentality in the next song, "The Victim of Tyranny," reprinted from the *Press* and set to the tune "Mary's Dream." That tune was appropriate because it was from a popular sentimental song of that title written in 1750 by a Scotsman named John Lowe. He had written lyrics in both Scots dialect and in "elegeant English" telling the story of how a dead lover's ghost appeared three times in a dream to his beloved to tell her "Sweet Mary, weep nae mair for me" (Johnson 1962, 2:39). The United Irishmen's "Victim of Tyranny" is equally sentimental. Pat, the "victim," laments injustices of his "tyrant landlord," the burning of his house, the loss of his wife and children, and the imprisonment of his friends. Subject and style changed radically in the next song, "Glee— In Praise of Liberty," to the tune "Drink to Me Only with Thine Eyes," from Ben Jonson's famous song "To Celia." The high style of the short "Glee," like its threat to die for liberty if necessary, is far different from the sentimental ballad that preceded it:

> Let Freedom's sacred name resound
>   Thro' earth from shore to shore;
> So shall the Rights of man be found
>   When tyrants are no more.
> Let's drink the beauteous nymph with thee,
>   Fill, fill the Goblet higher,
> Before we lose blest LIBERTY—
>   We'll in her cause expire.

Several of the new songs in the collection also deserve analysis. According to contemporary accounts, two of the songs, "Paddy Evermore" and "Plant, Plant the Tree," were sung frequently. Both songs were written in a lively style with enough wit and popular ideas to enliven the patriotic dogma about unity. The text of "Paddy Evermore" in the 1798 *Paddy's Resource* is reprinted in appendix B. The song's pun "just asses" for justices suggests that the song was meant to be circulated in print, but it clearly obtained an oral circulation as well. A version of "Paddy Evermore" on a printed ballad sheet in the Sirr Papers at Trinity College Dublin (869/7. f. 209), evidently confiscated by Major Charles Henry Sirr in the late 1790s, exhibits the changes, referred to as "verbal corruption" by folklorists, that occur in a song when it has entered popular oral tradition: "dares" in line two of the *Paddy's Resource* version becomes "bares" on the ballad sheet, "tell the world" in the fourth line of the second stanza becomes "all the world."

"Paddy Evermore" was certainly a popular song in United Irish circles. Charles Hamilton Teeling's *History of the Irish Rebellion in 1798:*

A Personal Narrative described how the song had animated the spirits of United Irishmen, even in prison. In September 1796, in his eighteenth year, Teeling had been arrested in Belfast with Thomas Russell and Samuel Neilson on charges of high treason and imprisoned in Dublin. Teeling described what happened when one of the United Irish prisoners was put in irons, referred to as "ironing," for wearing "a small knot of green riband" and defying the commander of the prison, referred to as "his Lordship" in the following passage. Other United Irish prisoners, in a gesture of unity and sympathy, asked to be put in irons, too. Then, according to Teeling,

> His lordship viewed the operation of ironing the prisoners with a cold and malignant composure, while they, with cheerful heart and animated voice, sung aloud a popular air of the day, and again and again rejoined in the chorus—
>
> > Though we to the dungeons go,
> > Where patriots dwelt before,
> > Yet in the cell, or on the sod,
> > We're Paddies evermore.
> > (1828, 37–38)

Similarly, R. R. Madden tells how a United Irish prisoner, Henry Downes, consoled a fellow prisoner shortly before his own execution in 1798 by singing "Paddies Evermore" (1858b, 2:245).

In the 1798 *Paddy's Resource*, "Plant, Plant the Tree," to the tune "Daffy Hi Down Dilly," was singled out for government notice in *The Report of the Secret Committee of the House of Commons* (1798, 276–78). The song predicted the coming of "Frenchmen to relieve us" and the abolition of tithes, but paid special attention to the punishment of the oppressors, mocking them in stanzas like these:

> Those nicknames Marquis, Lord and Earl,
> That set the crowd a gazing,
> We prize as hogs esteem a pearl,
> Their patents set a blazing;
> No more they'll vote away our wealth,
> To please a King or Queen, sirs,
> But gladly pack away by stealth,
> Or taste the Guillotine, sirs.

CHORUS:
Plant, Plant the Tree, fair Freedom's Tree,
    'Midst dangers, wounds and slaughter,
Erin's green fields its soil shall be,
    Her tyrant's blood its water.
Those Lawyers who with face of brass,
And wigs replete with learning,
Whose far fetch'd quibling quirks surpass,
Republicans discerning:
For them, to ancient forms be staunch,
'Twill suit such worthy fellows,
In justice spare one legal branch,
I mean reserve the gallows.

The song also promised the transfer of the oppressors' wealth to the people:

The useless baubles that adorn'd
Our late Viceroyal ninnies,
Now to the crucible return'd
Produce you useful guineas.

Historians have expressed surprise at the credulity of the peasants participating in the 1798 uprising in Wexford who expected an immediate transfer of wealth from the rich to the poor. It is clear, however, that the United Irish songs encouraged such expectations.

Such sarcasm and insult, which presumably had broad popular appeal, was part of a larger vein of satire in the 1798 collection. The song "The Chapter of Kings," to the tune "The Night Before Larry Was Stretch'd," presented a sarcastic, bawdy view of English history that began:

When William that son of a whore,
Took into his head to invade us,
Our liberty from us he tore,
And poor abject rascals he made us.

King John was a "serviling ass / Without honesty, wisdom, or courage." Henry VIII was portrayed as follows:

Hal the Eight was the boy of a prince
His conscience was wonderful tender,
He stepp'd forth his faith to evince
And was dubb'd by the Pope its defender;
But his holiness proving uncivil
Our Harry appear'd but an odd piece,
He kick'd the poor Pope to the devil
And founded the church in his cod-piece.

Catholicism fared no better than Anglicanism: "Queen Mary ascended the throne / Devoted to Rome and its maggots." Queen Elizabeth was "a high supercilious tyrant" and "at sixty she acted the whore / And she died of an itching at eighty." Neither William of Orange nor his rival James were held in high esteem: "Wou'd Will had been drown 'd in the Scheld / And James as he sailed out of Dover." The song concluded: "Since our Monarch's so wise and so good, / Let's hope we shall ne'er have another."

The song "The Spy," to the tune "Poll and Partner Joe," satirized government spies:

I am d'ye see, an Informer, Sirs,
        As horrid a dog as any;
At the Sessions-house and Castle-yard,
        Swore false for many a guinea:
. . . .
In tavern or in public house,
        You're always sure to find me;
I sit so mute to hear all chat
        That folks but seldom mind me;
If you on politics should talk,
        Or civic songs should sing,
I'll artfully provoke your words,
        And swear you've damned the King.

Significantly, both political "talk" and "songs" were of interest to informers. Contemporary accounts suggest that the authorities did view songs as sedition rather than harmless metaphor. For example, local folklore in Westmeath claimed a rebel named John Reilly was brutally tortured by a body of yeomen. The group who captured him after a

battle there in the summer of 1798 because they regarded as seditious
a piece of paper found in his pocket on which were printed the following lines:

> Far may the boughs of liberty extend,
> For ever cultured by the brave and free;
> For ever blasted be the impious hand
> That lops one branch from this noble tree!
> Patriots 'tis yours to make her verdure thrive,
> And keep the roots of liberty alive.
>
> (Cox 1969, 14)

These lines recall the more formal style of many United Irish
songs. Even when the United Irishmen used tunes from popular drinking songs, the new lyrics were often formal rather than colloquial, as
in the "Glee," to the tune "Why, Soldiers, Why?" that appeared in the
1798 *Paddy's Resource*. The formal lyrics of the "Glee" include some
phrases from the original drinking song "Why, Soldiers, Why?" discussed earlier in this chapter:

> Why, Erins, why,
>   Should you submit to tyranny?
> Why, Erins, why,
>   'Tis better far to die!
> When Nature cries!
>   And famine stares ye in the face,
>   'Tis time to rise,
>   Or else despise
> The RIGHTS OF MAN, and furnish Pitt
>   With more supplies!
>
> 'Tis but in vain,
>   Your PRIVILEGES bought and sold,
> 'Tis but in vain,
>   For Erins to complain!
> The next campaigne,
>   May thousands send to their graves,
>   Then they're free from pain;
>   But those who remain,
> Must kiss the rod of slavery,
>   And hug her chain!

R. R. Madden agreed with Thomas Davis that this "Glee" was probably written by Wolfe Tone because the line " 'Tis but in vain for soldiers to complain" was a repeated refrain in Tone's journal (Madden 1887, 126). I think it more likely, however, that Thomas Russell composed the song because Tone claimed he had learned the phrase from Russell's frequent use of it, and the song is in the ornate style favored by Russell.

A lurid sensationalism became more and more apparent in United Irish songs in the course of the 1790's. For example, the 1798 *Paddy's Resource* song "Union's Your Helm," to the tune "Lash'd to the Helm," appealed to emotions rather than to reason:

> Now Erin bleeds in ev'ry vein,
> The curst effects of George's reign;
> See, dungeon'd deep, her patriots lie;
> Oh see them for opinions die!
>
> Now tyrant, view your deadly ire;
> See there, the humble roof on fire;
> See from the flames the Peasant flies;
> Oh see—he on the bayonet dies!
>
> Now view among your bloody deeds,
> Where gracious ORR for Erin bleeds!
> "Be true, he cried, as I've been true."
> Oh Erins—think, he died for you!
> Oh sacred shade,
> Now purer made;
> Oh ORR—who died for ALL:
> While we have breath,
> And in our death,
> We will avenge your fall!

The conjunction of religion and violence in the last lines of "Union's Your Helm," with their Christ-like presentation of Orr dying "for all" and their call for vengeance, is significant. Here again Thomas Russell provides an index, albeit perhaps extreme, of United Irish views about the relationship between violence and religion. Russell's dedication to the United Irish cause, expressed in a letter he wrote on

10 December 1800 from Fort George in Scotland where he and other
United Irishmen were then imprisoned, also combined religious righteousness and violent vengeance:

> The number who have fallen and among them many great and
> good . . . imposes an obligation on the survivors to persevere in the
> great cause promoting the good of my country and the progress of
> liberty . . . I have no doubt of her ultimate and speedy success . . . [in]
> a contest which embraces every quarter of the globe, which em-
> braces the fate of the human race . . . the contest between two prin-
> ciples of Despotism and Liberty and can only terminate in the
> extinction of one or the other. Reason and religion leave one no
> doubt which will triumph and believe me, my brother and my friend,
> that so far as I am able of judging, the sacred volume, in which I
> have always found support and consolation, evidently points out the
> impending vengeance of Almighty God on those individuals and
> those nations who obstinately persist in supporting injustice and
> tyranny (TCD, Madden Papers 873/6551).

For other United Irishmen, such as William Drennan, violence remained an unacceptable alternative even in a righteous cause.

The 1798 *Paddy's Resource* concluded on a less violent religious
note, with "Liberty—a hymn to be sung or said in all churches and
chapels on PATRICK's Day," which had appeared in the *Press* on 15
February 1798 "by a Protestant clergyman." This "hymn" reverted to
the stylistic and philosophic high road with which the collection had
opened. The hymn praised Liberty as a "Sister of LOVE" and an
"ethereal flame" that "mov'st to soft harps . . . And wak'st to ecstasy
the soul!" The "Poet's strain" and "song" were to bring "raptures to
the ecstatic breast" and make Erin a "favour'd nation blest."

The publication date of what is presumably the fourth and final
United Irish songbook, which includes materials from all three earlier
songbooks as well as new songs referring to events of 1800, is uncer-
tain. The slightly revised title, *Paddy's Resource; or, the HARP OF
ERIN Attuned to Freedom; being a Collection of Patriotic Songs; Selected
for Paddy's Amusement*, stresses entertainment rather than the useful
didactic function alluded to in the earlier three titles. The bottom of
the title page reads as follows:

—Dublin Printed—
By the Printer Hereof
(Price an Irish Hog)

No date of publication is printed on the title page; however, a copy in the Joly Collection in the National Library of Ireland has "1803(?)" penned in on the title page. That tentative date is probably based on the following observation by R. R. Madden in *Literary Remains:* "the later edition of the same collection of songs without date or place of publication but concluding with a song called 'Jemmy O'Brien's Minuet,' in allusion to O'Brien's recent execution, which took place in 1800, that edition could not have been published prior to 1800, and in all probability must have appeared previously to Robert Emmet's attempt, in May 1803" (1887, 329).

However, unless Madden is referring to another edition that has not survived, his description of the songbook is inaccurate. There is indeed a place of publication, Dublin, indicated on the title page of the copy in the National Library. Moreover, "Jemmy O'Brien's Minuet" was not the concluding song, but the third from the last song. It is possible that Madden saw a copy that was missing the final two songs. For example, the copy of the 1796 *Paddy's Resource* in the Linen Hall Library is missing the final two songs; were it not for the presence of an index at the beginning of that collection, the presence of the last two songs in that collection would not be known. The fact that so few copies of *Paddy's Resource* have survived, and the well-used condition of those that have, suggest that the songbooks were very popular and were indeed "used" by the people for whom they were printed.

I agree with Madden that the final *Paddy's Resource* was probably published in connection with Emmet's Rising in 1803, and I will refer to it as the 1803 edition hereafter. Robert Emmet himself was known to have had a strong literary bent and he and his associates in 1803 printed huge bundles of proclamations prior to the uprising (Landreth 1948, 191). Mary Ann McCracken gave R. R. Madden several poems written and signed by Emmet. The following stanzas from one of them, "Genius of Erin," demonstrate that Emmet was well versed in the imagery of United Irish songs:

> Genius of Erin, tune thy harp
>   To freedom, let its sound awake
> Thy prostrate sons, and nerve their hearts
>   Oppression's iron bonds to break.
>
> Long and strong then strike the lyre—
>   Strike it with prophetic lays,
> Bid it rouse the slumbering fire
>   Bid the fire of freedom blaze.
>   . . . .
>
> Show her fields with blood ensanguined,
>   With her children's blood bedewed—
> Show her desolated plains,
>   With their murdered bodies strewed.
>
> Mark that hamlet—how it blazes!
>   Hear the shrieks of horror rise—
> See—the fiends prepare their tortures—
> See! a tortured victim dies.

The endless sufferings catalogued by the harp of Erin were a call for action, as is evident in the concluding stanza:

> Erin's sons, awake!—awake!
>   Oh! too long, too long, you sleep;
> Awake! arise! your fetters break,
>   Nor let your country bleed and weep.
>   (Madden, 1846, 3:495–502)

Emmet had clearly been a careful reader of United Irish songbooks and of the lurid verse in the *Press*, the publication of which his brother Thomas Addis Emmet was so closely involved in.

Robert Emmet's use of the motif of the "Harp of Erin" is significant because the print used to highlight that phrase in the title of the 1798 and 1803 *Paddy's Resource* songbooks made it more prominent than the words "Paddy's Resource" in the title. Moreover, the symbolic devices on a seal that Robert Emmet designed and wore on his watch, and which eventually came into the possession of R. R. Madden, also echo major motifs on the title pages and frontispieces of the

1798 and 1803 *Paddy's Resource* songbooks. The seal depicted a harp with shamrocks, above which was the phrase "Tuned to Freedom" (a phrase that was added to the *Paddy's Resource* title in the 1803 edition) and below which was the phrase "Erin go Bragh," which had appeared on the frontispieces of both the 1798 and 1803 songbooks (Emmet 1915, 2:235).

Although none of this proves that Robert Emmet had anything to do with the actual publication of either songbook, the "Harp of Erin" was certainly one of his favorite symbols, and he clearly would have approved its use in any songbook produced in connection with his uprising in 1803. Moreover, Thomas Russell, one of Emmet's closest associates in planning the 1803 Rising, had been involved in the publication of poetry in the *Northern Star* and in the production of the first, if not the second, *Paddy's Resource* printed in Belfast. The song "Man Is Free by Nature," which manuscript evidence cited by Helen Landreth suggests might have been composed by Russell, appeared only in the songbooks published in 1795 (when Russell lived in Belfast) and in 1803 (when Russell was associated with Emmet in Dublin).

The likely printer of the 1803, and possibly the 1798, *Paddy's Resource* was John Stockdale, whose Dublin press had printed many issues of the *Press* newspaper during 1797–1798.[5] Whoever was responsible for its publication, the 1803 *Paddy's Resource* was clearly intended to be a continuation of the earlier songbooks. The opening pages reprinted the prefaces from the 1795 and the 1796 songbooks and the epigraph and the symbolic devices from the 1798 *Paddy's Resource*. One of the new songs in the collection, "Let Millions Be Wise," to the popular tune "Vicar and Moses," reiterated the United Irish goal of educating the people, proclaiming that ignorance aided tyrants who feared the power of "weapons of truth," namely the press and song.

The collection opened with the same song as the 1798 *Paddy's Resource*, Drennan's lovely and genteel "Erin." The 1803 collection as a whole, however, was markedly more popular and less literary in style, and more sensational and less philosophic in content, than the preceding collections had been. Although the sixty-four old songs reprinted in the new collection were generally representative of the broad range of literary styles that characterized United Irish verse, the twenty-one new songs, filled with the standard United Irish poetic images, were written in a much more popular style. The following discussion will focus on these new songs.

The broadside style and lurid and sentimental content of the second song in the collection, "The Maniac," suggests it was taken directly from popular oral tradition. The maniac is "Mary Le More," who has gone mad and wanders raving through Cork after seeing her brother beaten, her father slain, and her home burned by soldiers who then raped her. Her sufferings are recounted by the typical first-person broadside ballad narrator who observes the lurid events. "The Maniac" thus achieves the combination of sensational events and detached style common in such eighteenth-century ballads, and has the same inconsistencies of timing and plot common to such songs.

Most of the twenty-one new songs in this 1803 collection used the first person narrator. Although the narrator of "The Maniac" was merely an observer, fifteen of the other new songs used first-person participant narrators, thus enhancing the immediacy and power of the events described. In contrast, the majority of the songs in the first two *Paddy's Resource* songbooks had used either the imperative first-person plural "we" or the third-person imperative voice to preach abstract philosophical messages.

This maniac motif was very common in popular literature of the time. Robert Ashton's folk play *The Battle of Aughrim* had portrayed a young girl's hysteria and suicide after the death of her lover in battle. A series of ballads about a figure similar to "Mary Le More" named "Crazy Jane" was frequently reprinted in America and in Ireland in the 1790s (Upton 1964, 93–94, 103). The popular 1790s songwriter Charles Dibdin, the composer of several of the tunes used by the United Irishmen, such as "Poor Jack" and "Lovely Nan," had written a well-known song called "Mad Peg" in the 1790s (Upton 1964, 245). "The Maniac's" seditious implications were not lost on the authorities. On 1 January 1799 an informant sent the Home Office in England a copy of a printed ballad of "Mary Le More," which recounted atrocities committed by British soldiers in Ireland (Emsley 1979, 541). John Daly Burk's description of a song entitled "Ellen O'Moor" in *A History of the Late War in Ireland* matches the plot of "The Maniac" or "Mary Le More" exactly. According to Burk, at Vinegar Hill "enthusiastic United Irishmen, disdaining the command to await the attack, rushed upon their enemies singing the pathetic ballad of Ellen O'Moor" (1799, 107–8).

The horror of "The Maniac" was followed by the sentimental lyricism of "The Exiled Irishman's Lamentation" (reprinted in appendix B) to the old Irish air "Savourna Deelish [sic]," or "Erin Go Bragh." "Erin Go Bragh" was also the tune for the new song that followed, entitled "The Exile of Erin," which was in many ways a continuation of "The Exiled Irishman's Lamentation." The speaker in "The Exile of Erin" sings the "bold anthem of Erin Go Brah" and laments he would never again "cover my harp with the wild woven flowers, / And strike to the numbers of Erin Go Brah." Like the exiled Irishman of the earlier song, "The Exile of Erin" offers only words, a blessing to Ireland, rather than a call to arms:

> Green be thy fields, sweetest isle of the ocean,
> And thy harp striking bands sing aloud with devotion,
> Erin Ma Vorneen, Erin Go Bragh.

Other new songs called upon Irishmen to stay and fight, to avenge their fallen comrades. "Fly to Arms, Brave the Field," to the tune "The Wandering Sailor," commanded suffering Erin to cease sighing and instead "let your Country's wrongs inspire / Heroic deeds and martial fire." The song catalogued Erin's woes— "the purest men your dungeons fill," "bleeding peasants," "the houseless child and mother's tears," screaming "Virgins," and burning villages—and concluded with a call to action: "Then all the softer feelings spurn, / And for revenge and glory burn."

The song "Erin's Martyr's," to the tune "Molly Astore," which harpist Charles Fanning had performed at the Belfast Harp Festival in 1792, lamented "friends obliged to fly," but called upon Erin to "cease to weep" and her sons to "revenge" the "martyred" Oliver Bond and Edward Fitzgerald." Immediately following "Erin's Martyrs" was another new song, "The Dawning of the Day," to the tune "Shannon's Flowry Banks."[6] The "Dawning of the Day" offers practical advice about how to make violent retribution effective. At the beginning of the song the speaker, named "John Murphy," hears "the Bhvan Tigh's [banshee's] dismal yell" and observes "Orange Gang" atrocities revealed

"By dawning of the Day"—the burnt huts, the "piercing cries" of the "infant victim" and the "hideous screams" of "Fond Mothers," some of whom "madly find pure death in flames." Murphy calls for vengeance, "advance with PIKES," but advises "prudence"—"hunt your prey like nightly owls, / Before the dawn of Day," and warns not to "make our vengeance premature." His advice to "rise at once before the moon" anticipates the title of the popular nineteenth-century nationalist ballad, "The Rising of the Moon."

Like the banshee in the preceding song, St. Patrick himself became associated with the United Irish cause in the song "New St. Patrick's Day" in which St. Patrick appears to a group of United Irishmen observing the traditional St. Patrick's Day custom of "drowning the shamrock" to announce:

> By Almighty command, to this earth I came,
> Unto Erin's children aloud to proclaim,
> That their Brethren who died in LIBERTY's cause,
> Are crowned with glory and Heaven's applause.

After telling Patrick, "Since you've banished the serpents now banish the spies," the United Irishmen send a message with him to their United Irish comrades in heaven:

> Tell our brethren above, who triumph with thee,
> We swear by the Shamrock, we yet will be FREE.
> Shake hands with brave Orr, with brave Teeling and Tone
> And M'Cann, whom fidelity mark'd as her own;
> Tell Bond and our Martyrs their names are carress'd,
> And a blessing from Erin, by Erins are bless'd.
> Come boys let the liquor go merrily round,
> And cheer all our hearts 'till the Shamrock is drown'd,
> When drown'd may that Saint whom we fervently love,
> Waft it up to their souls in the regions above.

A new song entitled "The Rights of Man" was far different than the song of that title, set to the tune "God Save the King," that had appeared in the 1795 *Paddy's Resource*. The earlier song, which had been taken from an English radical songbook, had formally celebrated Reason, Truth, and Liberty in an impersonal third-person voice. The new song entitled "The Rights of Man," set to the popular tune from Charles Dibdin's song "Lovely Nan," was much more personal and concrete:

> When in a dungeon I was penn'd,
> By persecution murderous fiend!
>   And pimps and spies around me ran;
> No convert for the blackest crime,
> E'er met with punishment like mine:
>   Whipt, scourged, half-starved, and then half-hanged,
> Yet spite of persecutions [sic] wrath;
> Again I tread fair Freedom's path,
>   And sing of truth and Rights of Man.

The fact that both "Rights of Man" songs were used in the 1803 *Paddy's Resource* indicates the broad range of styles in the songbook, and also the diverse audience to which the collection was meant to appeal.

An even more colloquial, songlike tone is apparent in "The United Real Reformer," to the tune "The Jolly Tinker":

> I am a Patriotic Bard,
>   That loves the constitution,
> . . . .
> The PRESS is my Artillery
>   No hireling can debar me,
> . . . .
> How can the sons of Ireland
>   Endure this degradation?
> With England we in Union stand,
>   By scheming mechination;
> . . . .
> I'm an United Irishman,
>   And ne'er will act contrary,
> In Ninety-two, I join'd that plan,
>   Of tyrants being weary;
> Old Erin's rights I'll still defend,
>   And never will surrender,
> I am its persecuted friend,
>   A dauntless bold DEFENDER.

The song's reference to the Act of Union dates the collection as definitely after January of 1800. The song also offers evidence of the links between the United Irishmen and the Defenders.

Several songs singled out the notorious Major Charles Henry Sirr and his henchmen in the Dublin police for satiric abuse and condemnation. The speaker in "Jem Stag" declared "I'm the Major's own boy" and bragged of being an informer and the descendant of a long line of criminals. The song "Jemmy O'Brien's Minuet," to the tune "De night before Larry was stretch'd," used vivid dialect to celebrate the hanging of Jemmy O'Brien, one of Sirr's infamous assistants who had been involved in the arrest of the United Irish martyr Henry Downes. Downes's execution had been the subject of another new song in the 1803 *Paddy's Resource* entitled "Erin's Martyr." The stanzas were interspersed with prose commentary by an audience clearly in sympathy with the United Irishmen who made remarks such as,"Major jewel! leep up your spirits . . . Never lament for poor Jemmy, as he's only gone a step before you." Jemmy's ignominious end concluded the song:

> He gracefully pull'd down his cap,
>   And turned his mug tow'rds de Liffey,
> Den down fell de leaf with a flap,
>   And he dy'd, wid three kicks, in a jiffey.

The popular Dublin street song "The Night Before Larry was Stretched," on which Jemmy O'Brien's Minuet" was modeled, was supposedly written by Reverend Robert Burrowes of Trinity College Dublin. Burrowes who also wrote articles for the *Transactions of the Royal Irish Academy*, yet another indication of how writers in the 1790s wrote and appreciated both the "low" and "high" literary styles. Burrowes was Thomas Moore's first tutor at Trinity in 1794.

Major Sirr's most notorious crime, of course, had been the arrest and mortal wounding of Lord Edward Fitzgerald in 1798. The 1803 *Paddy's Resource* fittingly concluded with the popular ballad "Edward," reprinted in appendix B, which epitomizes the immediacy and the popular balladlike style of many later United Irish songs. "Edward's" artificial literary language and sentimental style are as typical of popular eighteenth-century songs as the Dublin street slang and rowdy humor of "The Night Before Larry Was Stretched." "Edward's" sentimentality and graphic violence were obviously designed to appeal to the masses for whom Edward Fitzgerald epitomized the patriot hero.[7] In "Edward," Sirr has replaced the abstraction of "Slavery" condemned in the first *Paddy's Resource* as the personification of evil, just as violent vengeance had replaced "Truth" as the means of achieving justice and freedom. In the same way that the violent rhetoric of the 1798 *Paddy's Resource* songbook anticipated the 1798 Rebellion, the 1803 songbook announced Emmet's.

The concluding songs in the 1803 *Paddy's Resource* thus indicate that the humorous and the sentimental modes eventually triumphed over the formal and philosophic style that had characterized many of the earlier United Irish songs. Although several such earlier songs were reprinted in the 1803 collection, the twenty-one new songs offered sentimental models for future nationalist songs. Thomas Moore and the Young Irelanders would intensify the sentimentality they found in many United Irish songs. Moore would emulate the moral righteousness and passivity of some United Irish verse, whereas the Young Irelanders would eventually embrace the physical force celebrated in many of the later United Irish songs.

· 6 ·

Thomas Moore's Songs and Satires

In the spring of 1798, Thomas Moore did not participate in the revo-
lutionary violence that he had called for in his inflammatory "Letter
to the Students of Trinity College" in the *Press* on 2 December 1797.
Moore did continue the United Irishmen's literary tradition, however.
His *Irish Melodies* are filled with motifs from United Irish songs and
echo the lyrical sentimentality of many of them. Moore's lesser known
Memoirs of Captain Rock (1824) recalls the prose satires of James
Porter, William Sampson, and Thomas Russell.

R. R. Madden pointedly dedicated his *Literary Remains of the
United Irishmen* (1887) to Thomas Moore. The dedication, dated
1846, emphasizes the literary relationship between Moore and the
United Irishmen that has subsequently been forgotten: "To one of
the few living contributors to 'the Press,' the first in merit of the
lyrists of our day, and among the last surviving friends of William
Corbet, Edward Hudson, and Robert Emmet, to THOMAS MOORE,
not merely 'in the beaten way of friendship,' but in token of homage
to his genius, and in remembrance of the constant devotion of his
talents to the service of his country, this volume is dedicated by the
editor."

Moore himself never forgot his personal and literary ties with the
United Irishmen. His memoirs stress how closely involved he and his
family were in the patriotism that animated Dublin during the 1790s
when Moore's earliest friends were ardent nationalists and included
many United Irishmen (Moore 1853). Moore's literary contributions
to the *Press* and the *Northern Star* (discussed in chap. 3) represent a
significant aspect of his early writing and are essential for a complete
understanding of his *Irish Melodies*.

The few commentators on Moore who mention his association with the United Irishmen emphasize the personal rather than the literary ties. Moore's anecdote about playing Bunting's airs for Robert Emmet has been frequently quoted, but as evidence of Emmet's ardent political nationalism rather than of Moore's literary nationalism. Moore's *Memoirs, Journal, and Coorespondence* is the source of his famous anecdote about Robert Emmet: "He was altogether a noble fellow, and as full of imagination and tenderness of heart as of manly daring. He used frequently to sit by me at the piano-forte, while I played over airs from Bunting's Irish collection; and I remember one day when we were thus employed, his starting up as if from a reverie while I was playing the spirited air 'Let Erin remember the Day,' and exclaiming passionately, 'Oh that I were at the head of twenty-thousand men marching to that air' " (1853, 58).

However, Moore's *Memoirs*, which focuses largely on his ardent nationalism during the 1790s and his ties with the United Irishmen, provides much additional information that deserves to be as well known as the Emmet anecdote. Yet, significantly, when John Russell's 1853 edition of Moore's *Memoirs* was reissued in 1983 as *The Journal of Thomas Moore*, the editor announced at the outset that everything was included "except for the short, unsatisfactory document entitled 'Memoirs of Myself' " (Dowden 1983, 9). Why Moore's memoirs of his life in the 1790s were "unsatisfactory" is not explained. Perhaps they focused too exclusively on the literary and political nationalism of the day and on popular music, theater, and magazines to suit the image of Moore that the editor wished to present.

Moore himself clearly considered those activities the most important part of his life during the 1790s. Early in the *Memoirs*, Moore declared "I must try my reader's patience with some account of my beginnings in music,—the only art for which, in my opinion, I was born with a real natural love; my poetry, such as it is, having sprung out of my deep feeling for music" (1853, 17). Moore always insisted his poems were actually songs, and for many years refused to allow his *Irish Melodies* to be published without the music. He was introduced quite early to the popularization of Irish music; at the age of thirteen, during summer theatricals, he played the role of Patrick in the popular play *The Poor Soldier*, the songs of which were set to old Irish airs like "Savourneen Deelish" and harp tunes by Carolan.

Recalling the "animated" politics of the early 1790s, Moore wrote: "Some of the most violent of those who early took a part in the proceedings of the United Irishmen were among our most intimate friends; and I remember being taken by my father to a public dinner in honour of Napper Tandy, where one of the toasts, as well from its poetry as its politics, made an indelible impression upon my mind— 'May the breezes of France blow our Irish oak into verdure!' I recollect my pride too, at the hero of the night, Napper Tandy, taking me, for some minutes, on his knee" (1853, 18). Moore's nationalist friends included "a clever, drunken attorney, named Matthew Dowling, who lived in Great Longford Street, opposite to us, and was a good deal at our house. . . . I recollect . . . his having engraved upon the buttons of his green uniform a cap of liberty surmounting the Irish harp instead of a crown" (18–19). Dowling was secretary of the Dublin United Irish Society for a time in 1793 and defended William Drennan at his trial for libel in 1794. He was arrested for treason in 1798.

While at Samuel Whyte's famous Dublin school, Moore was the protege of "the Latin Usher" Donovan, who, "together with the Latin and Greek which he did his best to pour into me, infused also a thorough and ardent passion for poor Ireland's liberties, and a deep and cordial hatred to those who were then lording over and trampling her down" (Moore 1853, 21). Moore continued, "Finding his pupil quite as eager and ready at politics as at the classics, he divided the time we passed together pretty well equally between both. And though from the first I was naturally destined to be of the line of politics which I have ever since pursued,—being, if I may so say, born a rebel,—yet the strong hold which the feeling took so early, both of my imagination and heart, I owe a good deal I think to those early conversations, during school hours, with Donovan" (21–22).

Sometime in 1793–1794, Moore organized "a debating and literary society" composed of himself, Tom Ennis, and Johnny Delany, his father's two clerks with whom he shared a room (Moore 1853, 27). Moore described Ennis as follows: "This honest fellow was (like almost all those among whom my early days were passed) thoroughly, and to the heart's core, Irish. One of his most favourite studies was an old play in rhyme, on the subject of the Battle of Aughrim, out of which he used to repeat the speeches of the gallant Sarsfield with a true national relish. Those well-known verses, too, translated from the Florentine bishop, Donatus, 'Far westward lies an isle of ancient fame,' were ever ready on his lips" (28–29). Moore's comment is further evidence of the influence of the famous Ulster folk play and Donatus's lines celebrating early Ireland that were discussed earlier.

Moore's first tutor when he entered Trinity in 1794 was Reverend Burrowes, of whom Moore noted: "There are some literary papers of his in the *Transaction of the Royal Irish Academy*; and he enjoyed the credit, I believe deservedly, of having been the author, in his youth, of a celebrated flash song, called 'The night before Larry was stretched,' i.e. hanged" (1853, 31). Moore also recalled his literary friendship with Mrs. Henrietta Battier, whose political satires he very much admired at the time (40–45). Both Moore and Mrs. Battier contributed to the *Press*, of which Moore recalled: "I can answer from the experience of my own home for the avidity with which every line was devoured. It used to come out, I think, three times a week; and on the evenings of publication, I always read it aloud to my father and mother during supper" (55).

Because his mother's anxiety about his future was "far more active than her zeal for the public cause," Moore did not tell her that his "Ossianic Fragment" had been published in the *Press* in October 1797. However, the day after his "Letter to the Students of Trinity College" appeared in December 1797, his friend Edward Hudson let slip the secret of his authorship and Moore "pledged the solemn promise she required of me" to "never again venture on so dangerous a step" (Moore 1853, 56–57).

Edward Hudson and Robert Emmet were Moore's closest friends at Trinity. Moore recalled Hudson, who was one of the United Irishmen seized in the midst of planning the rebellion at Oliver Bond's house in March 1798, as "full of zeal and ardour for everything connected with the fine arts; he drew with much taste himself, and was passionately devoted to Irish music. He had with great industry collected and transcribed all our most beautiful airs, and used to play them with much feeling on the flute. I attribute, indeed, a good deal of my own early acquaintance with our music, if not the warm interest which I have since taken in it, to the many hours I passed at this time of my life tête-à-tête with Edward Hudson,—now trying over the sweet melodies of our country, now talking with indignant feeling of her sufferings and wrongs" (Moore 1853, 49).

Unlike Hudson and Emmet, Moore was evidently never active within the United Irish societies that existed within Trinity, but when their existence was investigated by the authorities Moore steadfastly refused to give any evidence against his friends who were involved (61–66). Moore's other United Irish friends at Trinity included the William Corbet alluded to in Madden's dedication, and John Brown, who contributed a translation from the Irish to Bunting's 1809 *General Collection of the Ancient Music of Ireland*.

Moore explained in his *Memoirs* that he was "confined with illness" when "the long and awfully expected explosion of the United Irish conspiracy took place" (1853, 66). But his remarks about the 1798 Rebellion in *The Life and Death of Lord Edward Fitzgerald* (1831) indicate that he was haunted by the event for many years:

> Meanwhile affairs in Ireland were hurrying to their crisis; and events and scenes crowded past, in fearful succession, of which,—if personal feelings may be allowed to mingle themselves with such a narrative,—so vivid is my own recollection, I could not trust myself to dwell upon them. Though then but a youth in college, and so many years have since gone by, the impression of horror and indignation which the acts of the government of that day left upon my mind is, I confess, at this moment, far too freshly alive to allow me the due calmness of a historian in speaking of them. Not only had I myself, from early childhood, taken a passionate interest in that struggle which, however darkly it ended, began under the bright auspices of a Grattan, but among those young men whom, after my entrance to college, I looked up to with most admiration and regard, the same enthusiasm of national feeling prevailed. Some of them, too, at the time of the terror and torture I am now speaking of, were found to have implicated themselves far more deeply in the popular league against power than I could ever have suspected; and these I was now doomed to see, in their several ways, victims,—victims of that very ardour of patriotism which had been one of the sources of my affection for them, and in which, through almost every step but the last, my sympathies had gone along with them. (1831, 1:300–301).

Moore went on to recall his visit to Edward Hudson "in the jail of Kilmainham, where he had then laid immured for four or five months, hearing of friend after friend being led out to death, and expecting every week his own turn to come. As painting was one of his tastes, I found that, to amuse his solitude, he had made a large drawing with charcoal on the wall of his prison, representing the fancied origin of the Irish Harp, which, some years afterward, I adopted as the subject of one of the Melodies" (1831, 1:301–2). The melody in question was "The Origin of the Irish Harp" in the third number of the *Irish Melodies*. In his footnote to that song, however, Moore, who refrained from broadcasting his United Irish ties in his annotations to the *Irish Melodies* because the songs were continually accused of sedition by Tory reviewers, omitted all reference to the drawing's Kilmainham origin: "This thought was suggested by an ingenious design prefixed to an ode upon St. Cecilia, published some years since, by Mr. Hudson of Dublin" (Moore 1843, 328). Edward Hudson was banished rather than executed, and emigrated to Philadelphia where he married the daughter of Dublin bookseller and United Irishman Patrick Byrne, who had also been arrested and banished in 1798.

Moore also used the occasion of his biography of Edward Fitzgerald to defend and eulogize his United Irish friends and to proclaim his own continued devotion to their cause. Moore's lengthy and moving celebration of Emmet included the following remarks: "Were I to number, indeed, the men, among all I have ever known, who appeared to me to combine, in the greatest degree, pure moral worth with intellectual power, I should among the highest of the few, place Robert Emmet" (1831, 1:303). Moore placed the responsibility for the violence on the government: "Such, in heart and mind, was another of those devoted men, who with gifts that would have made them the ornaments and supports of a well-regulated community, were yet driven to live the lives of conspirators and die the deaths of traitors, by a system of government which it would be difficult even to think of with patience, did we not gather a hope from the present aspect of the whole civilized world, that such a system of bigotry and misrule can never exist again" (1:305–6).

Moore then concluded the first volume of his biography of Fitzgerald by remarking that, although he never knew Fitzgerald personally, he vividly recalled seeing him once in 1797 on Grafton Street. This sighting was "as present and familiar to my memory as if I had intimately known him. Little did I then think that, at an interval of four-and-thirty years from thence,—an interval equal to the whole span of his life at that period,—I should not only find myself the historian of his mournful fate, but (what to many will appear matter rather for shame than of boast) with feelings so little altered, either as to himself or his cause" (1831, 1:306–307). Those eloquent statements defending the United Irishmen and proclaiming his own continued allegiance to their cause contradict the stereotype of Moore as a coward singing for his supper in English drawing rooms and fearing to offend his patrons. This stereotype is further undermined by the biography itself, which Moore completed and published against the wishes of some of his most prominent English patrons.

Moore certainly did not deserve William Butler Yeats's criticism that he was "an incarnate social ambition" (Yeats 1954, 447). A more accurate assessment of Moore is that, although he did not participate in the revolutionary violence that represented the dimension of the United Irish movement best known today, he continued the literary program of the United Irishmen in his *Irish Melodies* and in his prose writings. In the course of the nineteenth century, however, it became increasingly difficult to be considered an Irish patriot unless one was a revolutionary. Yet violence had not been a part of the original United Irish program, and it was only one of many doctrines preached in their songs. Moore wrote songs in the nostalgic and sentimental mode that had been a key feature in many United Irish songs.

Moore used the imagery of United Irish songs even before he began writing the *Irish Melodies*. His Ossianic fragment, reprinted in appendix C, which had appeared in both the *Northern Star* and the *Press* in 1797, was filled with bombastic and lugubrious sentimentality such as had characterized some United Irish songs. It also contained the motifs common to all United Irish verse: bards, silenced and resounding harps, imprisoned patriots, corrupt oppressors, the darkness of tyranny, the light of freedom, slavery, exile, burning peasant cottages, and the lament for the glorious heroic past. One reason Moore's Ossianic fragment seems so excessive is that he managed to use so many of the standard United Irish images in one poem.

Moore's 1808 poem "Corruption," which depicted Britain as a slave sleeping in chains until reform was accomplished, placed Britain in the position that Ireland had assumed amidst the same images in early United Irish verse. Likewise, Moore's urging in the poem's preface that Britain seek reform without revolution applied the original

United Irish agenda to Britain. Moore also used the poem to castigate Whigs and Tories alike for treating Ireland with equal cruelty. He closed the poem with the observation that Ireland now had some revenge "for centuries of wrong, for dark deceit / And withering in-sult" in being able to watch "the grand artizan of Mischief," Pitt, "whose whips and chains" had once terrorized Ireland, now ruining England (Moore 1843, 222–23).

Similarly, in his poem "Intolerance" (1808) Moore used lines that were indistinguishable, except for their greater lyricism, from many that appeared in United Irish songs in the 1790s:

> Oh! turn awhile, and, though the shamrock wreathes
> My lonely harp, yet shall the song it breathes
> Of Ireland's slavery, and of Ireland's woes,
> Live, when the memory of her tyrant foes
> Shall but exist, all future knaves to warn,
> Embalm'd in hate and canonized by scorn!
> (Moore 1843, 224)

Moore criticized the English government for reneging on its promise that Catholic Emancipation would follow the Act of Union in 1800. But his most vitriolic anger in the poem was reserved for Robert Stewart, Viscount Castlereagh.

Moore's lifelong fury at Castlereagh originated in the 1790s when Stewart, whom many believed had actually taken the United Irish oath early in the 1790s, received strong and indispensable electoral support from the Belfast Volunteers and United Irishmen, only to abandon his liberal principles once in office and eventually to become Chief Secre-tary in 1798. Castlereagh was notorious for his prosecution of the United Irishmen and for his support of the Act of Union. In his journal for 14 September 1820, Moore gleefully recorded receiving from the poet Byron the following "excellent" epitaph for Castlereagh, who actually did not commit suicide for another two years:

> Posterity shall ne'er survey
> A monument like this;
> Here lie the bones of Castlereagh,
> Stop, stranger, and piss!
> (1983, 1:343)

Shortly after the publication of the first number of his *Irish Melodies* in 1808, Moore talked of publishing a collection of political songs to Irish airs. Although that project never materialized, many of the *Irish Melodies* are indeed political songs to Irish airs. The political messages in many of the songs echo themes in earlier United Irish songs, a fact that answers the common charge that Moore's songs are shallow, offering only empty rhetoric and no substance or context. Moore's images and themes have substance when viewed within the context of United Irish political songs. Moore, however, was always aware that he would be suspected of seditious writing by his Tory reviewers, one of whom in 1820 referred to Moore's songs as "the melancholy ravings of the disappointed rebel" (Jordan 1975, 158). Therefore, he understandably did not broadcast his literary and thematic debt to the United Irishmen, knowing it would be obvious to anyone familiar with their songs and that it had best remain unknown to others. For example, the significance of Moore's use of a tune entitled "Paddy's Resource" in the third number of the *Irish Melodies* (1810) would have been readily apparent to any reader familiar with United Irish songbooks.

Many of the images, themes, and tunes that Moore used in the *Irish Melodies* derived from United Irish songs. Like his celebration of Irish music as the voice of the soul of Ireland, Moore's images of bards, harps, green flags, shamrocks, slaves, chains, martyred heroes, of the dawning light of freedom, and of the weeping, slumbering, enchanted Erin, all originated in the songs of the United Irishmen. The United Irishmen's ideology, if not their call to violent revolution, also echoed throughout the *Irish Melodies*. The necessity for "Unity" among all Irishmen was the most common theme in United Irish songbooks. All United Irish songs, whether they celebrated moral or physical force, agreed on the need for Irish unity. Likewise, Moore called for unity among all shades or "tints" of Irish social classes and religion in this stanza from "Erin! The Tear and the Smile in Thine Eyes":

> Erin! thy silent tear never shall cease,
> Erin! thy languid smile ne'er shall increase,
>> Till, like the rainbow's light,
>> Thy various tints unite,
>> And form, in Heaven's sight,
>>> One arch of peace!
>>>> (Moore 1843, 317)

A similar vague Utopian vision of peace had concluded many United Irish songs, even the ones that urged violent revenge.

A moving plea for an end to religious prejudice animates Moore's "Come, Send Round the Wine," which recalls the many United Irish drinking songs that celebrated justice and toleration:

> Shall I ask the brave soldier, who fights by my side
> In the cause of mankind, if our creeds are one?
> Shall I give up the friend I have valued and tried,
> If he kneel not before the same altar as me?
> From the heretic girl of my soul shall I fly,
> To seek somewhere else a more orthodox kiss?
> No! perish the hearts and the laws that try
> Truth, valour, or love, by a standard like this!
>   (Moore 1843, 322)

Moore, a Catholic, had married a Protestant. After describing many of his United Irish friends in his *Memoirs* and in his biography of Edward Fitzgerald, Moore carefully pointed out that these ardent Irish nationalists had been Protestants.

Many of Moore's lyrics in *Irish Melodies* could have been printed in any edition of *Paddy's Resource*, where only their artistry, not their message, would have set them apart. For example, "The Song of Fionnuala" contains the following lines:

> Yet still in her darkness doth Erin lie sleeping,
> Still doth the pure light its dawning delay!
> When will that day-star, mildly springing,
> Warm our isle with peace and love?
>   (Moore 1843, 321)

"Erin! Oh Erin!" describes the appearance of the "bright" spirit of Erin "through the tears of a long night of bondage" and declares: "And though slavery's cloud o'er thy morning hath hung, / The full moon of freedom shall beam round thee yet" (Moore 1843, 325).

Like the United Irishmen before him, Moore preferred the simplicity of Freedom to the ostentation of tyrannic Power, a theme that had been especially prominent in many songs by Ulster Presbyterians in the two Belfast *Paddy's Resource* songbooks. In "Oh, the Sight Entrancing," Moore declared:

> Leave pomps to those who need 'em—
> Adorn but Man with freedom,
> And proud he braves
> The gaudiest slaves
> That crawl where monarchs lead 'em.
> (Moore 1843, 346–47)

The same song contained lines celebrating violence in the muted and ambiguous manner of many United Irish songs:

> Oh, the sight entrancing,
> When morning's beam is glancing
> O'er files, array'd
> With helm and blade,
> And in Freedom's cause advancing!
> When hearts are all high beating,
> And the trumpet's voice repeating
> That song whose breath
> May lead to death,
> But never to retreating!
> (Moore 1843, 346–47)

Indeed, individual lines in Moore's songs often celebrated violence, but the historical context of the song generally placed such rebellion and violence safely in the past. The second song in the first number of the *Irish Melodies* was "War Song," which, as Moore's footnote carefully pointed out, celebrated Brian Boru's victory and death at Clontarf. However, the song's celebration of fallen heroes and its condemnation of tyranny inevitably recalled the much more recent United Irish attempts to expel the invaders.

> Remember the glories of Brien the brave,
> Though the days of the hero are o'er;
> Though lost to Mononia and cold in the grave,
> He returns to Kinkora no more!
> That star in the field, which so often has pour'd
> Its beam on the battle is set;

But enough of its glory remains on each sword
    To light us to victory yet!

Mononia! when nature embellish'd the tint
    Of thy fields and thy mountains so fair,
Did she ever intend that a tyrant should print
    The footstep of Slavery there?
No, Freedom! whose smile we shall never resign,
    Go, tell our invaders, the Danes,
That 't is sweeter to bleed for an age at thy shrine,
    Than to sleep but a moment in chains!

Forget not our wounded companions who stood
    In the day of distress by our side;
While the moss of the valley grew red with their blood
    They stirr'd not, but conquer'd and died!
The sun that now blesses our arms with his light,
    Saw them fall upon Ossory's plain!—
Oh! let him not blush, when he leaves us tonight,
    To find that they fell there in vain!
                (Moore 1843, 317)

The Danes were also the "proud invader" from whom Malachi won "the collar of gold" in "Let Erin Remember the Days of Old" (Moore 1843, 321). Similarly, the ancient tale of Deirdre was the setting for "Avenging and Bright," which celebrated how "Avenging and bright fell the swift sword of Erin" and declared "Revenge on a tyrant is sweetest of all!" (Moore 1843, 332)

Moore's caution about his songs sounding too seditious evidently waned with time. By the fifth number of the *Irish Melodies* in 1813, his "Song of O'Ruark, Prince of Breffni" described the arrival of the English in Ireland and concluded with this stanza:

Already the curse is upon her,
    And strangers her vallies profane;
They come to divide—to dishonour,
    And tyrants they long will remain!
But, onward!—the green banner rearing,
    Go, flesh every sword to the hilt;

On *our* side is VIRTUE and ERIN!
On *theirs* is THE SAXON and GUILT.
(Moore 1843, 335)

In the same number, "The Minstrel Boy," which celebrated the "war-rior-bard" who died tearing the strings from his "wild harp" and his declaration, "Thy songs were made for the pure and free / They shall never sound in slavery!", had no specific historical setting.

By the sixth number in 1816, Moore no longer set his battle poems and eulogies for fallen heroes several centuries safely in the past. No setting is given in "Where Is the Slave?" as Irish soldiers mock "slaves" who prefer bewailing Ireland's woes to fighting for their freedom. The soldiers march off to battle with these words:

We tread the land that bore us,
Her green flag glitters o'er us,
The friends we've tried
Are by our side,
And the foe we hate before us!
Farewell Erin!—farewell all
Who live to weep our fall!
(Moore 1843, 388)

The references to the green flag and to defeat evoke the spirit of the United Irishmen. Likewise, the United Irishmen are the likely subject of "Tis Gone, and For Ever" in the same number, a song that is filled with the rhetoric about Truth, Liberty, and Freedom and the images of light and bloodshed so common in United Irish songs (Moore 1843, 339). Moreover, Moore set the song to the tune "Savournah Deelish [*sic*]" which the United Irishmen used for several of their most popular songs.

Moore wrote several *Irish Melodies* about Robert Emmet. His elegy for Emmet, "Oh! Breathe Not His Name," lyrically evoked Emmet's famous speech from the dock in which he supposedly asked that his epitaph not be written until Ireland had taken her place among the nations of the world (Moore 1843, 317). Moore's portrait of Emmet's beloved Sarah Curran (the daughter of John Philpot Curran, who frequently defended United Irishmen at their trials) in "She Is Far from the Land" commemorated Emmet's love of Irish music: "She sings the wild songs of her dear native plains, / Every note which he loved awaking" (Moore 1843, 331). Emmet himself is the speaker addressing Ireland in Moore's "When He Who Adores Thee":

> Oh! blest are the lovers and friends who shall live
>   The days of their glory to see;
> But the next dearest blessing that Heaven can give
>   Is the pride of thus dying for thee!
>   (Moore 1843, 317)

Once Moore's United Irish frame of reference is recognized, his "Forget Not the Field" in the seventh number of the *Irish Melodies* in 1818 can be read as a deeply personal and powerful elegy for all of his United Irish friends:

> Forget not the field where they perish'd,
>   The truest, the last of the brave,
> All gone—and the bright hope they cherish'd
>   Gone with them, and quench'd in their grave.
>
> Oh! could we from death but recover
>   Those hearts, as they bounded before,
> In the face of high Heaven to fight over
>   That combat for freedom once more:—
>
> Could the chain for an instant be riven
>   Which Tyranny flung round us then,
> Oh! 't is not in Man nor in Heaven,
>   To let tyranny bind it again!
>
> But it is past—and, though blazon'd in story
>   The name of our Victor may be,
> Accursed is the march of that glory
>   Which treads o'er the hearts of the free.
>
> Far dearer the grave or the prison,
>   Illumed by one patriot name,
> Than the trophies of all who have risen
>   On liberty's ruins to fame!
>   (Moore 1843, 342–43)

There is nothing vague, shallow, or trivial about that song when it is read as a eulogy for the United Irishmen in 1798 and 1803 and as an apologia for Moore's own rise to fame. Although Moore's fame has been derided by literary critics and militant nationalists, it unquestionably ensured the United Irish message a wider audience than it had ever received in the 1790s.

Moore himself recognized that his audience included even the "masters" of Ireland in his eloquent defense of the patriotic purpose of his songs in "Oh! Blame Not the Bard":

> Oh! blame not the bard, if he fly to the bowers,
>   Where Pleasure lies carelessly smiling at Fame;
> He was born for much more, and in happier hours
>   His soul might have burn'd with a holier flame.
> The string, that now languishes loose o'er the lyre,
>   Might have bent a proud bow to the warrior's dart,
> And the lip, which now breathes but the song of desire,
>   Might have pour'd the full tide of a patriot's heart.
>
> But, though glory be gone, and though hope fade away
>   Thy name, lov'd Erin! shall live in his songs;
> Not even the hour when his heart is most gay
>   Will he lose the remembrance of thee and thy wrongs!
> The stranger shall hear thy lament on his plains;
>   The sigh of thy harp shall be sent o'er the deep,
> Till thy masters themselves, as they rivet the chains,
>   Shall pause at the song of their captive, and weep.
>   (Moore 1843, 326)

As explained in that song, the rationale behind Moore's songs was the same as much of the verse that had appeared in United Irish newspapers and songbooks.

Given the close ties that exist between many of Moore's supposedly vague songs and the harsh political realities of the United Irish uprisings of 1798 and 1803, the reservations that Thomas Kinsella expresses about Moore's *Irish Melodies* in his introduction to the *New Oxford Book of Irish Verse* are without foundation: "None of this popular poetry bears close scrutiny. Its grasp on actuality is slight" (Kinsella 1986, xxvi). Robert Welch is much closer to the heart of Moore's *Irish*

Melodies when he remarks that their "images hint at the burning political core" of the poetry (Welch 1988, 53). Kinsella, however, dismisses Moore's position in "Oh! Blame Not the Bard," saying Moore only "partly forestalls criticism" because "in the time of testing he has proved inadequate, withholding his talents from the service of the oppressed and choosing to entertain the oppressor" (Kinsella 1986, xxvii).

Even Moore's use of tunes has not been without criticism, which has centered mostly on his not giving immediate credit to Edward Bunting for the tunes he used from Bunting's collections. But Moore's use of tunes must be seen in a wider context. A study of the printed sources for his tunes has revealed that of the 124 tunes, twenty-one came from Bunting's 1796 collection, seventeen from his 1809 collection, twenty-nine from Smollet Holden's *Collection of Irish Slow and Quick Tunes* (1806), five from O'Keeffe's *The Poor Soldier* (in which Moore had acted as a boy), and the rest from a wide variety of eighteenth-century and early nineteenth-century collections (Jordan 1975, 148). However, the value of such a study is limited, given the hundreds of printed sources available to Moore, in addition to the many tunes he simply heard from friends like Edward Hudson.

For example, in his *Irish Melodies*, Moore also used many of the same tunes that the United Irishmen had used for their songs: "Alley Croker," The Black Joke," "The Boyne Water," "The Girl I Left Behind Me," "Langolee," "Limerick's Lamentation" (for which the United Irishmen had used the Scottish title "Lochaber"), "Moll Roe," "Paddy Whack," "Patrick's Day," "Savourneen Deelish," and "Sios agus sios liom" (for which the United Irishmen had used an English title "Shepherds I Have Lost My Love").

Although much of the scholarly focus has been on the origin and antiquity of Moore's tunes, it is important to note that, contrary to many later literary nationalists, he did not emphasize their antiquity. In his dedication to the third number in 1810, Moore wrote, "Though much has been said of the antiquity of our music, it is certain that our finest and most popular airs are modern; and perhaps we may look no further than the last disgraceful century for the origin of most of those wild and melancholy strains, which were at once the offspring and solace of grief." Moore added, "However heretical it may be to dissent from these romantic speculations, I cannot help thinking it is possible to love our country very zealously, and to feel deeply interested in her honour and happiness, without believing that Irish was the language spoken in Paradise" (Moore 1843, 323).

Moore was thus much closer in attitude to the United Irishmen in this regard than he was to later literary nationalists. Despite the fact that the United Irishmen extolled the Irish language and the antiquity of much Irish music in the *Northern Star* and in *Bolg an tSolair*, theirs was a pluralistic conception of Irish culture and they made no attempt to use either ancient or Irish airs exclusively. Nor did Moore. Although eight of the twelve tunes Moore used in the first number of his *Irish Melodies* in 1808 were from Edward Bunting's 1796 *General Collection of Ancient Irish Music*, the publication of which had been supported by many Belfast United Irishmen, Moore used tunes from a variety of sources, including many contemporary ones, throughout *Irish Melodies*. Therefore, Moore's pluralistic sense of the origin and transmission of tunes probably explains his supposed failure to credit Bunting as the source of so many of his tunes. Moore undoubtedly acquired some of his tunes from now lost oral sources, such as the tunes he credited to his friend Edward Hudson as having collected. Like the United Irishmen, he rightly considered such tunes to be the common cultural property of all Irishmen.

Imagery, themes, and tunes were not the only links between Moore's *Irish Melodies* and United Irish songs. The rude woodcut that adorned the first number of the *Irish Melodies* was said to have first appeared on a Dublin broadside ballad of 1803 commemorating Robert Emmet (O Casaide 1935, 8–9). Howard Mumford Jones described the woodcut as follows: "the Muse of Ireland, chastely clad, pensively at ease under a willow tree, her right arm negligently resting on a Celtic harp" (1937, 105). Jones's description would also apply to the woodcuts at the beginning of the first two *Paddy's Resource* songbooks and on the 1790s broadside ballad of "Paddy Evermore" in the Linen Hall Library. Even iconography connects Moore and the United Irishmen.

Another important link between Moore and the United Irishmen is the ambiguity and unresolved tensions, especially about violence, that their songs shared. Norman Vance, who ignores Moore's literary debt to the United Irishmen in his 1990 analysis of Moore, presents a description of Moore's poetry that could easily be applied to United

Irish songs as a group. Defending Moore, Vance argues we should avoid any condemnation of Moore that "trivializes the tensions and ambivalence of Moore's poetry, encompassing without reconciling rebellion and quiescence, hope and despair, atavistic blood-sacrifice and the rational prospect of daylight and liberty" (1990, 111).

Moore's commemoration of the United Irishmen and emulation of their literary works extended beyond his *Irish Melodies*. For example, the phrase "so link'd together" in the song "Oft, in the Stilly Night" in his *National Airs* (1818) suggests that song too refers to the "United" Irishmen:

> Oft, in the stilly night,
>   Ere Slumber's chain has bound me,
> Fond Memory brings the light
>   Of other days around me;
> . . . .
> When I remember all
>   The friends, so link'd together
> I've seen around me fall,
>   Like leaves in wintry weather;
>   I feel like one
>   Who treads alone
>   Some banquet-hall deserted,
>   Whose lights are fled,
>   And all but he departed!
>   (Moore 1843, 353)

Moore also incorporated the history of the United Irishmen, especially that of Robert Emmet, into his famous Oriental romance *Lalla Rookh* (1817), which was composed of four long poems, interspersed with song, and connected by a prose frame story in which Lalla Rookh is entertained by the four poetic tales told her on her journey to Cashmere for her wedding. In the end, the young poet who told her the stories happily turns out to be the king she is traveling to marry. The third poem, "The Fire-Worshippers," tells of the struggle of the Ghebers, or Fire-Worshippers, of Persia against their Moslem rulers. The history of Iran (an evident pun on Erin) parallels that of Erin: "Fierce invaders pluck the gem / From Iran's broken diadem, / And bind her ancient faith in chains" while the "poor exile" is "cast alone on foreign shores, unlov'd, unknown." The exile is

Yet happier so than if he trod
His own belov'd but blighted sod,
Beneath a despot stranger's nod!—
Oh! he would rather houseless roam
    Where Freedom and his God may lead,
Than be the sleekest slave at home
    That crouches to the conqueror's creed!
Is Iran's pride then gone for ever,
    Quench'd with the flame in Mithra's caves?—
No—she has sons that never—never—
    Will stoop to be the Moslem's slaves,
    While heaven has light or earth has graves.
                (Moore 1843, 61)

As a plea for religious toleration, Moore's fable echoes the United Irish hope for the same.

The Persian rebel Hafed is described to the tyrannical Moslem Emir as follows:

Is one of many, brave as he,
Who loathe thy haughty race and thee;
Who, though they know the strife is vain—
Who, though they know the riven chain
Snaps but to enter in the heart
Of him who rends its links apart,
Yet dare the issue—blest to be
E'en for one bleeding moment free,
And die in pangs of liberty!
                (Moore 1843, 61)

A heroic but doomed rebel in the tradition of Emmet, Hafed is betrayed much as Emmet had been, and his death, too, is that of a political martyr. When Moore wrote the lines cursing Hafed's betrayer, he could well have been writing of the betrayal of the United Irish leaders meeting at Oliver Bond's in 1798 or of the betrayal of Emmet in 1803:

Oh for a tongue to curse the slave,
    Whose treason, like a deadly blight,
Comes o'er the councils of the brave,
    And blasts them in their hour of might!
                (Moore 1843, 64)

Moore's lines about "Rebellion" in *Lalla Rookh* provide a moving commentary about the United Irishmen:

> Rebellion! foul, dishonouring word,
>   Whose wrongful blight so oft has stain'd
> The holiest cause that tongue or sword
>   Of mortal ever lost or gain'd.
> How many a spirit, born to bless,
>   Hath sunk beneath that withering name,
> Whom but a day's, an hour's, success
>   Hath wafted to eternal fame!
> As exhalations when they burst
> From the warm earth, if chill'd at first,
> If check'd in soaring from the plain,
> Darken to fogs and sink again;—
> But if they once triumphant spread
> Their wings above the mountain-head,
> Become enthron'd in upper air,
> And turn to sun-bright glories there!
>   (Moore 1843, 61)

The structure of *Lalla Rookh* recalls similar combinations of verse and prose in several United Irish satires. Its Oriental mode suggests the several "Oriental" works in the *Northern Star* that the United Irishmen used to comment on contemporary events, especially the "Chinese Journal," which was serialized in 1795 and which evidence in the Drennan letters suggests was written by Thomas Russell (PRONI, Drennan Letters no. 540 and no. 544).

Moore's satire *Memoirs of Captain Rock, The Celebrated Irish Chieftain, with Some Account of His Ancestors, Written by Himself* (1824) is also a reminder that the romantic mode of United Irish songs was not the only literary model that he adopted from the United Irishmen. Like so many United Irish satires in verse and prose, *Memoirs of Captain Rock* is a history of English stupidity and misrule in Ireland. Moore assumed the character of an Irish outlaw to make his point, much as James Porter had adopted the pose of an informer to a landlord in *Billy Bluff* and as United Irish songs had satirically portrayed their enemies' points of view.

The "editor" of Captain Rock's memoirs had been sent to Ireland as a missionary despite his "horror" of Ireland, which, prior to reading Captain Rock's work, he believed was peopled by "savages" (Moore 1824, iii). He meets Captain Rock who, disguised as a gentleman, entrusts the "editor" with his manuscript and entreats him to publish it. The "editor" does publish it, and thus Captain Rock himself addresses the reader. Rock's thesis is that violence in Ireland is the result of English oppression: "The object of the following history and biographical sketch is to show how kindly the English government has at all times consulted our taste in this particular—ministering to our love of riot through every successive reign" (9). According to Captain Rock, whenever the English began, temporarily, to act with justice towards the Irish, his family of outlaws experienced "diminished opportunities" and lacked popular support (186). Like the United Irishmen, Captain Rock believes reform would have ended Irish dissension once and for all.

Captain Rock, whose ancestors had been the anonymous leaders of the earlier revolts all the way back to the time of Henry VIII, says he was born in 1763, yet he nevertheless claims *Paddy's Resource* was one of the texts at the hedge school he had attended (Moore 1824, 187). He claims that the Act of Union had joined tithes and parliamentary corruption as guarantees to his continued successful career. His survey of Irish history emphasizes that all Irish rebellions, including 1798, were part of a larger historical pattern. One could not "expect moderation from a people kept constantly on the rack of oppression," especially in a country where the "lower orders" had been "broken down and barbarized" and the upper classes "so demoralized and denationalized" (251, 289). The "bayonet" had been the government's repeated remedy when reform had been what was needed (294–95). When Captain Rock emigrates at the end of the book, wearing an old green coat that had originally been made for United Irishman Napper Tandy and leaving his son to assume the sobriquet of "Captain Rock," he advises the "editor" that the best means of converting the Catholics to Protestantism would be to transfer the payment of tithes to the Catholic clergy (375–76).

In a similar manner, Moore impersonated the "Orange" point of view in his poem "The Petition of the Orangemen of Ireland," arguing as follows:

> That, forming one seventh, within a few fractions,
> Of Ireland's seven millions of hot heads and hearts,

We hold it the basest of all base transactions
To keep us from murd'ring the other six parts.
(Moore 1843, 410–11)

Moore's poem is very similar to the United Irish poem *Lysimachia*, which had impersonated the "Orange" point of view in 1797. Moore thus emulated the sarcastic satire as well as the sentimental romanticism of the United Irishmen. When one considers Moore's United Irish literary backgrounds, Moore the satirist is not hard to reconcile with Moore the romantic songwriter.

Significantly, however, Norman Vance, whose *Irish Literature: A Social History* has offered the most objective analysis of Moore to date in that it sees beyond many of the prejudices and stereotypes about Moore, has difficulty reconciling the romantic and the satiric aspects of Moore's work because he does not recognize either the United Irish literary tradition or Moore's connection to it. According to Vance, "Moore the satirist seems to belong in a different context and tradition from Moore the elegist of Ireland" (1990, 105). The United Irishmen provide the necessary context and tradition. Likewise, Vance is surprised at how "Moore rises above narrowly national feeling" (117). However, once one realizes that Moore is actually more representative of the United Irish literary tradition than of the narrow and sectarian literary nationalism that succeeded him, Moore's inclusive Irish nationalism is not surprising.

· 7 ·

Young Ireland Poetry

The Young Ireland movement of the 1840s takes on a new significance when analyzed in the context of United Irish literary nationalism and of Thomas Moore's poetry, rather than in the usual political context of Daniel O'Connell's Repeal movement. Although the "news" in the Young Ireland newspaper, the *Nation*, was largely devoted to O'Connell and Repeal, Young Ireland verse continued the literary nationalism of the United Irishmen's political songs and Moore's *Irish Melodies*.

The Young Ireland writers clearly believed that their United Irish predecessors had created a significant literary tradition as well as an ideology. Despite Daniel O'Connell's habitual disparagement of the United Irishmen and their espousal of violent revolution, the Young Ireland writers, especially Thomas Davis and Charles Gavan Duffy, read and studied United Irish literary works and modeled their own publications upon them. Young Ireland songs imitated the United Irish practice of writing new, politically charged words to traditional Irish melodies. The *Nation* is strikingly similar in format and content to the United Irish newspapers. There were many personal and literary links between the United Irishmen and the Young Irelanders. It was no coincidence that Young Irelander John Mitchel, the son of a United Irishman, named his newspaper the *United Irishman*, or that images and phrases from United Irish writings echo throughout his *Jail Journal*. John Blake Dillon, who, along with Thomas Davis and Charles Gavan Duffy, founded the *Nation* in 1842, was the grandson of a United Irishman (O'Cathaoir 1990, 1–6). William Drennan, the son of United Irish poet William Drennan, contributed verse to the *Nation*. Robert Emmet's brother-in-law was John Mitchel's defense attorney. Emmet's nephew, also Robert Emmet, the son of United Irishman Thomas Addis Emmet, assisted John Blake Dillon when he fled to New York in 1848.

Charles Gavan Duffy's Ulster origins had given him direct contact with the literary remains of the United Irishmen. In his autobiography, Duffy recalled reading United Irish songbooks and prose satires as he grew up (1898, 1:1–37). He claimed that his first mentor and patron was the former United Irishman Charles Hamilton Teeling, who had been arrested and imprisoned in 1796 along with Samuel Neilson, the editor of the *Northern Star*, Thomas Russell, and others, and whose brother had been executed in 1798 (19).

In 1838, Teeling, who became a prominent newspaper editor in Ulster, gave the twenty-two-year-old Duffy a copy of his book, *History of the Irish Rebellion of 1798: A Personal Narrative* (1828). Teeling's book was a romanticized account of the 1798 rising that emphasized the literary and musical dimensions of the United Irish movement. The example of the United Irishmen's use of songs was not lost on Charles Gavan Duffy. He recalled in his autobiography that as a young journalist he realized that "song was an immense though greatly underrated force" and that "Swift, who was as little as possible of a Celt, seems to have divined this passion in the race, and his political songs were almost as powerful stimulants of opinion as his pamphlets" (Duffy 1898, 1:55). Thanks to Teeling's help and influence, Duffy began a career as a journalist. Duffy claimed that while he was editor of the *Belfast Vindicator*, he had tried to "appeal to an old bardic people in passionate verse" (1898, 1:64), a phrase that could also describe much of the verse that had been published in the *Northern Star* during the 1790s. Duffy said that he and Davis continued that program in the *Nation* (1898, 1:57).

The popular Young Ireland *Spirit of the Nation* songbooks (1843–1845), which contained songs and poems originally published in the *Nation*, are modeled upon the United Irishmen's *Paddy's Resource* songbooks, which had anthologized songs first published in United Irish newspapers. Duffy's own anthology of popular nationalist poetry, *The Ballad Poetry of Ireland* (1845), which ran through fifty editions in as many years, included several United Irish songs. Significantly, in his introduction to that anthology, Duffy surveyed the popular literary tradition that had preceded the poetry of the Young Irelanders and described it as encompassing the political ballads of Jonathan Swift; the songs of the Volunteers; popular literature such as the play *The Battle of Aughrim*; and the United Irishmen's songs, which, according to Duffy, "are continually republished, and have run through endless editions, their circulation in Ulster alone counts by tens of thousands" (1869, 22).

Literary historians, however, have ignored the United Irish context in which Duffy and other Young Irelanders placed their writings. For example, Leonard Ashley's introduction to the 1973 facsimile reproduction of the fortieth edition of Duffy's *Ballad Poetry*, though it mentions that the Young Irelanders were inspired by the political doctrines of the United Irishmen, omits all reference to the United Irishmen's literary works, which Duffy's own introduction had argued were an important influence on him. Instead, Ashley places the Young Ireland writers in a literary context of purely antiquarian dimensions: "Before the *Nation* came along, there had been for some years a growing interest in the ancient poetry of Ireland and translation of Gaelic poetry had followed the first significant published collection of the Ancient Songs and Ballads in Bishop Thomas Percy's *Reliques of Ancient English Poetry* (1765) and the less reliable so-called 'Ossian' poems in the 'translations' of James Macpherson" (Ashley 1973, vii). Ashley also omits all reference to the popular literature that Duffy credited as an influence. Clearly, "popular literature," whether by the United Irishmen or produced earlier in the eighteenth century, was not a worthy cultural antecedent to the Young Irelanders if their literary reputation was to be elevated.

Although United Irish verse is the most significant point of origin for Young Ireland poetry, Moore's songs were the Young Ireland poets' most immediate model, in both a positive and negative sense. Many, but not all, of the Young Ireland poems were songs set to traditional melodies in the general manner of Moore's *Irish Melodies* and the United Irish songbooks. However, whereas Moore had taken up the mournful sentimental strain of United Irish verse, the Young Ireland poets sought the more energetic and optimistic tone that had characterized many United Irish political songs. In the view of the most important Young Ireland poet, Thomas Davis, the best *Paddy's Resource* song was "God Save the Rights of Man." That song, from the first *Paddy's Resource* songbook in 1795, was energetic and passionate in tone, but it was also quite formal and philosophic in style. Most Young Ireland verse, including that of Thomas Davis, is at once less formal than the more philosophic United Irish songs and less colloquial than many later United Irish songs. It is more like the poems of William Drennan and, melancholy aside, the popular middle-class songs of Moore.

Moreover, most Young Ireland verse attempted an energy and passion of a more historical, personal, and localized kind. In that sense, Young Ireland verse resembles later United Irish verse such as William Drennan's "Wake of William Orr" and George Nugent Reynold's "The Exiled Irishman's Lamentation," both of which Thomas Davis greatly admired. Some of the Young Ireland songs were set to traditional tunes, whereas others were set to "original" music that represented the larger Young Ireland effort to stimulate Irish art.

The first issue of the *Nation*, edited by Thomas Davis, John Blake Dillon, and Charles Gavan Duffy, appeared on 15 October 1842 and was an immediate popular success. The newspaper's epigraph was: " 'To create and to foster public opinion in Ireland—to make it racy of the soil.'—Chief Baron Woulfe." The source and meaning of the epigraph are significant. Stephen Woulfe (1787–1840), a Catholic, had been named the Chief Baron of the Irish Exchequer in 1838, succeeding Henry Joy, the first cousin of Henry Joy McCracken, who had defended Thomas Russell at his trial for treason in 1803. Woulfe had actively participated in O'Connell's campaign for Catholic Emancipation, but he was noted for his positions not always being in accord with those of O'Connell. The fact that he was the source of the *Nation's* motto thus foreshadowed the Young Irelander's independence from O'Connell on several major issues in the years ahead.

Charles Gavan Duffy described the origin of Woulfe's remark that became the *Nation's* motto: "When Municipal Reform was before Parliament Peel asked contemptuously what good corporations would do a country so poor as Ireland? 'I will tell the right honourable gentleman' said Stephen Woulfe, afterwards Chief Baron, 'they will go far to create and foster public opinion and make it racy of the soil" (Duffy 1881, 63). Duffy went on to point out the similarity between Woulfe's remark and a sentence in Macaulay's essay on Boswell's *Life of Samuel Johnson:* "We know no production of the human mind which has so much of what may be called the race, so much of the peculiar flavour of the soil from which it sprung" (63).

Duffy claimed that Davis's close friend Daniel Owen Maddyn had suggested Woulfe's remark for the motto. Maddyn was probably the author of an article about Woulfe that had appeared in the *Dublin Monthly Magazine* in the autumn of 1842. The article quoted Woulfe's famous remark, declaring that its "words embody with inimitable terseness the objects of an Irish patriot-statesman," and called Woulfe "a powerful and accomplished Celt" (Maddyn 1842, 293, 280). The *Dublin Monthly Magazine* was the successor of the *Citizen*, founded by Davis's friend Thomas Clarke Wallis, who had been Davis and Dillon's nationalist tutor at Trinity. Davis published his famous "Udalism and Feudalism" essay in the *Citizen*, which was largely subsidized by Davis's friend William Elliott Hudson (a relative of Moore's friend Edward Hudson). William Hudson, an expert on traditional Irish music, contributed to both magazines an ongoing series of articles entitled "The Native Music of Ireland," which Davis had bound separately and studied carefully. Wallis and Maddyn were no doubt among Davis's friends at Trinity whom Duffy described in his *Short Life of Thomas Davis* as "a little knot of generous Protestants in college who talked to each other the old doctrine of Tone and Emmet" (1895, 7).

Both the *Citizen* (1838–1841) and the *Dublin Monthly Magazine* (1842) were important literary antecedents to the *Nation* because they published stories, poems, and essays about the United Irishmen, as well as verse in the tradition of both Moore and the United Irishmen. The tradition of literary and cultural nationalism fostered by the United Irishmen in the 1790s flourished in the period between 1803, the year that marked both Emmet's Rising and the final collection of *Paddy's Resource* songs, and 1842 when the *Nation* was launched. Thomas Moore's songs were the best known, but not the only, example of that tradition. John Power's annotated *List of Irish Periodical Publications (Chiefly Literary) from 1729 to the Present Time* (1866) provides ample evidence of magazines that combined literature and politics in the manner of United Irish newspapers and songbooks. Power lists over 100 Irish periodical publications for the period between 1800 and 1842. Most had a "national" focus on literature and political events (1866, 6–18).

Some of the most important pre-1840 examples of the continuation of the United Irish model of literary and political journalism were: the *Belfast Magazine* (1808–1814), edited by William Drennan in Belfast; *The Rushlight* (1824–1825), described by Power as "a liberal weekly literary publication," edited in Belfast by Luke Mullen Hope, the eldest son of United Irishman Jemmy Hope, a close associate of Thomas Russell and Henry Joy McCracken; *Bolster's Quarterly Magazine* (1826–1830), published in Cork by John Windele, which was in Thomas Davis's personal library; the *Ulster Magazine* (1830–1832), edited by former United Irishman Charles Hamilton Teeling; the *Irish Rushlight; or Magazine of Politics and Miscellaneous Information for the Millions* (1831), edited by Luke Mullen Hope in Dublin; the *Irish Monthly Magazine of Politics and Literature* (1832–1834) which was published in Dublin; and *Ancient Ireland: A Weekly Magazine*, edited by Philip Barron of County Waterford for several months in 1835. Barron's *Ancient Ireland* focused on the Irish language and Irish antiquities, and resembled the United Irishman's *Bolg an tSolair: or, Gaelic Magazine*.

Poetry written in Ireland during the early nineteenth century often resembled United Irish verse. For example, J. J. Callanan's earliest recorded poem, merely entitled "Song" and written about 1818, recalled United Irish songs in style and subject. In the tradition of United Irish emigration ballads, the speaker, bidding farewell to "my own dear Erin . . . my own green Isle / Ye fields where heroes bounded / To meet the foes of Liberty," hopes that "still the day may brighten" when the "shouts of freedom" will be heard in Ireland (Windele 1829, 283).

Although the peasantry's songs about 1798 were pessimistic and despairing (Thuente 1989, 51), the rebellion was romanticized and heroicized in the many novels about the United Irishmen published in the first half of the nineteenth century. A list of these novels is given in Stephen Brown's *Ireland in Fiction: A Guide to Irish Novels, Tales, Romances, and Folk-Lore* (1919, 327–28). Similarly, the *Dublin Monthly Magazine*, a precursor of the *Nation* with which many of Davis's friends had been associated, serialized a tale entitled "Gerald Kirby: A Tale of the Year 1798" in 1842, as well as a lengthy article that defended the United Irishmen by arguing that they were more than "merely a military organization," and that they had achieved "political and social triumphs" (1919, 81).

John Cornelius O'Callaghan, who joined the staff of the *Nation* in 1842, had published poems and essays about the United Irishmen in the 1830s. His "Song for United Irishmen; or, Irishmen United" (1837) was a drinking song in the tradition of many United Irish songs. This song and others that resembled United Irish verse were collected and published by O'Callaghan in *The Green Book; or, Gleanings from the Writing-Desk of a Literary Agitator* in 1841. O'Callaghan also praised and included some of the United Irishmen's own songs, claiming such songs provided the best evidence about United Irish ideology available to historians and suggesting they "be collected from old music books" and reprinted in "a regular work, like the *Jacobite Minstrelsy of Scotland*. If Ireland is ever to attempt a resumption of her former legislative independence, those lyrical effusions would form no bad democratic Scriptures of poetical nationality, for circulation by a Bible Society of patriotism" (1841, 132–36).

Perhaps in response to O'Callaghan's suggestion, James McCormick included numerous songs from *Paddy's Resource* songbooks in *The Irish Rebellion of 1798, with Numerous Historical Sketches, Never Before Published* (1844), which is more a literary anthology than a political history of the United Irishmen. McCormick also reprinted James Porter's *Billy Bluff and the Squire*, and even Drennan's plan for a secret "Irish Brotherhood," although he did not credit it to Drennan, saying merely that this "original plan" for the United Irish Society had been circulated in Dublin in June of 1791 (1844, 151). McCormick's *Irish Rebellion* was only one title in the "National Library for Ireland" series of popular books, mostly about the United Irishmen, which he published in the 1840s. McCormick's books were cheaper and more popular than the Young Ireland series edited by Charles Gavan Duffy, which was entitled "Library of Ireland" and which also included several books about the United Irishmen ("The National Library for Ireland" 1921, 16).

Several poets who contributed verse to the *Nation* had previously published verse in the *Citizen* and the *Dublin Monthly Magazine*. For example, "To the Harp" appeared in the fourth volume of the *Citizen* in 1841 under the pseudonym "T. C. D.," a pseudonym later used by several of Thomas Davis's Trinity College friends who contributed verse to the *Nation*. "To the Harp," using the motif of the harp popularized by the United Irishmen and Moore, called upon the harp of Erin to exchange its "notes of woe" for a happier tune: "Tell us of spirits that for Erin are glowing." That appeal would become the main poetic agenda of the *Nation*, whose literary nationalism was at least partially derived from these two Dublin magazines and from the other earlier nineteenth-century publications that had continued the literary nationalism of the United Irishmen.

The Young Ireland movement, however, followed the example of the United Irishmen and, instead of founding a magazine, established the *Nation* and published collections of its verse. The first Young Ireland anthology of verse that appeared in the *Nation* was published in March 1843. Entitled *The Spirit of the Nation*, it contained sixty-one poems, thirty-two of which had tunes. A second part, published in November 1843, contained fifty-five new poems, thirty-three of which were songs. In 1844, a new edition of *The Spirit of the Nation* appeared in six numbers that contained a total of 147 poems, sixty-five of which had tunes. Forty-nine of the tunes were traditional tunes and sixteen were "original." In 1845, the 147 songs that had appeared in the six numbers in 1844 were published in one volume entitled *The Spirit of the Nation*.

The *Nation* also attempted to foster a native Irish literary tradition which encompassed more than political verse. Thus, in 1845, it also sponsored two anthologies of Irish poetry and song that had not appeared in its pages: Charles Gavan Duffy's *Ballad Poetry of Ireland* and Michael Joseph Barry's *Songs of Ireland*, which was dedicated to "Thomas Moore, the National Bard of Ireland." Both collections were very popular. Duffy's was in its sixth edition by 1846 and its thirty-ninth edition in 1866; Barry's was in a fourth edition by 1849.

Thomas Davis had begun to compile *The Songs of Ireland* as a complement to the largely narrative poems in Duffy's *Ballad Poetry*. Michael Joseph Barry took the project over from the busy Davis, who gave him his source materials, and completed it shortly after Davis's sudden death on 16 September 1845. *The Songs of Ireland* contained Davis's "Essay on Irish Songs" in which he outlined the Young Irelanders' relationship to earlier Irish literary tradition and described their own literary agenda. The contents of *The Songs of Ireland* reflected Thomas Davis's and the movement's image of a national Irish literary tradition. Frequently evoking the memory of Swift and Carolan, the collection included songs by United Irish poets (William Drennan, Edward Lysaght, James Orr, and John Philpot Curran), by nineteenth-century Irish writers (Thomas Moore, John and Michael Banim, Gerald

Griffin, Lady Morgan), and by writers for the *Nation* (J. J. Callanan and Thomas Davis), in addition to thirty-eight anonymous songs.

Thomas Davis wrote his "Essay on Irish Songs," which appeared anonymously in the *Nation* on 21 December 1844 and 4 January 1845, to mark the publication of the newest edition of *The Spirit of the Nation*, of Duffy's *Ballad Poetry of Ireland*, and of Barry's *Songs of Ireland*. The essay is the Young Ireland movement's most important statement about its relationship to previous Irish poetry and its own poetic agenda, and thus provides an important context for an analysis of the Young Ireland movement's relationship to Thomas Moore and to the United Irishmen.

Davis's essay makes clear that Thomas Moore was one of the Young Irelanders' most important literary models, in both a positive and a negative sense. Davis's praise of Moore included some important reservations:

> It may be said that Moore is lyrist enough for Ireland. We might show that though he is perfect in his expression of the softer feelings, and unrivalled even by Burns in many of his gay songs, yet, that he is often deficient in vehemence, does not speak of the stronger passions, spoils some of his finest songs by pretty images, is too refined and subtle in his dialect, and too negligent of narrative; but to prove these assertions would take too great space, and perhaps lead some one to think we wished to run down Moore. He is immeasurably our greatest poet, and the greatest lyrist, except Burns and Beranger, that ever lived; but he has not given songs to the middle and poor classes of Ireland. (Davis 1914, 269)

Many years later, Charles Gavan Duffy aptly summed up the difference between Moore's poetry and that of the *Nation*: "His melodies dating from the unsuccessful insurrection of '98 and the Union were the wail of a lost cause; while the songs of the *Nation* vibrated with the virile and passionate hopes of a new generation" (1881, 181). Young Ireland verse echoed the optimism of United Irish verse rather than the sorrows of Moore's songs.

The *Nation* publicly declared its emulation of Moore's poetry on many occasions. On 15 July 1843, the newspaper proudly and defiantly quoted part of a *Belfast Newsletter* review of *The Spirit of the Nation* that had objected to its seditious materials: "We strongly suspect that MOORE must have had a hand in some of the productions. SEVERAL OF THE SONGS ARE SO DECIDEDLY IN MOORE'S STYLE, that nothing less than his own solemn declaration will, in our esteem, acquit him of their authorship, and he is a pensioner of the government." A few weeks earlier, a *Nation* editorial by Charles Gavan Duffy entitled "Thomas Moore's Treason," which referred to the same review, had declared that the editors might publish many things by Moore "without anybody discovering the smallest incongruity" between Moore's works and the usual *Nation* verse (24 June 1843).

Many songs published in the *Nation* indeed sounded very much like Moore, such as "The Harp of the Nation" (4 November 1843):

> Dear harp though around thee yet glisten
> The last links of slavery's chain,
> And tyrants too watchfully listen,
> We'll tune thee to freedom again.

The song, which also echoed the United Irish motto of tuning the Irish harp to freedom, was signed "Montanus," the pseudonym that Thomas Addis Emmet had used in the *Press*. It appeared in a *Nation* column entitled "Songs of the Bog-Trotters," the title of which recalls the United Irishmen's sarcastic use of epithets such as "the swinish multitude" and "Paddy."

The first issue of the *Nation* promised a literary portrait of Moore that appeared two weeks later as the first in a series of essays about distinguished Irish writers entitled the "National Gallery." Thomas Davis's essay on Moore emphasized Moore's literary nationalism, repeating all the anecdotes about Moore's close associations with the United Irishmen that had appeared in his biography of Lord Edward Fitzgerald and focusing on Moore's most nationalistic works, such as his *Memoirs of Captain Rock* and the *Irish Melodies*. According to Davis, the latter work's popularity in Ireland was second only to that of the short lives of Edward Fitzgerald and Robert Emmet (*Nation*, 29 November 1842). Davis repeatedly cited Moore's *Memoirs of Captain Rock*, *The Life and Death of Lord Edward Fitzgerald*, and his *History of Ireland* in his essays. Even Davis's list of suggested historical sources for a series of paintings based on Irish history, "Hints for Irish Historical Painting" (29 July 1843), included Moore's *Irish Melodies*.

Davis's appreciation of Moore was partly French in its inspiration. Augustine Thierry, the Frenchman whose literary nationalism had been a major influence on Davis's, had celebrated three aspects of Ireland—its ancient music, the United Irishmen, and Thomas Moore. In his essay "A Ballad History of Ireland" (30 November 1844), Davis praised Thierry's treatment of the United Irishmen: "his vindication of the 'men of 98' out of the slanderous pages of Musgrave is a miracle of historical skill and depth of judgment." Davis's essay on Thierry, which appeared in the *Nation* on 26 November 1842, quoted extensively from Thierry's 1820 essay on the national character of the Irish as displayed in their music and in the songs of Thomas Moore:

> There are some people who have long memories, whom the thought of independence never abandons in their slavery, and who, holding out against long habit, elsewhere so potent, still detest and strive to shake off, after centuries, the yoke which superior power has imposed on them. Such is the Irish nation. This nation, reduced by conquest beneath the English sway, refuses for these six centuries to consent to this government and give it its sanction; it spurns it as it did the first day; it protests against it as the Ancient Irish protested—by unsuccessful battles. Its revolts it does not regard as rebellions, but as just and legitimate war. . . . Old Ireland is still the only country that true Irishmen will acknowledge; 'tis for her sake they have clung so closely to her creed and tongue; and whenever insurrection frees their voices 'tis her they invoke by the ancestral name—Erin! Erin! To maintain this chain of manners and traditions unbroken against all the efforts of the conqueror, the Irish have made monuments which neither fire nor sword can destroy—their music.

Thierry went on to extol the bards whose harps had celebrated "the freedom of days gone by, and the glory of the patriot." Thierry's views on Irish music, as quoted and translated by Davis, recalled the editorials about the connection of traditional music and national character that had appeared in the United Irishmen's *Northern Star* on the occasion of the Belfast Harp Festival. They also foreshadowed the views of the Young Irelanders: "The words of the national songs to which Ireland has narrated her long tale of suffering have for the most part perished; the music alone has been saved. The music may serve as a comment on the history of the country. It paints the inside of souls, as well as narrative paints action" (*Nation*, 26 November 1842).

Although O'Connell, whose frequent quotes from Moore enhanced his own ambiguity about the use of violence, gladly embraced the mournful passivity that always prudently enveloped even the most potentially seditious of Moore's songs, the Young Irelanders condemned Moore's melancholy and embraced a vigorous tone similar to many United Irish political songs. The Preface to *The Spirit of the Nation* (1 January 1845) declared: "The greatest achievement of the Irish people is their music. It tells their history, climate, and character; but it too much loves to weep. Let us, when so many of our chains have been broken, when our strength is great and our hopes high, cultivate its bolder strains—its raging and rejoicing; or, if we weep, let it be like men whose eyes are lifted, though the tears fall" (1981, vi). Young Ireland songs were often set to tunes that Moore had used in his *Irish Melodies*. I have noted twenty-seven different tunes from Moore's *Irish Melodies* in songs in the *Nation* in 1843 and 1844.

When there were not enough "bolder strains" among traditional Irish tunes, the Young Irelanders wrote "original" music. Twenty-five percent of the tunes in the 1845 *Spirit of the Nation* were original and described in the preface as "of a proud and fierce character" (1981, vi). Several of these original airs were written by Davis's close friend William Elliot Hudson. Many of the poems and songs published in the *Nation* and later in *The Spirit of the Nation* could be described as very similiar to those of Moore except that they lacked his typical melancholy. Many of them also contained more narrative than was generally found in Moore's vague lyrics. Young Ireland poetry thus embodied the new poetic formula advocated by Davis in his criticism of Moore's songs as "deficient" in "vehemence" and "the stronger passions" and "negligent of narrative."

Narrative is what distinguishes ballads from songs, which are largely lyrical. Duffy's *Ballad Poetry of Ireland* contains mostly ballads. The two songs by Moore, "The Desmond" and "The Return of O'Ruark," that Duffy included in his collection have a stronger narrative line than most of Moore's songs and do indeed qualify as ballads. Duffy described "The Desmond," in which the Earl of Desmond spoke of his love for a woman of lower social station, as expressing "violent passion" (1869, 177). Many of the songs in Duffy's anthology concerned love, but most were ballads rather than love songs because of their plots and specific historical settings. The passion in the songs often had a political significance, as when they were spoken by heroic Irish rebels such as the Earl of Desmond. In a similar manner, Moore's "Return of the O'Ruark" recounted Devorgilla's husband's discovery that she had fled, an infidelity that, according to tradition, prompted the Norman invasion of Ireland.

O'Ruark's final lines were among the most energetic Moore ever wrote:

> But onward!—the green banner rearing,
>   Go, flesh every sword to the hilt;
> On our side is VIRTUE and ERIN!
>   On theirs is the SAXON and GUILT.
>   (Duffy 1869, 103)

For Moore, and for Daniel O'Connell, who used the lines as an epigraph for his history of Ireland, the historical setting of the ballad, which made the words O'Ruark's and not Moore's or O'Connell's, answered any charge of seditious intent. Young Ireland poetry was frequently in the vein of Moore's "Song of O'Ruark." Indeed, one suspects that in addition to the energy, passion, and narrative interest offered by ballads, their historical setting and dramatic nature also offered the Young Ireland poets an important defense against charges of sedition. In any event, by intensifying the sentimental sedition and vague story lines in Moore's songs, the Young Ireland poets developed a new dimension in Irish political poetry.

Thomas Moore was only one of several potential literary models discussed by Davis in his essay on Irish songs. Davis identified a similar tendency to weep too much in the native Irish tradition: "The Irish-speaking people have songs by the thousand, but they (especially the political ones) are too despairing" (1914, 269). The songs of the English-speaking poor were likewise defective. Davis described songs of the last century, whether in Irish or English, as follows: "Their structure is irregular, their grief slavish and despairing, their joy reckless and bombastic, their religion bitter and sectarian, their politics Jacobite, and concealed by extravagant and tiresome allegory" (271). He argued that although the old songs deserved to be.preserved for scholars in "libraries," and the best of the older native songs could be condensed and edited in the manner of Ramsay and Burns for popular consumption in "cabins," there were nevertheless "great gaps in Irish song to be filled up" (270–71).

In addition to Moore's songs, Davis looked to the best of the United Irish songs and to the historical Anglo-Irish ballads of Gerald Griffin for models. In Davis's view, which he had already expressed six months previously in an essay in the *Nation* entitled "Irish Music and Poetry" (29 June 1844), "Save for one or two by Lysaght or Drennan, almost all the Irish political songs are too desponding or weak to content a people marching to independence as proudly as if they had never been slaves" (*Davis* 1914, 162). In his new essay on Irish songs, Davis praised the most energetic and assertive political songs of the 1790s:

> Great opportunities came with the Volunteers and the United Irishmen, but the men were wanting. We have but one good Volunteer song. It was written by Lysaght, after that illustrious militia was dissolved. Drennan's "Wake of William Orr" is not a song; but he gave the United Men the only good song they had—"When Erin first rose." In "Paddy's Resource," the text-book of the men who were "up," there is but one tolerable song— "God save the Rights of Man"; nor looking beyond these, can we think of anything of a high class, but "The Sean Bhan Bhocd" [*sic*], "The Wearing of the Green," Lysaght's "Island," and Reynolds' "Erin-go-bragh" ["Exiled Irishman's Lamentation"], if it be his. (1914, 274)

Davis's remarks deserve comment. Lysaght's "Volunteer Song," to the popular and lively eighteenth-century march tune "The British Grenadiers" (reprinted in Madden's *Literary Remains of the United Irishmen*), had used standard Volunteer and United Irish motifs to vigorously celebrate Grattan, "The gallant man who led the van of the Irish Volunteers" and "broke oppression's chain." The only further information that I have been able to discover about the song Davis refers to as Lysaght's "Island" is in Duffy's introduction to *The Ballad Poetry of Ireland*: "His [Lysaght's] song of 'Our Island' is a fine speci-men of political verse—rough, strong, and impulsive, without much attention to method, but clear and simple as water. Here is a speci-men of it:—

> May God in whose hand
> Is the lot of each land,
> Who rules over ocean and dry land,
> Inspire our good King
> Ill advisers to fling,
> Ere destruction they bring on our Island!
> Don't we feel 'tis our dear little Island,
> A fertile and fair little Island!
> May Orange and Green
> No longer be seen
> Distained with the blood of our Island!"
>   (1869, 22–23)

All five stanzas were included in O'Callaghan's *Green Book* and in *Barry's Songs of Ireland* under the title "No Union for our Dear Native Island" (O'Callaghan 1841, 134–35; Barry 1845, 221–23).

Lysaght's song "Advice to Paddy," which first appeared in the 1795 *Paddy's Resource* to the tune "Larry Grogan," was also evidently popular in Young Ireland circles. Davis's close friend John O'Hagan, who wrote under the pseudonym "Sleivegullion" (Gaelicized to "Sliabh Cuilinn" in the 1845 *Spirit of the Nation*), used the opening lines of "Advice to Paddy," which he simply attributed to an "Old Song," as an epigraph to his "The Irish Catholic to His Protestant Brother" (*Nation*, 24 December 1842). Rejecting the stage Irish brogue of Lysaght's song, O'Hagan's song advised the standard United Irish and now Young Ireland doctrine of "UNION" in terms of the old United Irish motifs of chains, dawning freedom, and green banners. The United Irishmen had used a few Irish phrases in their songs, but they had more generally used dialect to provide an Irish note, as in the opening line of Lysaght's song, "Arrah, Paddy, my boy." The Young Ireland poets preferred phrases in Irish to such brogue, which to them smacked too much of the stage-Irishmen whose presence in the novels of Charles Lever they condemned. Other verse by O'Hagan, an Ulsterman who displayed a large knowledge of and debt to United Irish songs, will be discussed later in this chapter.

The second writer from the 1790s whom Davis praised in his essay on Irish songs was the United Irish poet William Drennan. Davis's favorite poems by Drennan, "Erin" and "The Wake of William Orr" (both reprinted in appendix B), were among the most popular of all United Irish poems. The fact that only one was actually a song, and that it was set to "its own tune" rather than to a traditional tune, no doubt influenced the Young Ireland practices of writing poems as well as songs and of composing original music for their songs. Both of Drennan's poems represented the combination of lyricism, energy, and optimism that Young Ireland poets sought to achieve. "Erin" called upon the people to "awake" and be ready "to strike." The Orr elegy directed Orr's Irish brothers to "wake not him with women's cries," but instead to "arise" in the manner of the dawning light of freedom at the end of the poem. Commands to Erin's sons to "awake" and "arise," which had originated in Drennan's famous *Letters of Orellana* in 1785, were among the most common motifs in Young Ireland poetry, as they had been in United Irish songs.

Davis's praise of two of the most popular songs of 1798, "The Wearing of the Green" and the "Shan Van Vocht," also suggests that Davis considered vigor an essential ingredient for a truly national song. Both songs lamented Ireland's sad plight, yet they also celebrated spirited defiance. Although we today think of "The Wearing of the Green" in terms of the lugubrious version by Dion Boucicault that became popular in the course of the nineteenth century, Davis was clearly referring to earlier versions, variously entitled "Green Upon My Cape" or "The Wearing of the Green," which, unlike many songs of the people around 1798, were quite upbeat. In a version printed in Dundalk in 1802, a year before Emmet's rising, a United Irishman, exiled because "they knew I was United by the green upon my cape," meets Emmet in France, rather than Napper Tandy in America as in the later sentimental version. Emmet (whether it is Thomas Addis or Robert is unclear) tells the United Irishman to return to Ireland: "A convoy must go with you and not be cut down, / We'll reap the justice and merrily we'll sing / And show authority for wearing of the green" (Zimmermann 1967, 168).

Likewise, "The Shan Van Vocht," the first printed version of which appeared in the second issue of the *Nation* on 29 October 1842, celebrated not only the French being on the sea, but also "the boys," including "Lord Edward," with "their pikes in good repair" on the Curragh of Kildare. Davis, an avid collector of oral and printed versions of traditional Irish songs, was familiar with such popular songs and rightly recognized early *Paddy's Resource* songs such as "God Save the Rights of Man" as being in an entirely different tradition.

Davis's reference to *Paddy's Resource* as the "text-book" of the United Irishmen aptly captures the formal, philosophic quality of many of those songs. Evidence suggests that Davis knew only the first *Paddy's Resource* songbook of 1795, in which "God Save the Rights of Man" had appeared. He refers to Reynold's "Erin Go Bragh" by its popular title rather than as "The Exiled Irishman's Lamentation," the title under which it had appeared in the 1796, 1798, and 1803 *Paddy's Resource* songbooks. Nor does Davis associate either of Drennan's poems specifically with *Paddy's Resource*, although both had appeared in the 1798 and 1803 *Paddy's Resource* songbooks, with "Erin" as the opening work in both collections.

Similarly, Charles Gavan Duffy seems to have been familiar with only the 1795 and 1796 *Paddy's Resource* songbooks. In his 1881 history of the Young Ireland movement, Duffy recalled that when he was a boy in Ulster *Paddy's Resource* was one of the popular books that "circulated most extensively in the provinces," and described it as "a collection of songs from the *Northern Star*," a description that only applies to the 1795 and 1796 Belfast editions (1881, 72, 74). In his autobiography, Duffy recalled his childhood reading as including "Moore's *Melodies* [which] soon passed permanently into my memory" and "cheap books printed at Belfast, of which the most popular were the *Battle of Aughrim* and *Billy Bluff*" (1898, 11). The numerous nineteenth-century Belfast editions of James Porter's *Billy Bluff and the Squire* had always included a generous selection of songs from *Paddy's Resource*, but only from the Belfast editions of 1795 and 1796. This suggests that Duffy's description of the popularity of the *Paddy's Resource* songs in Ulster in the first half of the nineteenth century probably refers to the joint publications of *Billy Bluff and the Squire* and *Paddy's Resource* and to songsheets based on the Belfast *Paddy's Resource* collections only: "It is a curious fact, that in Belfast, reputedly so anti-national, these songs are continually republished, and have run through endless editions. Printed on coarse paper, and sold at a few pence, their circulation in Ulster alone counts by tens of thousands. The collection is still called, as it was on its first publication in '97, *Paddy's Resource*; popularly Paddy's *Race-Horse*. The practice of printing them in Belfast was, no doubt, inherited from the time when that town was the chief seat of the United Irishmen" (Duffy 1869, 22).

If Duffy was only familiar with the songs from the first two Belfast editions of *Paddy's Resource* it would explain his description of *Paddy's Resource* songs: "For the most part they were frigid in style, French in sentiment, and inflated or prosaic in language. When they were addressed to the body of the people it was in a diction too pedantic to be familiar, or too cold to be impressive" (1869, 22). Duffy immediately went on to praise Drennan's poems but, like Davis, he did not associate them with *Paddy's Resource*. This is not surprising, as Drennan's work did not appear in either of the Belfast editions of *Paddy's Resource*.

Duffy's *Ballad Poetry of Ireland* included Drennan's "Wake of William Orr" and a poem by Drennan, which Duffy entitles the "Wild Geese" but which had appeared in Drennan's *Fugitive Pieces in Verse and Prose* (1815) as "Verses for Old Irish Melodies." Duffy also included another popular United Irish ballad "Mary Le More," which had appeared in the 1803 *Paddy's Resource* as "The Maniac." Duffy mistakenly attributes "Mary Le More" to George Nugent Reynolds, whom he describes as having written "several rough, strong, popular songs in the national interest" (Duffy 1869, 106), presumably a reference to Reynold's "Exiled Irishman's Lamentation," which Thomas Davis also praised highly.

Although neither Davis nor Duffy evidently realized Reynold's song had appeared in any *Paddy's Resource* songbook, it was clearly an important model for Young Ireland poetry, which often followed its example in using Irish phrases. Moreover, the vigorous tone of the supposed lament, which Mary Ann McCracken had recounted United Irish prisoners singing defiantly in Belfast in 1796, epitomized the "bolder strains" that Young Ireland poetry hoped to achieve. Reynold's line "Too long have we suffered and too long lamented" was a cornerstone of the Young Ireland poetic agenda.

Thomas Davis's third literary model for would-be national poets was Anglo-Irish ballads. His essay on Irish songs cited fiction-writer Gerald Griffin's ballads as an example. Four ballads by Griffin appeared in Duffy's *Ballad Poetry*. His "Orange and Green" demonstrates how ballad narrative could propagate political doctrine. The ballad recounts how, as the Orange bands victoriously played the "Battle of the Boyne," an Orangeman gives refuge to a Catholic soldier after a battle, even after he finds out the man has just killed his son. Years later in 1798, as the United Irishmen are victoriously playing "Granua Uile" in Wexford, the same Catholic peasant returns the favor by giving refuge to the now elderly Orangeman (Duffy 1869, 85–89).

Duffy's anthology of Irish ballads offered a new model, whom Davis's essay had not even mentioned, for the Anglo-Irish ballad; Duffy included more ballads by Samuel Ferguson than by any other poet. The *Nation* poets, J. J. Callanan, Thomas Davis, and Edward Walsh, were each represented by six songs, whereas there were ten, including three translations from the Irish, by Ferguson. Davis's review essay on Duffy's collection, which appeared in the *Nation* on 2 August 1845, heartily approved the prominence that Duffy had given to Ferguson. Although he had not even mentioned Ferguson in any of his earlier essays on Irish songs and ballads, Davis now had the highest praise for both Ferguson's translations and his original Anglo-Irish ballads. Davis referred to Ferguson's translation "O'Byrne's Bard to the Clans of Wicklow" as his "Wicklow War Song." In the tradition of "rousing" laments such as Drennan's elegy on Orr and Reynold's "Exiled Irishman's Lamentation," Ferguson's "translation" deserved Davis's description as being as "crashing as anything we know of" (*Davis* 1914, 371). Ferguson attended the Belfast Academical Institution where he must have been influenced by the literary and educational policies of the United Irishmen, which had survived in many of its founders. Although Drennan and others never accepted armed rebellion, they continued to pursue nonviolent United Irish principles and policies in popular education and publications.

Davis had even higher praise for Ferguson's poem "Willy Gilliland," calling it the "best" of the ballads in Duffy's collection, surpassing anything in either Percy's *Reliques of English Poetry* or Scott's *Minstrelsy of the Scottish Border* (Davis 1914, 372). Although Davis emphasized the fact that "Willy Gilliland" was "vigorous," the subject of Ferguson's song, subtitled "An Ulster Ballad," was also significant in that it added to the collection an important Protestant dimension reminiscent of days when Ulster had been the center of Volunteer and United Irish activity. (This is also true of the other "Orange ballads" that Duffy, an Ulster native, included in his anthology.) Ferguson's song celebrated the Presbyterian Willy Gilliland, who, landless and reduced to being an outlaw as a result of injustices by both the king and the Anglican church, successfully defies both oppressors. Ferguson's final lines could be read as a call for Protestant support of the Repeal movement, such as frequently appeared in the pages of the *Nation*: "Yet so it was; and still from him descendants not a few / Draw birth and lands, and, let me trust, draw love of Freedom too" (Duffy 1869, 176).

Davis's high praise for Ferguson's "Orange" ballad and the diverse religious and social backgrounds of the contributors to Barry's and Duffy's anthologies underscore how inclusive Young Ireland national-ism was. Despite the fact that Davis and the Young Ireland poets are sometimes inaccurately identified with the narrow and sectarian forms of nationalism that succeeded them, their nationalism is actually much closer to that of the United Irishmen. Davis's essay "United Irishmen" (8 July 1843) reminded readers of the *Nation* that the United Irishmen's purpose, in addition to "Parliamentary reform and Catholic equality," had been "to unite Irishmen of all creeds and classes for the service of their country."

Young Ireland verse repeatedly promoted the United Irish goal of "Union." Michael J. Barry's "Gael and the Green," to the tune "One Bumper at Parting," a drinking song similar to many such United Irish songs, declared:

> Here, under our host's gay dominion,
>   While gathered this table around,
> What varying shades of opinion
>   In one happy circle are found!
> What opposite creeds come together—
>   How mingle North, South, East, and West;
> Yet, who minds the diff'rence a feather?—
>   Each strives to love Erin the best.
>   (*The Spirit of the Nation* 1981, 43)

Although the song's tune, "One Bumper at Parting," indicates that Moore's song of that title was Barry's source (which Moore's song called by the name "Moll Roe," the title of a tune used by the United Irishmen), Barry's "Gael and the Green" bears little resem-blance to Moore's lugubrious song. In a similar manner, Thomas

Davis's song "Penal Days" declared that such days should be forgotten because "All creeds are equal in our isle." Unity and song could now replace division and bitterness: "Let us unite / For Ireland's right, / And drown our griefs in Freedom's song" (*The Spirit of the Nation* 1981, 199).

Even Davis's notorious poem "Celt and Saxon," which has so often been cited as an example of xenophobic nationalism, actually pleads for and promises unity. The opening lines are indeed deceptive when quoted out of context:

> We hate the Saxon and the Dane,
> We hate the Norman men—
> We curs'd their greed for blood and gain,
> We curse them now again.

Yet Davis immediately retracted those lines in the ones that followed:

> Yet start not, Irish born man,
> If you're to Ireland true,
> We heed not blood, nor creed, nor clan—
> We have no curse for you.

The song is actually a celebration of "How every race and every creed /Might be by love combined—" (*The Spirit of the Nation* 1981, 193).

Davis's essay on Thierry had also been the occasion for a spirited criticism of any racially based nationalism. Davis warned his readers of Thierry's "one fault"—"a too exclusive notice of the distinctions arising from race, and occasionally attributing to alienage in blood, differences arising from legal or personal incidents." Davis then voiced an impassioned plea for his readers to "lay down" negative racial distinctions: "We must sink the distinctions of blood as well as sect. The Milesian, the Dane, the Norman, the Welshman, the Scotchman, and the Saxon, naturalised here, must combine, regardless of their blood. . . . This is as much needed as the mixture of Protestant and Catholic. If a union of all Irish-born men ever be accomplished, Ireland will have the greatest and most varied materials for an illustrious nationality, and for a tolerant and flexible character in literature, manners, religion, and life, of any nation on earth" (*Nation,* 26 November 1842).

The Young Irelanders' widespread use of epithets such as "Saxon," which emphasized racial distinctions but which had seldom been used in United Irish verse, did indeed introduce an unfortunate racial connotation into nationalist verse. However, these poetic stereotypes have too often obscured the Young Irelanders's political ideology, which promoted a unity of all races.

The *Nation's* obituary for Thomas Davis was appropriately entitled "The Union of Parties" (27 September 1845), which by coincidence had also been the title of a United Irish song in the 1795 *Paddy's Resource.* Charles Gavan Duffy pointed out how fitting it was that Davis was buried in Mount Jerome, located on the former grounds of John Keogh's home where Keogh and Wolfe Tone, his fellow United Irishman and associate in the Catholic Association in the 1790s, had frequently walked and talked of politics and union among all Irishmen. The Fenian John O'Leary declared in 1886 that the Irish could never go astray in thinking and feeling with Thomas Davis (1886, 12). Likewise, F. S. L. Lyons wrote in *Ireland Since the Famine,* "If the reality of Irish life came to bear little relation to Davis's dream, the fault may be in the reality not the dream" (1971, 112). Once Davis's debt to the United Irishmen's original political ideology of "union" among all parties and religions is appreciated, and the United Irishmen are seen as more than violent rebels, O'Leary's and Lyons's appreciation can be extended to them as well.

The Young Irelanders certainly conceived of the United Irishmen as more than violent, misguided rebels. They launched the *Nation* shortly after the publication of R. R. Madden's first volume in his series *The Lives and Times of the United Irishmen.* The first number of the *Nation* promised to "deal with the silly and malignant article on Dr. Madden's *Lives of the United Irishmen,*" which had appeared in a recent issue of the *Dublin University Magazine.* The promised defense of Madden, written by Thomas Davis, appeared in the next issue. Entitled "An Irish Vampire," it claimed that "Next to *Wolfe Tone's Memoirs,* it is the most instructive book on that boldest attempt ever made to unite Irishmen and liberate Ireland" (22 October 1842).

Many essays and poems in the *Nation* championed Madden's argument that the United Irishmen had not been merely violent revolutionaries of whom Ireland should be ashamed. Davis's essay "United Irishmen," which appeared in the *Nation* on 8 July 1843, began: "United Irishmen!—what a glorious name. How nobly sounds the title of brotherhood in any land!" Davis lamented that theirs had unjustly become a name of reproach in Ireland. Echoing Madden, Davis declared the United Irishmen had been "a political association of our purest and ablest men," and when "forbidden to agitate, they were forced to conspire" and "driven to premature insurrection."

In contrast to Daniel O'Connell's repudiation of the United Irishmen, the *Nation* repeatedly celebrated their political doctrines and heroicized their rebellion as part of a larger Irish historical tradition of battles for freedom. The poetry and songs in the *Nation* celebrated the United Irishmen more often than they did Repeal. On 6 July 1844, the *Nation* proudly quoted *Tait's Magazine*'s assertion that there was as much of Tone as of O'Connell in the *Nation*. One popular anecdote of the time recounted how a Dubliner, when asked what the tone of the *Nation* was that day, had replied, "Wolfe Tone."

The editors obviously took great delight in being associated with the United Irish movement. Davis's article entitled "Hoche's Ghost" appeared in the *Nation* on 5 November 1842. General Lazare Hoche had commanded the French expedition Napoleon sent to Ireland in December 1796. Tone, who was a member of the expedition, recorded in his journal the frustration of seeing the coast of Cork only to have inclement weather prevent a successful landing. Here is the opening of Davis's article:

> The Editor of the *Mail* has seen, in a Vision, Hoche's ghost followed by the veterans of the Rhine, and Wolfe Tone's spirit at the head of the United Irish, issuing in dim array from our office, marching in Indian file, to the air of the *Shan van Vocht*, down the defile of Trinity-street, traversing with stealthy tread and closed ranks the valley of Dame-street. No sooner, however, had the two bodies crowned Cork-hill, than, concealment being no longer necessary, Wolfe Tone and his men dashed in at the Castle-gate, with a cry of *Faugh a Ballagh*, upset a sentry-box, made Lord De Grey turn white, and then vanished; while Hoche, wheeling suddenly into Parliament-street, raised the *ça ira*, stormed the house No. 27, seized the editor of the *Mail*.

"Ça Ira" was, of course, the French revolutionary tune frequently used in United Irish songs, while "Faugh a Ballagh" (Clear the Way) was the traditional Irish war cry celebrated in a poem of that title by Charles Gavan Duffy in the previous issue of the *Nation* on 29 November.

Davis concluded "Hoche's Ghost" with some "suggestions" about how the government might combat the current outbreak of songs that they found so seditious:

> The Parliament should be summoned and the watch called; and a short Act passed empowering a search through the book and music shops, lest treason be printed in Milliken's or Wiseheart's, or rebel harps be made, tuned, and repaired at Robinson's or Pigott's. Let Jews'-harps be broken, for they are constructive treason—let patrols of cavalry with bands (dangerous things those bands, for they some-times play "Patrick's Day") suppress whistling, and break hurdy-gurdy's which don't play orthodox or loyal tunes . . . thus shall the Music-and-Ballad plot (so providentially discovered) be put down— thus may the State be secured against the assaults of Blank Verse and the treachery of Rhyme . . . thus may Prose and Provincialism reign for ever. (*Nation*, 5 November 1842)

Davis's essay was in the tradition of United Irish satires by James Porter, whose grave Davis and Duffy had visited at Greyabbey in County Down when they toured Ulster and visited places associated with the United Irishmen. One such tour was completed shortly be-fore the *Nation* was launched. Davis's library contained a copy of Porter's famous satire *Billy Bluff and the Squire*, which had mocked an earlier government's paranoia about songs and poetry (Noonan 1913, 37–41). Davis's reference to breaking "hurdy-gurdy's" suggests he was also familiar with another famous United Irish satire, William Sampson's *Faithful Report of the Trial of Hurdy Gurdy*.

The Young Irelanders' most famous homage to the United Irishmen is, of course, the poem "The Memory of the Dead," by John Kells Ingram. Ingram was a native of Ulster, as were so many of the Young Irelanders who exhibited the strongest attachment to the United Irishmen. The poem appeared anonymously as a song with no tune in the *Nation* on 1 April 1843 in the series "Songs of the Symposiac," songs supposedly sung by the editors at their weekly dinners. It was reprinted in the first edition of *The Spirit of the Nation* to the tune of "Auld Lang Syne," but had its own "original" music in the 1844 and 1845 editions of *The Spirit of the Nation*. By then the song had become something of a battle cry, for it was the only Young Ireland poem named in the government's indictments against O'Connell and others during the State Trials of 1844. The poem, popularly known today by its first line, emulates the popular drinking song style of many United Irish songs and declares the Young Irelanders to be a continuation of the earlier movement:

> Who fears to speak of Ninety-Eight?
> > Who blushes at the name?
> When cowards mock the patriot's fate,
> > Who hangs his head for shame?
>
> He's all knave, or half a slave,
> > Who slights his country thus;
> But a true man, like you, man,
> > Will fill your glass with us.
>
> We drink the memory of the brave,
> > The faithful and the few—
> Some lie far off beyond the wave—
> > Some sleep in Ireland, too;
>
> . . . .
>
> And we will pray that from their clay
> > Full many a race may start
> Of true men, like you, men,
> > To act as brave a part.
>
> They rose in dark and evil days
> > To right their native land;
> They kindled here a living blaze
> > That nothing shall withstand.
> Alas! that Might can vanquish Right—
> > They fell and pass'd away;
> But true men, like you, men,
> > Are plenty here to-day.

> Then here's their memory—may it be
>   For us a guiding light,
> To cheer our strife for liberty,
>   And teach us to unite.
> Through good and ill, be Ireland still,
>   Though sad as theirs your fate;
> And true men be you, men,
>   Like those of Ninety-Eight.
>   (*Nation*, 1 April 1843)

Ingram's poem was one of several songs celebrating the United Irishmen in the early issues of the *Nation*. The second "National Ballad" to appear in the *Nation* was entitled "Song of the United Irishmen" (10 December 1842), set to the air "The Siege of Belleisle." The song appeared anonymously, but was by John Edward Pigot, one of Davis's closest friends. In the 1845 *Spirit of the Nation* it was set to the popular 1798 tune "The Wearing of the Green" and given a new title, "Up for the Green," which echoed the United Irish slogan of being "Up," with the subtitle remaining "A Song of the United Irishmen." The date "A.D. 1796" was added, as if to suggest the song had actually been sung by the United Irishmen. The motifs of "the martyred dead" and "the green flag" certainly echoed many United Irish songs. The militant chorus proclaimed:

> Then up for the green, boys, and up for the green!
> Shout it back to the Sassenagh, "We'll never sell the green!"
> For our TONE is coming back, and with men enough, I ween,
> To rescue, and avenge us and our own immortal green.

The song called upon the people to remember Limerick, Benburb, and Fontenoy, exemplifying the Young Irelanders' effort to present the United Irishmen as part of a larger and heroic historical tradition.

The poem "Ninety-Eight" by Edward Walsh, who also published many translations from the Irish in the *Nation*, appeared on 5 August 1843. Its tone was more melancholy than militant, which probably explains why it was reprinted in the 1843 *Spirit of the Nation*, but dropped in later editions. Walsh's poem used metrical and rhyme patterns reminiscent of poetry in Irish:

In memory save the martyr'd brave, who fell in conflict
vain,
By soldier's sword, or shameful cord, or in the convict's
chain;
And those whose gore the red lash bore, when tyrants
strode elate,
And pitchcaps clung, and tortures wrung, strong hearts
in Ninety-Eight!

Walsh's more somber approach to 1798 was much closer in spirit to
the popular songs of the peasantry, among whom Walsh collected
songs, than most Young Ireland verse was.

The United Irishmen were too frequently a subject in the *Nation*
for all the songs and poems about them to be discussed in detail. The
following list of some of the articles and poems that I have not yet
mentioned suggests how constant a theme the memory of the United
Irishmen was in the *Nation*: an article entitled "Some of the Opinions of a United Irishman," which quoted from William James
MacNeven's 1807 memoirs *Pieces of Irish History* (12 November 1842);
a reprint of United Irishmen's "famous" song "Union Forever" by
request (18 February 1843); an editorial by Charles Gavan Duffy entitled "Did the Government Foster the Insurrection of '98?" (18 March
1843); an essay by Thomas Davis on Drennan's "Wake of William
Orr," the second in a series entitled "Illustrations of Irish History" (25
March 1843); a review article by Davis on the newest work in R. R.
Madden's *Lives and Times of the United Irishmen* series (29 April 1843);
an essay by Davis on "The Martyrdom of William Orr" (16 September
1843); Davis's poem "Tone's Grave" to the tune "Savourneen Deelish,"
popularized by the United Irishmen (25 November 1843); Davis's
ballad "The Bride of Mallow," which celebrated the wedding of a
United Irishman who "had worn a green coat and born a pike . . . with
the patriots brave" in 1798 (30 December 1843); an obituary for
United Irishman James Porter's son Alexander, a U.S. Senator and
judge (9 March 1844); Davis's song "The Green Above the Red,"
which celebrated Owen Roe O'Neill, Patrick Sarsfield, Wolfe Tone,
and Edward Fitzgerald (12 October 1843); Carroll Malone's ballad of
1798 "The Croppy Boy" (4 January 1845); and an article about United
Irishman John Sheares (27 September 1845). In addition, several of
the books in the "Library of Ireland" series published by the Young

Irelanders focused on the United Irishmen. Thomas Davis was in the process of writing a life of Tone for the series when he died. His outline for it is now in the National Library of Ireland (NLI, Davis Papers, 1791/2).

Even when the contents of the *Nation* were not explicitly about the United Irishmen, their influence was often obvious. Many features of the *Nation* were modeled on the United Irish newspapers, most notably the inclusion of political verse. The first issue of the *Nation* contained James Clarence Mangan's song "The Nation's First Number," to the rousing traditional march tune of "Rory O'More." The song echoed earlier United Irish songs when it declared how, through the power of the press and the "weapon" of the pen, "The Nation comes forth . . . [to] achieve things undreamed of as yet, save in song." Its command to "arise! fling aside your dark mantle of slumber" repeated the rhetoric of much United Irish writing. Yet, from the beginning, the *Nation* included a focus on the peasantry and the land that had not been central in the United Irish movement except among the lower classes:

> We announce a New Era—be this our first news—
> When the serf-grinding Landlords shall shake in their shoes;
> While the ark of a bloodless yet mighty Reform
> Shall emerge from the flood of the Popular Storm!
> (15 October 1842)

Similarly, "The Song of the Poor" (9 March 1844) declared the harp of Erin would now sing of the peasantry.

The Young Irelanders generally emphasized the poverty and the grievances of the peasantry more than their political rights. Such a practical approach undoubtedly had broader popular appeal. For example, four of the six objects of the "Repeal Rent," as outlined in a *Nation* article of that title on 19 November 1842, were economic (revival of Irish manufacture and trade, abolition of tithes, fixity of tenure, and repeal of the poor law), and the repeal of the Union was listed last.

In addition to Mangan's promise of a "bloodless" revolution, the first issue also displayed an ambiguity about violence that had been central to Irish literary nationalism since the days of the Volunteers.

The first song in a series entitled "Songs of the Nation" was entitled "We Want No Swords," but it was set to an "air" entitled "Oh for the swords of former times!" Thomas Moore had included a song entitled "Oh for the Swords of Former Times" in the seventh number of his *Irish Melodies* that began:

> Oh for the swords of former times!
> Oh for the men who bore them,
> When, armed for Right, they stood sublime,
> And tyrants crouched before them!
> (Moore 1808–1834)

Even when verse in the *Nation* promoted peaceful means, the tone was never melancholy as it had been in Moore's work. As the editors put it when they rejected a poem entitled "Sighs for Erin" in the "Answers to Correspondents" column on 5 November 1842, "WE are not of the whining school of politicians." Even Thomas Davis's famous "lament" for Owen Roe O'Neill opened on a note of outraged defiance:

> "Did they dare, did they dare, to slay Owen Roe O'Neill?"
> 'Yes, they slew with poison him, they feared to meet with
> steel.'
> "May God wither up their hearts! May their blood cease
> to flow!
> May they walk in living death, who poisoned Owen Roe!"
> (19 November 1842)

There was no ambiguity in the militant tone of Charles Gavan Duffy's "Faugh a Ballagh," which first appeared in the third issue of the *Nation* (29 October 1842) as "The Charter-Song of the Contributors" and was reprinted in 1843, 1844, and 1845 in *The Spirit of the Nation*. In the *Nation* it was subtitled thus: "A National Hymn, chaunted in full chorus at the last Symposiac of the Editors and Contributors of The Nation." By 1845, it was still subtitled as "a national hymn," but its title had been Gaelicized to "Fag An Bealach." The translation in Duffy's notes in all reprintings of the poem was "Clear the road," which Duffy claimed was "the cry with which the clans of Connaught and Munster used in faction fights to come through a fair with high hearts and smashing shillelahs," and had also been used by Irish regiments fighting on the continent (29 October 1842). Duffy's militant hymn declared "WE preach a land awoken." Or, as the title of a song to the tune "Savourneen Deelish" had put it in the previous issue, "Awake, and Lie Dreaming No More" (22 October 1842). Other song titles carried similar prohibitions against melancholy and despair such as "Weep No More— A National Ode" (11 February 1843) by Charles Meehan, who compiled R. R. Madden's *Literary Remains of the United Irishmen* later in the century. However, "war songs" published in the *Nation* usually had a definite "historical" context in order to prevent charges of sedition.

Several features and practices in the *Nation* recalled those of the United Irish newspapers. An international, especially a European, emphasis included articles on "Continental Literature" (26 November 1843), on Goethe's poetry (12 November 1842), and on contemporary European political events. The *Nation* also encouraged readers to contribute verses, and even tunes. Early on, the editors themselves posed as "contributors" to encourage such submissions. The "Answers to Correspondents" column for 3 December 1842 declared "R. L.'s lines in imitation of Burns' 'She is a winsome wee thing' are only middling." The "lines" in question were actually Thomas Davis's poem "My Land," which begins, "She is a rich and rare land." That Davis wrote poetry in imitation of Burns is another link between the poetic practices of the *Nation* and the *Northern Star*, which had frequently included poetry in imitation of Burns. Some Young Ireland verse echoed the religious strain of United Irish verse. The poem "Brothers Arise!" began: "Brothers arise! the hour has come / To strike the blow for truth and God" (*The Spirit of the Nation* 1981, 76).

As in United Irish verse, the common bardic motifs were testimony to the great influence and popularity of Macpherson's bard Ossian. Some Young Ireland verse even emulated Macpherson's style. Although it is in verse rather than poetic prose, "The Awakening of the Sleepers" by "Eva" on 20 February 1847 is very similar to the Ossianic effusion that Thomas Moore had published in the *Northern Star* and in the *Press*:

Yes!—the time is come!—it is the hour,
Warrior chiefs of Eire, now for your pow'r!
    Lift those mail'd hands from your brow—
        Now!—now!
Now, for your shimmering swords, and with'ring shout—
    On!—on!—from the dark cave out!
        On!—on!—no hour more meet;
        Thousands pant your rise to greet,
        From North to South, with footsteps fleet.
            Arise!

"The Stricken Land" (23 January 1847) by "Speranza" (Jane Francesca Elgee, later Oscar Wilde's mother) displayed a lurid sensationalism similar to that which characterized verse in *The Press* in the months leading up to the 1798 uprising. One "popular" note that was quite subdued in the *Nation* was the use of dialect. The few songs in Irish dialect that were published were not reprinted in *The Spirit of the Nation* collections. For example, "Granu Waile—A National Ballad," published on 17 June 1843, clearly lacked the "elevating influence" of the nationality celebrated by Davis in his inaugural editorial in the *Nation* (15 October 1842) and was never reprinted:

> John Bull was a bumpkin—devil a doubt—
> A royster, a bully at ball or a rout;
> Yet, soft at the heart, he made love like a whale,
> And he cast a sheep's eye at sweet Granu Waile.

Popular music, however, was another matter, for it could be used as an effective background for any "elevating" message that the Young Irelanders wished to preach. Like the United Irishmen, Bunting, and Moore, the Young Ireland poets believed Irish music expressed the soul of Ireland. They did use many traditional tunes for their verse, but their "original" tunes underscore how their vision of Irish literature and nationality was not frozen in some mythical Irish past. They used a broad range of tunes for their verse, including many tunes used by the United Irishmen.

The song "Why, Gentles, Why?" by "L.N.F." in the *Nation* on 29 June 1844 was to the tune of the soldiers' drinking song "Why, Soldiers,

Why?" that had been so popular among the United Irishmen. "L.N.F."
has subsequently been identified as Mrs. Ellen Bridget O'Connell
Fitzsimmons, the eldest daughter of Daniel O'Connell (MacGrath
1948, 211). Likewise, when two "New Year's" songs for 1844 were
published in the *Nation*, the first was to the tune "Patrick's Day" (21
December 1843), a tune Michael Joseph Barry has used for his song
"St. Patrick's Day and Garryowen" in the 21 September 1844 issue.
Such politically charged "New Year's" songs had also been a regular
feature in the *Northern Star*. The second "New Year's Song" (13 January 1844) was to the United Irish tune "Paddies Evermore" and included these lines:

> No whining tone of mere regret,
> Young Irish bards, for you;
> But let your songs teach Ireland yet
> What Irishmen should do!

Young Ireland poet John O'Hagan even wrote a song entitled
"Paddies Evermore," which used the refrain "We're Paddies evermore"
from the earlier United Irish song. O'Hagan's song was published in
the *Nation* on 26 August 1843 and was reprinted in the 1843, 1844,
and 1845 editions of *The Spirit of the Nation*. The following stanza
opened and closed the song:

> The hour is past to fawn or crouch
> As suppliants for our right;
> Let word and deed unshrinking vouch
> The banded millions' might;
> Let them who scorned the fountain rill,
> Now dread the torrent's roar,
> And hear our echoed chorus still,
> We're Paddies evermore.

Like the United Irishmen, the Young Irelanders believed that the
best way to awaken Ireland was through choruses of songs and through
"Cheap Literature—Popular Education," which was the title of an
editorial on 17 December 1842. As Charles Gavan Duffy's song "Watch
and Wait" (14 December 1844) put it, Ireland's "trance" was "ignorance." An article entitled "Philosophy for *The Nation*. Lesson #3,"

examined the "Political Value of Knowledge" (10 December 1842). Davis wrote five essays for the *Nation*, including "Educate that You May Be Free" (5 October 1844), which argued that education was to nationality as a match was to a fire. Verse, especially songs and ballads, was considered the most effective way of educating the people because it appealed to their intellects as well as their emotions.

The inaugural editorial in the *Northern Star* had promised that political reform would bring "prosperity" to Ireland, whereas the inaugural editorial in the *Nation* took a more stridently nationalist approach, declaring that the new paper's task would be to "demonstrate that National feelings, National habits, and National government, are indispensable to individual prosperity" (15 October 1842). The United Irishmen had sought to integrate native Irish literature into English literary tradition, whereas the Young Irelanders emphasized a more distinctly Irish note. Irish phrases became increasingly common in their verse. The 1845 *Spirit of the Nation* contained a nineteen-page index and glossary of Gaelic names, places, and phrases that had occurred in the verse. As Davis declared in 1841 in his "Udalism and Feudalism" essay, "give us the worst wigwam in Ireland and a dry potato rather than anglicize us" (1914, 75). Yet Davis, though he defended the Irish language and encouraged its revival, had no qualms about anglicizing Irish tunes with English words and championed a literary nationalism that blended the Irish and English traditions.

In his essay "Ballad Poetry of Ireland" (*Nation*, 2 August 1845) Davis rejected a nationality that excluded the Norman and Saxon elements in Irish national identity and any nationality of only political dimensions that sought "nothing but a parliament in College Green." He praised Duffy's *Ballad Poetry of Ireland* for integrating Irish and English, and quoted Duffy's assertion that his materials were "just as essentially Irish as if they were written in Gaelic."

Like the United Irishmen before them, the Young Irelanders considered the ancient literature and culture of Ireland as a means of achieving a national unity that would transcend subsequent sectarian and political divisions. John Cornelius O'Callaghan's article on "Ancient Irish Literature" in the first issue of the *Nation* argued that no subject was more worthy of attention in the effort to unite "every party and every creed of Irishmen" than "the ancient history

and literature of the country," which would "promote intellectual
nationality" (15 October 1842).

The image of ancient Ireland popularized in the *Nation* was the
same one of bards and harps that United Irish verse had celebrated in
a militant energetic style. Thus, a poem entitled "The Bard's Appeal"
(16 December 1843) called upon the "Youth of Erin" to "arise" and
become "brave, erect, self-righted men!" Similarly, in a poem entitled
"The Expulsion," translated by Edward Walsh "from the Irish of Owen
Roe O'Sullivan," who is described as "a Munster Bard of the last
Century," the eighteenth-century "bard's" vision of the lovely Erin has
her telling him to "arise" and "let joy possess thee." The poem concludes with a command to "Shout loud amen to the bard!" who has
inspired "Erin's brave, 'mid war's wild thunder" and has caused "Saxon
power [to] be crush'd and broken" (27 April 1844). "A Minstrel's
Address to the Bards of the Nation" on 16 March 1844 declared:

> We yet must pour the strain of gladness
>   To drown the clanking of our chain,
> Or memory may be swayed to madness
>   By brooding o'er our wrongs in vain.

Thomas Davis's description of Frederick W. Burton's highly symbolic design for the title-page and cover of *The Spirit of the Nation*
demonstrates how completely the Young Irelanders' iconography and
their conception of their verse continued the literary nationalism of
Thomas Moore and of the United Irishmen, whose philosophic ratio-
nalism had been imbued with the romantic conception of Ireland they
had inherited from eighteenth-century antiquarianism. Davis called
Burton's total design "a monument to bardic power, to patriotism, to
our music and our history," and described the "main" design as follows:

> On the one side of the picture is a young bard, harp-bearing. The
> hills of Ireland are behind him, he has come down full of strength,
> and wisdom, and faith. He played with the fair hair of the cataract
> till his ears grew filled with its warnings—he has toiled up the
> mountain till his sinews stiffened and his breath deserted him, for
> he was full of passion and resolve—he has grown strange among the
> tombs, and perchance has softened, to, in the hazel glen; but now

he has another, or rather his one great mission, the dream of his childhood before him, and he moves along through the land. . . . He has awakened the slumbers of ages, and he treads on a broken chain, . . . An old bard, vast, patriarchal, rigid with years (for he might have harped at the landing of Owen Roe) sat tranced and clutching his harp of broken chords. The singing of the minstrel of the Nation has broken the old harper's spell, and his hand is rising, and there is life coming into his huge rocky face. Two young brothers in arms (friends and patriots) are looking wildly at the passing bard, and as his song swells louder, there is fierce daring in their eyes and limbs. They are in old Irish costume, barred, cloak and trews; one wears the gold torque of an Irish knight, the other grasps a yet sheathed sword—it will be drawn. (1914, 163-65)

The United Irishmen's bardic "harp of Erin" clearly had taken on new life, as well as intensified its romanticism in the *Nation*.

Although much verse in the *Nation* took the form of ballads the narratives of which had a much more dramatic impact than the vague philosophic odes more common in United Irish verse, some Young Ireland verse was indistinguishable from the earlier, more abstract United Irish verse. For example, on 7 June 1845, the *Nation* published "Ireland's Vow," which celebrated Liberty in the manner of much United Irish verse. Similarly, "The Song of Liberty" (18 May 1844) sounded like many United Irish songs:

> See! see! the morning breaks,
>   And light is dawning o'er us!
> Hark! hark! a spirit wakes
>   Throughout the land that bore us!
> And Freedom's sun that darkly set,
>   In shame and gloom and sorrow,
> Shall rise in kindly brightness yet
>   Upon a cloudless morrow.
>   On, On, 'tis Freedom's Cry!
>   Our ancient sunburst rearing!
>   Live free, or bravely die
>   For Liberty and Erin!

The next stanza of that song introduced the motif of "dead" fathers whose "spirits linger still around / To rouse, to guide, to cheer us." This was clearly a reference to the United Irishmen and was an appropriate image because several Young Ireland writers, such as John Blake Dillon and John Mitchel, were descendants of United Irishmen.

The word "spirit" echoes throughout Young Ireland verse and is prominent in the title of *The Spirit of the Nation* songbooks. "Spirit," in the sense of life principle, of animating force, of vigor and enthusiasm, was the most obvious meaning of the word in the title "spirit of the nation." John O'Hagan's poem "Our Hopes" refers to the United Irishmen in this regard:

> Oh! many a nobler heart than ours
> Hath perished that dream to gain;
> And many a mind of Godlike powers
> Was wasted—not all in vain!
> They've left us a treasure of pity and wrath—
> A spur to our cold blood set—
> And we'll tread their path with a spirit that hath
> Assurance of triumph yet.
> (*The Spirit of the Nation* 1981, 235)

However, many references are also made in Young Ireland verse to "spirits" in the sense of the "martyred dead" motif of United Irish verse. For example, "Repeal Song," to the "air" of "Cruiskin Lan" (20 January 1844), declared, "Ye Dead! / We'll have Freedom by your life blood shed!" "Weep No More" (11 February 1843) commanded:

> Weep not for the glorious dead—
> Their spirits cannot die:
> They're with us wheresoever we tread;
> They watch us from on HIgh—
> They watch us from the realms of light—
> The regions of the free;
> And on their harps, in Heaven's sight,
> Strike chords of liberty.

The poem "Emmet's Death" also proclaimed the spiritual presence of United Irishmen like Emmet:

Nay, wail him not; with the harp's sad string,
Let him sleep with the mournful past;
His spirit is here, like an earth-pent spring,
And will sparkle to light at last!
(*The Spirit of the Nation* 1981, 244)

The most famous example of this idea is, of course, John Kells Ingram's "The Memory of the Dead," in which the memory of 1798 was a living force in the present: "In true men, like you, men, / Their spirit's still at home" (*The Spirit of the Nation* 1981, 46).

The "spirit" of United Irish literary nationalism animated the writings of the Young Irelanders. This literary connection between the two movements was clearly recognized in the 1840s and later in the nineteenth century. In 1845, a joint collection of songs from *Paddy's Resource* and from *The Spirit of the Nation* was published in Cork. John Savage, a Young Irelander who was the son of a United Irishman and was later a Fenian, published a book entitled *'98 and '48: The Modern Revolutionary History and Literature of Ireland* in 1856. Savage's use of the word "literature" in his title demonstrates that he, like many of his contemporaries, recognized a literary as well as an ideological continuity between the two movements. Likewise, when the editors of the *Nation* in 1879 compiled *Penny Readings for the Irish People*, literary works by and about the United Irishmen, Thomas Moore, and the Young Ireland poets were intermingled in the two volumes.

The fact that the United Irishmen, Thomas Moore, and the Young Irelanders manifested a single literary tradition has, however, been ignored by twentieth-century literary and political historians. This collective neglect of the literary and cultural dimensions of the United Irishmen is unfortunate because, in view of the xenophobic forms that later Irish literary nationalism assumed, a recognition of its origins in the United Irish movement could have provided an antidote.

The United Irishmen's literary nationalism, subsequently eclipsed by their influential political ideology, was also central to their movement and to the development of modern Irish nationalism. The United Irishmen failed as reformers and as revolutionaries, but they succeeded in creating a significant literary tradition. The origin, development and influence of United Irish literary nationalism provide an essential context for understanding the United Irish movement, subsequent Irish history, and the ongoing cultural debate in Ireland today.

United Irish songs and satires illuminate the development of their ideology and the transformation of the movement's goals from reform to revolution. United Irish literary works enlarge our appreciation of the United Irishmen by qualifying stereotypes of them as merely rationalist reformers or violent revolutionaries. The complexities and tensions in United Irish literary themes continued to reverberate in later nationalist verse and prose and remain central issues today. United Irish literary nationalism provides an especially important context for understanding Thomas Moore and the Young Ireland writers.

The existence of cultural and literary dimensions within the United Irish movement extends the origins of Irish literary nationalism back into the eighteenth century. Like their political ideology, the United Irishmen's literary nationalism was a synthesis. The United Irishmen drew upon a wide array of literary, scholarly, political and musical traditions to create a pluralistic literary tradition that was a paradigm of their political goal of unifying all aspects of Irish society. United Irish literary nationalism thus provides an important antidote to the more xenophobic and sectarian forms of nationalism that later evolved.

The mingling of politics and literature evident in the United Irish movement has indeed had many unfortunate consequences in subsequent Irish history. Popular national literature created for the purpose of political propaganda created inaccurate and divisive views of Irish history and inferior literary works. However, that does not justify ignoring the important and influential symbiotic relationship between politics and literature that existed within the United Irish movement. Many of the divisive "myths" of Irish national identity that have been the subject of so much recent revision did indeed originate in the United Irish movement, but there, significantly, they were part of a pluralistic conception of Irish culture.

Appendix A
Appendix B
Appendix C
Notes
Bibliography
Index
Song and Tune Index

Appendix A

United Irish Literary Publications

Northern Star (Belfast), 2 January 1792–19 May 1797. Each issue contained poems and songs, often of a political nature. The Northern Star Office also published an Irish magazine, *Bolg an tSolair; or, Gaelic Magazine*, only one issue of which survives, and other literary works.

National Journal (Dublin), 26 March 1792–7 May 1792(?). The prospectus, written by Wolfe Tone, issued in Dublin on 5 October 1791, declared that publication would begin on the first Tuesday in January. The first surviving issue is number 4 and is dated Monday, 2 April 1792, which indicates that publication did not actually begin until the last week in March 1792. Few copies of this newspaper survive. The last surviving issue is number 19 and dated Monday, 7 May 1792.

Press (Dublin), 28 September 1797–13 March 1798. Several anthologies of articles and poems from the *Press* were subsequently published: *Beauties of The Press* (London, 1800) and *Extracts from The Press* (Philadelphia, 1802, 1804).

The Harp of Erin (Cork), 7 March 1798–17 March 1798.

UNITED IRISH SONGBOOKS

Songs on the French Revolution that took place at Paris, 14 July 1789. Sung at the Celebration thereof at Belfast, on Saturday, 14 July 1792. Belfast, 1792. (Six songs)

Paddy's Resource: Being a Select Collection of Original and Modern Patriotic Songs, Toasts, and Sentiments, Compiled for the Use of the People of Ireland. Belfast, 1795. Contained sixty songs, ten of which had previously been published in the *Northern Star*, including three songs that had originally appeared in *Songs on the French Revolution*. This collection was reissued in Philadelphia in 1796, the only change being that the phrase "People of Ireland" was replaced by "All Firm Patriots."

Paddy's Resource: Being a Select Collection of Original Patriotic Songs for the Use of the People of Ireland. Belfast, 1796. Contained forty-three songs, all new, except for three previously published in the *Northern Star*.

A collection of thirty-two songs from the 1795 and 1796 Belfast *Paddy's Resource* songbooks was published in New York in 1798 under the title *Paddy's Resource, Being a Select Collection of Original and Modern Patriotic Songs Compiled for the Use of the People of Ireland, to which is added Arthur O'Connor's Address,* followed by the notes: "From an Irish edition—with corrections" and "At the request of a number of Hibernians in this country who were desirous of having copies of them." No extant Irish edition survives that corresponds to the contents and arrangement of the materials in this 1798 New York edition.

Paddy's Resource; or, the Harp of Erin, Attuned to Freedom. Being a Collection of Patriotic Songs Selected for Paddy's Amusement. Dublin, 1798. Contained sixty-four songs, twenty-seven of which are from the 1795 and 1796 Belfast *Paddy's Resource* songbooks, in addition to thirty-seven new songs, twelve of which had appeared in the *Press* and the *Harp of Erin*.

Paddy's Resource; or, the Harp of Erin, Attuned to Freedom; Being a Collection of Patriotic Songs; selected for Paddy's Amusement. Dublin: n.d. It can be assumed that the collection was published after January 1800 because one song refers to the Union with England as accomplished fact. National Library of Ireland copy has "1803?" written on title page. Contained eighty-five songs, sixty-four of which are from the three earlier *Paddy's Resource* songbooks, in addition to twenty-one new songs.

Songs from *Paddy's Resource* were published throughout the nineteenth century. According to Charles Gavan Duffy in his introduction to *The Ballad Poetry of Ireland*, United Irish songs from *Paddy's Resource* "are continually republished, and have run through endless editions . . . their circulation in Ulster alone counts by tens of thousands" (1869, 22). Few copies have survived, but they include the following: *Billy Bluff and the Squire, with a Selection of Songs from Paddy's Resource*. Belfast: Joseph Smith, 1812. United Irishman Jemmy Hope's son, Luke Mullan Hope, was foreman printer for Joseph Smith. This edition contained sixty-four songs, all from the 1795 and 1796 *Paddy's Resource* songbooks. In 1840, a Belfast edition with the same title and contents claimed to be the thirteenth edition.

UNITED IRISH SATIRES

Review of the Lion of Old England; or, Democracy Confounded. Anon. Belfast, 1794 (2 editions). Published in serial form in the *Northern Star* from September to December 1793; written by William Sampson and Thomas Russell.

A Faithful Report of the Trial of Hurdy Gurdy: Tried and Convicted of Seditious Libel in the Count of the King's Bench on the Testimony of French Horn. Anon. Belfast, 1794; New York, 1806. Published in serial form in the *Northern Star* as "The King vs. Hurdy Gurdy" from July to August 1794; written by William Sampson.

Billy Bluff and the Squire; or, A Sketch of the Times. Anon. Belfast, 1796. Published in serial form in the *Northern Star* from May to November 1796; written by Reverend James Porter. Numerous editions were published in the nineteenth century, as late as 1879 in Belfast and 1886 in Glasgow. A Belfast edition in 1840 claimed to be the thirteenth edition. An American edition was published in New York in 1868 under the title *Billy Bluff and the Squire. A Relic of the United Irishmen*, with the note "Reprinted from the text of 1796, by the son of a United Irishman."

Lysimachia. A Poem Addressed to the Orange or Break-of-Day Men in the Counties of Armagh and Down. Belfast: Public Printing Office, 1797. The United Irishman Thomas Storey owned and operated the Public Printing Office at this time. Attributed to "Reverend James Glass," which was perhaps the pseudonym of Reverend James Porter.

Appendix B

United Irish Poems and Songs

"IERNE UNITED"

by Wolfe Tone

When Rome, by dividing, had conquer'd the world,
And land after land into slavery hurl'd,
Hibernia escaped, for 'twas Heaven's decree,
That Ierne United, should ever be Free,
    With her Ballinamoney, &c.
Her harp then delighted the nations around,
By its music entranc'd, their own suff'rings were drown'd,
In Arts, and in Learning, the foremost was she,
And Ireland United was Happy and Free,
    With her Ballinamoney, &c.
But soon—ah! too soon, did fell discord begin;
Our domestic dissensions let foreigners in,
Too well they improv'd the advantage we gave,
Whom they came to protect they remain'd to enslave.
    Poor Ballinamoney, &c.
From that fatal hour, our Freedom was lost,
Peace, Virtue, and Learning, were banish'd our coast,
And the Island of Saints, might more fitly be nam'd
The Land of Tormentors, the place of the damn'd.
    Poor Ballinamoney, &c.
Then let us remember our madness no more,
What we lost by dissension, let Union restore;

Let us firmly Unite, and our covenant be,
Together to fall, or together be Free,
For Ballinamoney, &c.

"THE EXILED IRISHMAN'S LAMENTATION"

by George Nugent Reynolds

GREEN were the fields where my forefathers dwelt, O;
*Erin ma vorneen! slan leat go brah!
Though our farm it was small, yet comforts we felt O.
Erin ma vorneen! slan leat go brah!
At length came the day when our lease did expire,
And fain would I live where before liv'd my Sire;
But, ah! well-a-day! I was forced to retire.
Erin ma vorneen! slan leat go brah!

Though all taxes I paid, yet no vote could I pass, O;
Erin ma vorneen! slan leat go brah!
Aggrandiz'd no great man—and I feel it, alas! O;
Erin ma vorneen! slan leat go brah!
Forced from my home, yea, from where I was born,
To range the wide world—poor, helpless, forlorn;
I look back with regret—and my heart strings are torn.
Erin ma vorneen! slan leat go brah!

With principles pure, patriotic and firm,
Erin ma vorneen! slan leat go brah!
To my country attached, and a friend to reform,
Erin ma vorneen! slan leat go brah!
I supported old Ireland—was ready to die for it;
If her foes e'er prevailed, I was well known to sigh for it;
But my faith I preserv'd, and am now forc'd to fly for it.
Erin ma vorneen! slan leat go brah!

But hark! I hear sounds, and my heart strong is beating,
**Boie yudh ma vorneen! Erin go brah!
Friendship advancing—delusion retreating.
Boie yudh ma vorneen! Erin go brah!
We have numbers—and numbers do constitute power:

Let's WILL TO BE FREE—and we're Free from that hour:
Of Hibernia's Sons—yes—we'll then be the flower.
        Boie yudh ma vorneen! Erin go brah!

In the North I see friends—too long was I blind, O,
        Boie yudh ma vorneen! Erin go brah!
The cobwebs are broken—and free is my mind, O,
        Boie yudh ma vorneen! Erin go brah!
North and South here's my hand—East and West here's
    my heart, O;
Let's ne'er be divided by any base art, O;
But love one another and never more part, O.
        Boie yudh ma vorneen! Erin go brah!

Too long have we suffer'd and too long lamented;
        Boie yudh ma vorneen! Erin go brah!
By courage undaunted it may be prevented,
        Boie yudh ma vorneen! Erin go brah!
Nor more by oppressors let us be affrighted,
But with hearts and with hands be firmly United;
For by ERIN GO BRAH! 'tis thus we'll be righted,
        Boie yudh ma vorneen! Erin go brah!

    *Ireland my darling! for ever adieu!
    **Victory to you my darling Ireland! for ever!

"ERIN"

by William Drennan

When Erin first rose from the dark-swelling flood,
God bless'd the green island, He saw it was good:
The Emerald of Europe, it sparkled, it shone,
In the ring of this world the most precious stone!

In her sun, in her soil, in her station, thrice blest,
With back turn'd to Britain, her face to the West,
Erin stands proudly insular, on her steep shore,
And strikes her high harp to the ocean's deep roar.

But when its soft tones seem to mourn and to weep,
The dark chain of silence is cast o'er the deep;
At the thought of the past, tears gush from her eyes,
And the pulse of the heart makes her white bosom rise.

"O, sons of green Erin! lament o'er the time
When religion was—war, and our country—a crime;
When men, in God's image, inverted his plan,
And moulded their God to the image of man.

"When the int'rest of state wrought the general woe;
The stranger—a friend, and the native—a foe;
While the mother rejoic'd o'er her children distress'd,
And clasp'd the invader more close to her breast.

"When with pale for the body, and pale for the soul,
Church and state join'd in compact to conquer the whole;
And while Shannon ran red with Milesian blood,
Ey'd each other askance, and pronounc'd it was good!

"By the groans that ascend from your forefathers' grave,
For their country thus left to the brute and the slave,
Drive the Demon of Bigotry home to his den,
And where Britain made brutes, now let Erin make men!

"Let my sons, like the leaves of their shamrock, unite,
A partition of sects from one footstalk of right;
Give each his full share of this earth, and yon sky,
Nor fatten the slave, where the serpent would die!

"Alas, for poor Erin! that some still are seen,
Who would dye the grass red, in their hatred to green!
Yet, oh! when you're up, and they down, let them live,
Then, yield them that mercy that they did not give.

"Arm of Erin! prove strong; but be gentle as brave,
And, uplifted to strike, still be ready to save;
Nor one feeling of vengeance presume to defile
The cause, or the men, of the EMERALD ISLE.

"The cause it is good, and the men they are true;
And the green shall outlive both the orange and the blue;

And the daughters of Erin her triumph shall share,
With their full-swelling chest, and their fair-flowing hair.

"Their bosoms heave high for the worthy and brave,
But no coward shall rest on that soft swelling wave;
Men of Erin! awake, and make haste to be blest!
Rise, arch of the ocean! rise, queen of the West!"

"THE WAKE OF WILLIAM ORR"

by William Drennan

Here our worthy brother lies,
Wake not him with women's cries;
Mourn the way that mankind ought;
Sit, in silent trance of thought.

Write his merits on your mind,
Morals pure, and manners kind;
On his head, as on a hill,
Virtue placed a citadel.

Why cut off in palmy youth?
Truth he spoke, and acted truth;
"Countrymen, Unite!" he cried,
And died, for what his Saviour died!

God of Peace, and God of Love,
Let it not thy vengeance move!
Let it not thy lightnings draw,
A nation guillotin'd by law!

Hapless nation! rent and torn,
Early wert thou taught to mourn!
Warfare of six hundred years!
Epochs marked by blood and tears!

Hunted through thy native grounds,
And flung reward to human hounds,
Each one pull'd, and tore his share,
Emblem of thy deep despair!

Hapless nation, hapless land,
Heap of uncementing sand!
Crumbled by a foreign weight,
Or by worse, domestic hate!

God of mercy, God of peace,
Make the mad confusion cease!
O'er the mental chaos move,
Through it speak the light of love!

Monstrous and unhappy sight!
Brothers' blood will not unite.
Holy oil, and holy water,
Mix—and fill the Earth with slaughter.

Who is she, with aspect wild?
The widow'd mother, with her child;
Child, new stirring in the womb,
Husband, waiting for the tomb.

Angel of this holy place!
Calm her soul, and whisper, Peace!
Cord, nor axe, nor guillotine,
Make the sentence, not the sin.

Here we watch our brother's sleep;
Watch with us, but do not weep:
Watch with us, through dead of night—
But expect the morning light.

Conquer Fortune—persevere—
Lo! it breaks—the morning clear!
The cheerful cock awakes the skies;
The day is come—Arise, arise!

"THE SOCIAL THISTLE AND THE SHAMROCK"

by Henry Joy McCracken

Come all you valiant heros, now unto me draw near,

On my Highland pipes, I'll play a tune, will every bosom cheer.
    Shea da wea ma wallagh, ma wallagh, ma wallagh,
    Shea da wea ma wallagh, come listen unto me.
Highlandmen, and Irishmen, how happy we will be,
When like brethren, we're dancing, and singing Gramachree.
    Shea da wea ma wallagh, . . .
Then o'er the misty mountains, and through the rushy glens,
The poor industrious labourers will find us trusty friends.
    Shea da wea ma wallagh, . . .
The Scotch and Irish friendly are, their wishes are the same,
The English nation envy us, and over us would reign.
    But shea da wea ma wallagh, . . .
The auld gill stoups, we'll gie a coup, and drink prosperity,
To the ancient clans, in Scottish lands, that fought right manfully.
    Shea da wea ma wallagh, . . .
Our historians and our poets, they always did maintain,
That the origin of Scottishmen and Irish were the same.
    Shea da wea ma wallagh, . . .
Now to conclude and end my song, may we live long to see,
The Thistle, and the Shamrock, entwine the olive tree.
    Shea da wea ma wallagh, ma wallagh, ma wallagh,
    Shea da wea ma wallagh, a hearty health to thee.

"PADDY EVERMORE"

In concert join each soul that loves the Patriotic tye,
Who dares the test of UNION take, free for to love or die,
Unite your notes, they'll echo strong, they'll make the rafters roar,
With him who boasts himself to be a PADDY and no more.

UNITE, UNITE, UNITE, my boys, quell discord, live in peace;
Forget your Feuds in mutual love, and brotherly embrace,
Let each man freely chose his way, our maker to adore,
And tell the world as Irishmen, we are PADDIES and no more.

Our Patriots the best of men, in galling chains lie;
Hush, hark my friends, don't you think you hear the imprison'd
        Patriot's sigh,
But even that sigh will not be lost, it shall be found from shore to shore;
And wake the spirits of Freemen in the PADDY'S island o'er.

Our Patriots tho' in irons lie, their voices must be mute,
For who with Irish just asses dare venture to dispute,
And now we're to the dungeon brought, our friends came here before,
For in the Cell or on the Sod, we're PADDIES and no more.

Times are bad, and must be worse ere LIBERTY can reign;
Some yet must bleed, some yet must die, some grind the tyrant's chain:
And when all tyrants bite the dust, stain'd with their filthy gore;
Our children then will PADDIES be, from that day evermore.

The ever-green of Liberty, exotic in our isle;
Tho' such a noble plant should be a native of our soil;
And now its planted in our land, with garlands covered o'er,
We'll dance around with vive joy, like PADDIES evermore.

Our Patriotic Virgin band, have hoist their green Cockades,
Our charmers say they'll ne'er be won, by tolls of death afraid;
Assert your rights as freemen boys, we ask this and mo more;
And then we'll grasp you in our arms, and keep you evermore.

"EDWARD"

What plaintive sounds strike on my ear!
        They're Erin's deep-ton'd piteous groans,
Her harp attun'd to sorrow drear,
        In broken numbers joins her moans.
In doleful groups around her stand,
        Her manly sons (her greatest pride),
In mourning deep, for by the hand
        Of ruthless villain, EDWARD died.

Th'assassin horde had him beset,
        As slumb'ring on a bed he lay,
Arise my Lord, Swan cries up get,
        My prisoner, you I make this day.
Unaw'd our gallant CHIEF up steps,
        And in his vengeful hand he takes
His dagger keen—quite hard it gripes,

Then to the savage crew he speaks.
"Come on who dare—your courage shew,
    'Gainst Erin's steady children's CHIEF,
Your burthen'd soul at single blow,
    I'll from your body soon relieve."
Fear-sticken at his manly form,
    The blood-stain'd tribe, save Swan, back drew;
Who from our Chieftain's potent arm,
    Receiv'd a stroke that made him rue.
Aloud he shriek'd, then Ryan came
    Unto his aid with trembling step;
Mean Caitiff Ryan, lost to shame,
    With deeds most foul was full your cup.
Like vivid light'ning at him flew
    With well-aimed point, our Hero sweet,
The dastard's blood he forthwith withdrew,
    And left his bowels at his feet.

So wide the gash, so great the gore,
    That tumbling out his entrails came:
Poor grov'ling wretch! you'll never more
    Attempt to blast unsullied fame;
A baser death should you await,
    The hangman's rope—not EDWARD'S hand,
The gallows-tree should be your fate,
    Your like deserv'd a shameful end.

Next came on Sirr, half dead with fear,
    Deep stain'd with crimes his guilty mind,
He shook all through, (by EDWARD scared),
    Like Aspin-leaf before the wind;
With coward step, he advanc'd slow,
    Dreading to feel our EDWARD'S might,
'Tho eager to strike a blow,
    Yet fearful to appear in sight.
Assassin-like, he took his stand,
    Behind the door—and there he stood,
With pistol charg'd, in either hand,
    So great his thirst for EDWARD'S blood;
Upon his brows stood imp of hell,

Within his heart a Devil foul,
Dire murder dire, and slaughter fell,
    Had full possession of his soul.

His bosom-friend suggested then,
    A bloody deed—a Devil's act—
An hell-fram'd thought******ARISE YE MEN,
    Revenge, revenge the horrid fact.
Sound, sound aloud the trump of war,
    Proclaim that EDWARD'S blood is spill'd!
By traitor's hand, by coward Sirr,
    Revenge! revenge! for EDWARD'S kill'd.

Appendix C

Extract for a Poem in Imitation of Ossian

by Thomas Moore

O! why, my soul, rollest thou on a cloud? O! why am I driven from thy side, Elvira—and ye, beams of love, to to wander the night on the lonely heath? But why do I talk; Is not Erin sad, and can I rejoice? She waileth in her secret caves, and can I repose? The sons of her love are low, the mural hand of love is over them—and can my bed, though my love be there, afford me comfort? Yet not with their Fathers do they lie—then indeed would I joy—for their souls would exult in their clouds, and their names in freedom be blessed; but hard is the fate of the low—no beams of the Sun cheer their frames—but the putrid damps consume! No eddying breezes lighten their souls—but depressing are the airs which surround!—Nor can those, yet like me unconfined to the gloom, boast of fortune a choicer regard—for Usurpers prevail, and partial are thy courts, O! Erin; and corruption is the order of the day! That Freedom, O! Brethren of Woe, which once was yours, is driven from your isle, and now cheereth some nations abroad—but Britannia commands and Oppression is joined to your fate! Armies are bound to oppose your peace, and their ranks are filled from the land of strangers;—even your brethren of the soil are against you:—from your green hills are you driven, and your hamlets are strewed on the earth! like the dun Roe off the pale, which the grey dog hath chas'd to the heath and desisteth—its accustomed haunts are afar, as they think that the hunter is nigh, and therefore approach not the strange! Thus wander my brethren dispoiled, whose cots are no longer their home, for the flames of the foe have devoured them, and their ashes are given to the winds! nor dare the beholder assist, the hand of the spoiler is also his fear; and at bay must the friendless be kept tho' his heartstrings are sharing their woe! Nor dare we, unhappy, complain, or resist the recomplished

247

decree—for the dungeon awaits, and the hulk of the tender appears—so bound are our tongues, and our hands must desist from redress!—Our voice is unheard in the state, and our groans pass our court in the winds—there the voice of the stranger is free, and oppression devolves from his vote—but thy voice, O Erin! is condemned in thy senate, and Slavery dwells with thy sons!—Unimpartial is the throne of thy isle, smiles fall unequal around! Not so was the court of Fingal—not so were the Halls of Selma! there council'd the Chiefs of Innisfail—there sang sweet Ossian, sacred Bard of Jura!—for just was the soul of Fingal, and noble were the heroes of Morven;—noble also were our fathers:—their fame like that of your's dwelt behind them, like beams of the parting sun, when it looks through surrounding clouds over Collin of the mounded summit:—as these beams their fame also is gone, and no more swelleth the soul to their praise from the songs of the bands of heroes! but now Tyranny strides o'er our land dreadful as the gloom on his brow; and the pangs of despair are beneath him as he treads the subjected soil!—'tis therefore I am driven from they side, O! Elvira, of love; and 'tis therefore I wander the midnight snows and sigh forth my woes to the wind! thy beams, O, moon! fall in vain on my frame; they illumine not the breast of the wretched! Thy blasts, O, Wind! of the North, are futile to me—they disperse not the mist from my soul! O! children of Erin! you'r robb'd; why not rouse from you slumber of Death?—Oh! why not assert her lov'd cause, and strike off her chains and your own—and hail her to freedom and peace? Oh! that Ossian now flourished and here; he would tell us the deeds of our Sires, and swell up our souls to be brave!—for his Harp flow'd a torrent around, and incitement enforc'd as the stream!—but silence now reigns o'er its wires!—it met the fate of Jura!

The Northern Star, 12 May 1797
The Press, 19 October 1797

Notes

1. None of the four major *Paddy's Resource* songbooks or any of the United Irish satires is mentioned in Rosamond Jacobs's book-length study of the United Irishmen, in any of R. B. MacDowell's numerous works about the United Irishmen, or in Marianne Elliott's recent biography of Wolfe Tone. McDowell's most recent discussion of the United Irishmen, in his essay "Reform and Reaction, 1789–1794" in *A New History of Ireland*, *IV*, continues his limited approach to their literary activities. He mentions only that their newspaper the *Northern Star* "paid some attention to literature" and "published a fair quantity of well meaning verse" (1986, 323). Rosamond Jacobs's chapter entitled "The Northern Star" focuses on the political and ideological dimension of the newspaper and makes no mention of the songs and poems that appeared in each issue (1937, 173–91). Moreover, considering the *Northern Star's* promotion of the Irish language and Irish music, the following statement by Jacobs suggests a limited knowledge of the newspaper's contents: "At a time when Irish was the everyday language of the great majority of the people the *Northern Star* seemed unaware of its existence. All references were to English history, English literature, English tradition" (1937, 186). In truth many of the editorials, essays, poems and untitled songs published in the *Northern Star* focused on Irish history, Irish literature, and Irish tradition, and this Irish emphasis intensified as time went on. Historian J. C. Beckett's survey of "Literature in English, 1691–1800" in *A New History of Ireland*, *IV* ignores the extensive literary activities of the United Irish movement, and raises the question of why a literary historian was not assigned that topic.

This neglect of the United Irishmen's literary productions has limited the historians' perspective on the United Irishmen in several ways. For example, the contents of the first volume of *Paddy's Resource* in 1795 provide illuminating evidence concerning the movement at the time it became a secret organization. Many of the songs in it are clearly aimed at recruiting the Defenders and the lower classes, yet one looks in vain for mention of *Paddy's Resource* in essays by Nancy Curtin (1985) and Marianne Elliott (1978) concerning the development of the United Irish Society into a revolutionary organization and their ties with the Defenders.

249

A few historians have considered isolated examples of United Irish literary works as evidence to buttress their arguments about the political ideology of the United Irishmen. James S. Donnelly's article, "Propagating the Cause of the United Irishmen," which acknowledges the importance of literary propaganda in the movement and discusses a few United Irish songs, is nevertheless flawed in its literary analysis of those materials (1980, 5–23). For example, Donnelly ignores developments in the successive editions of *Paddy's Resource* songbooks and critical distinctions among rural folk songs, urban political street ballads, and the United Irish songs and, consequently, weakens his argument that United Irish songs were an index of the popular mind. Tom Dunne uses United Irish songs to support the opposite argument in his essay "Popular Ballads, Revolutionary Rhetoric, and Politicisation," in which he analyzes how the ideology of the French Revolution failed to be absorbed among the people, despite the many United Irish songs propagating it (1990, 139–55). Dunne's and Donnelly's selective use of a few songs for the purpose of argument illustrates the problems of generalizing about the *Paddy's Resource* songbooks on the basis of token songs.

Historians who have surveyed Irish cultural nationalism, rather than just the political nationalism of the United Irishmen, have offered two extreme positions concerning the United Irishmen and cultural nationalism. John Hutchinson, in *The Dynamics of Cultural Nationalism: The Gaelic Revival and the Creation of the Irish Nation State* (1987), recognizes the cultural dimensions of the United Irish movement, but he exaggerates the revivalist dimensions of eighteenth-century antiquarianism and consequently the role of cultural nationalism in the United Irish movement. At the other extreme, Joseph Leerssen does not include the United Irish movement and its literary publications in his monumental study *Mere Irish and Fíor-Ghael: Studies in the Idea of Irish Nationality, Its Development and Literary Expression Prior to the Nineteenth Century* (1986). According to Leerssen's schema, eighteenth-century "patriotic antiquarianism," which originated in the sympathy between the political thought of "patriots" such as Grattan and Flood and scholarly and literary antiquarianism, evolved into cultural nationalism in the nineteenth century. Leerssen makes no mention of the United Irishmen's seminal and transitional role in that process.

2. Many decades later Mary Ann McCracken told R. R. Madden she had heard Tone's daughter Maria sing "Ierne United" to the tune of the popular drinking song "Cruiskeen Lawn" (Cruiscin Lan) (Madden 1858b, 2:145). The song had also been published anonymously in a United Irish songbook in 1792 under the title "A New Song Addressed to Irishmen." In 1795, Tone's song appeared anonymously, as did all songs, in the first *Paddy's Resource*.

3. Following Yeats's lead, Malcolm Brown's study of Irish literary nationalism, *The Politics of Irish Literature: From Thomas Davis to W. B. Yeats* (1972), focuses on the Young Irelanders and considers the tradition that preceded them only insofar as Young Ireland poetry represented a reaction against Thomas Moore. Brown summarizes the political ideology of the United Irishmen and, like other scholars, considers Tone's prose writings and Robert Emmet's speech from the dock as the only United

Irish literary works of note. He never mentions the many songs and satires published in the four United Irish newspapers or the several songbooks entitled *Paddy's Resource*. Subsequent literary histories by Richard Fallis (1978), A. N. Jeffares (1982), and Roger Mchugh and Maurice Harmon (1982) have observed the parameters imposed by Yeats on the discussion of Irish political poetry.

Most music historians have also ignored the United Irish songs. For example, Brian Boydell, in his survey of eighteenth- and nineteenth-century music in *A New History of Ireland, IV*, claims that the tradition of writing patriotic songs in English to traditional Irish melodies was a nineteenth-century development (1986, 606). In fact, it preceded even the United Irishmen. Georges-Denis Zimmermann's invaluable *Songs of Irish Rebellion: Political Street Ballads and Rebel Songs, 1780–1900* is the only musical history to include United Irish political songs from *Paddy's Resource*.

Several recent studies have greatly expanded our knowledge of the eighteenth-century origins of nineteenth-century Irish literature, but they too neglect the literary works of the United Irishmen. Seamus Deane's *Field Day Anthology of Irish Writing* (1991) ignores the literary works of the United Irishmen, never mentions the *Paddy's Resource* songbooks, and includes only one United Irish poem, "The Wake of William Orr" by William Drennan. Patrick Rafroidi's two-volume survey *Irish Literature in English: The Romantic Period (1789–1850)*, published in 1972 and translated into English in 1980, discusses William Drennan but no other United Irish poet. Rafroidi mentions only two of Drennan's many poems and downplays Drennan's United Irish connections. For example, according to Rafroidi, Drennan's poem "Erin" first appeared in 1815; in fact, it had first appeared in the United Irish newspaper the *Press* in 1797. Rafroidi claims that the first body of poetry that is "wholly Romantic and national" came from Thomas Moore in his *Irish Melodies* (1808–1834), and that Maria Edgeworth and Lady Morgan were the first writers to romanticize "the nation's present" (Rafroidi 1980, 1:99–109). In truth, the poetic output of the United Irishmen between 1791 and 1803 included a large number of poems that were indeed "romantic and national," and many of their songs, especially those about heroic United Irish "martyrs," romanticized the present.

Similarly, Norman Vance's article, "Celts, Carthaginians and Constitutions: Anglo-Irish Literary Relations, 1780–1820," published in 1981, mentions only William Drennan (228–30). Likewise, in Seamus Deane's wide-ranging discussion of eighteenth-century literature and culture in *A Short History of Irish Literature* (1986), Tone's *Autobiography* is the only United Irish literary work mentioned. Terence Brown's opening chapter, "Poetry in a Colony," in *Northern Voices: Poets from Ulster* (1975), includes William Drennan and William Hamilton Drummond (5–28). Although Brown mentions that Drennan had been a United Irishman, he considers his poetry apart from its United Irish context. For example, according to Brown, Drennan's poem "To Ireland" first appeared in 1815; in fact, it had appeared twenty years earlier in the *Northern Star* in August of 1795. Brown makes no mention of Drummond having been a United Irishman or that his two early poems *Hibernia*, a poem infused with cultural nationalism, and *The Man of Age*, had both been published at the Northern Star Office in Belfast in 1797. Even Norman Vance's discussions of William Drennan and Thomas Moore in *Irish Literature: A Social History* (1990) ignore their United Irish backgrounds. Vance refers to *Paddy's Resource* only once, as the source of a toast, and gives incomplete and inaccurate bibliographic data for it.

4. The probable compiler was Charles Patrick Meehan (1812–1890), an eccentric clergyman and associate of the Young Irelanders, who was given a parcel of manuscripts bought by the publisher James Duffy at the sale of Madden's library ("Centenary of Father Meehan" 1912, 25–27). The "Publisher's Introduction," signed "C.P.M.," at the beginning of *Literary Remains* describes how the materials had been accumulated by Madden from printed sources and from people like Jemmy Hope, Mary Ann McCracken, and Anne Devlin, Robert Emmet's housekeeper. While "C.P.M." declares that "the notes on the poems throughout the volume are of course Madden's own" (Madden 1887, viii), the fragmentary notes and haphazard arrangement of materials indicate that Madden's editing and analysis of his materials was less successful than his accumulation of source material and oral testimony. Leon O'Broin has chronicled Madden's extraordinary efforts in that regard (1972, 20–33).

Perhaps if Madden had lived to actually organize and edit his own materials, the *Literary Remains* might have been more encouraging to the endeavors of future scholars. However, disorganization and inaccuracy are not the only problem. Despite his lengthy and arduous search for materials, Madden evidently did not have copies of the *Paddy's Resource* songbooks published in Belfast in 1795 and 1796. Moreover, Madden collected only poetry and songs and ignored the several popular prose satires produced by the United Irishmen.

5. The following is a list of some of the United Irish materials acquired by the government:

SPOI 620/19/87: a broadside ballad sheet printed in 1792 that contains two United Irish songs. The songs are anonymous on the ballad sheet, but other evidence indicates one was written by Samuel Neilson, the editor of the *Northern Star*, and the other was by Thomas Stott. Both men wrote many songs which appeared in the *Northern Star* and in the various *Paddy's Resource* songbooks.

SPOI 620/19/31,77,132: numerous manuscript poems presumably confiscated from individual United Irishmen upon their arrest or when offices of the United Irish newspapers were destroyed by authority of the government.

SPOI 620/20/16: four copies of the *Catalogue of the Books, Belonging to the Belfast Society for Promoting Knowledge*, compiled in 1795 by the society's librarian, the United Irishman Thomas Russell.

SPOI 620/20/35: songbook of the type known as a garland entitled *A New Song in Praise of the Sporting Plowman, with 1. The Negro's Lament; 2. A Drinking Song* (Belfast 1793). This songbook, along with a Latin pamphlet written by Whitley Stokes that was inscribed to Thomas Russell, were confiscated from Russell when he was arrested in September 1796. The bawdy songbook and the scholarly pamphlet typify the eclectic literary tastes of the United Irishmen.

SPOI 620/21: twenty copies of the second edition of the *Review of the Lion of Old England* by William Sampson and Thomas Russell.

SPOI 620/12/143: manuscript poems and printer's copy of poems that were among the papers seized when William Dowdall was arrested in 1803. Dowdall was a proprietor of the *Press* in the final weeks of its publication in the spring of 1798 and an associate of Robert Emmet in 1803.

620/22/61: *The Ascendancy Nosegay*, written by "one of the Swinish Multitude for the Amusement of his fellow animals in tribulation," a collection of satirical songs (1795).

4. UNITED IRISH NEWSPAPERS

1. Francis J. Bigger published a brief article on the *Northern Star* in 1895 that includes some interesting and some inaccurate details about the paper (33–35).
2. "The Exiled Irishman's Lamentation's" immense popularity made its authorship a subject of controversy in the nineteenth century. Mary Ann McCracken's response to R. R. Madden's inquiry concerning the song's authorship provided insight into the distribution and composition of United Irish songs. She wrote that Jemmy Hope, calling one day at the Northern Star Office, "found Samuel Neilson and Henry Joy McCracken correcting for the press and superintending the printing of a song called 'The Exiled Irishman's Lamentation,' and that he (Hope) was supplied with a large bundle of the printed songs for distribution." She also provided Madden with an important account of the adoption of the song by the United Irishmen: "I have no idea who the author of the song, 'Erin go bragh,' was. What I heard my brother say, was, that it was a joint composition of several; the first three or four verses having been heard sung through the streets of Dublin, called 'The Exiled Irishman's Lamentation,' was adopted by the United Irishmen with a view to the promotion of their objects" (Madden 1887, 341).

When the United Irishmen printed the song on broadside sheets they evidently used the title "Erin Go Bragh" instead of "The Exiled Irishman's Lamentation," because a broadside containing the song in the Linen Hall Library in Belfast is entitled "Erin Go Bragh!" Above the six stanzas of the song is a woodcut that is identical to that on the frontispiece of the 1795 edition of *Paddy's Resource*. At the bottom of the songsheet is printed: "Belfast—Printed at public Printing Office, 115, High-street where may be had a great Variety of Ballads, Pictures, Pamphlets etc." No date is given, but United Irishman Thomas Storey purchased the Public Printing Office in the summer of 1794.

The United Irishmen frequently distributed their songs on such ballad sheets. According to the *Report of the Committee of Secrecy of the House of Commons* in March 1799, which focused on the "propagation of those destructive principles" of the United Irishmen, "their proceedings and resolutions and the works of Paine and other seditious and impious publications, were distributed, throughout every part of the kingdom, with an activity and profusion beyond all former example" (9–10). W. H. Maxwell's History of the Irish Rebellion in the Year 1798 describes how bundles of United Irish publications were thrown into meetinghouse grounds on Sundays and left on the sides of public roads (1845, 13).

It was also the fashion for radical poetry to circulate in manuscript form. For example, Mary Leadbeater's Annals of Ballitore record the following entry for 1798 when soldiers came searching for seditious papers: "On the day of this search I was not at home, else I suppose I should have opened my desk in the security of conscious innocence, quite forgetting that I had thrown into it one of the squibs then privately circulated, which in a very tolerable poetry avowed disloyal sentiments. I started at the danger it was so near bringing upon us, and thankfully flung it into the fire" (1986, 61).

5. UNITED IRISH SONGS AND SONGBOOKS

1. J. R. R. Adams has credited Porter with "producing" Paddy's Resource in 1795 and 1796 (1987, 86, 180). I suspect that connection has been made largely because Billy Bluff and the Squire, known to have been written by Porter, was so often re-printed in the nineteenth century with selected songs from Paddy's Resource appended to it. Indeed, when I wrote to J. R. R. Adams, and to John Gray and John Killen, librarians at the Linen Hall Library who are experts on the period, to inquire about Porter's supposed association with the 1795 and 1796 Paddy's Resource songbooks, the only evidence any of them cited was "tradition." But it is a fairly recent "tradition" because contemporary sources and nineteenth-century experts on Porter and the period, such as W. T. Latimer (1897) and F. J. Bigger, never attributed Paddy's Re-source to Porter. For example, in his essay on Porter in The Irish Book Lover in 1922, Bigger posed the question: "It would be interesting to know who compiled Paddy's Resource." (128). Interestingly, R. R. Madden never even brings up the question of who compiled the Paddy's Resource songbooks in his extensive writings about the United Irishmen.

Porter could have been involved in publishing Paddy's Resource in 1795 and 1796, but such evidence as does exist is sketchy. One informant told Bigger that he thought Porter was the author of "The Exiled Irishman's Lamentation" because he had seen a manuscript of the song in Porter's hand (Bigger 1922, 127). However, there is no doubt that George Nugent Reynolds wrote that song, so the more likely explanation for the existence of a manuscript of it in Porter's hand was that Porter had copied it for his own use or for publication. The song did appear in the Northern Star in July 1796 and in the 1796 Paddy's Resource. Latimer reprints a letter dated 15 February 1796 from Porter to the Antrim poet Samuel Thomson, who frequently published poetry in the Northern Star, reminding Thomson to send Porter a song as promised (Latimer 1897, 167). As none of Thomson's Northern Star poems appeared in any Paddy's Resource, and his conservative political opinions prevented him from writing songs such as those that appeared in Paddy's Resource, the letter can only be viewed as evidence that Porter was involved in publishing poetry in the Northern Star.

In any event, Porter, who was hung on 2 July 1798, had nothing to do with the third and fourth *Paddy's Resource* songbooks, which were published in Dublin in 1798 and 1803(?).

2. Helen Landreth, who presents a great deal of information about Thomas Russell in her biography of Robert Emmet, quotes from a manuscript in Thomas Russell hand in which he wrote lines of poetry (which, I noted, are almost identical to the first stanza of "Man is Free by Nature") and then experimented with various choruses about "Death or Liberty" (1948, 164). Unfortunately, Landreth does not provide any information about the location of the manuscript, and I have not been able to trace it. Such a manuscript of the poem in Russell's hand suggests that either he was the author or he was revising it as he had other poems and songs.

"Gilly Crankey," the tune for "Man Is Free by Nature," provided a significant Scots-Irish historical context. The catchy tune of the Jacobite song "The Battle of Killiecrankie" had been popular in Scotland and in Ireland for over a century. In July of 1689, Highland forces, which included several hundred "raw, half-naked Irish auxiliaries sent by James," successfully attacked a larger force of William's soldiers in the narrow pass at Killiecrankie in Scotland and killed one half of them (Brander 1975, 180–84). "Killiecrankie" was yet another example of the confused origin of Scots and Irish tunes and songs. Although it celebrated a Scottish battle, the victors included numerous Irishmen and a 1694 Northumbrian manuscript of the song referred to it as "The Irish Gillcranky" (O'Neill 1913, 124). Most importantly, the United Irishmen's use of the tune recalled an important rebel victory against the forces of the crown at which Scottish and Irish forces had successfully *united* in their common grievances, much as they were being urged to do in Ulster in 1795.

3. "Larry Grogan" was a popular eighteenth-century jig tune. When Edward Bunting included "The Cuckoo's Nest" in his 1840 collection, he said it was a "very ancient Irish air" that he had found in "an old music book of 1723" (1869c, x). Two other songs were set to traditional Irish tunes that, according to Bunting, had been performed at the Belfast Harp Festival in 1792: "Hibernia in Woe" was set to "The County of Leitrim" and "The Hopes of Hibernia" was set to "Molly Astore."

4. R. R. Madden attributed the song to "Counsellor Lysaght," and included the following note when he reprinted the song in *Literary Remains*: "Mr. M., an intimate friend of Lysaght's, informed me this song was written by the latter, and frequently sung by him. The best of his songs, the same gentleman states, he knew to have been written off-hand by Lysaght, 'on the spur of the moment,' at convivial parties" (1887, 88). A good many United Irish songs probably originated in a similar manner.

5. Arthur O'Connor and Edward Fitzgerald often visited at Stockdale's house in early 1798 (Madden 1860, 3:334). After the Rising in 1803, Stockdale was arrested and charged with printing Emmet's proclamation, but was never brought to trial. Prior to the Rising, Robert Emmet and William Dowdall were frequent visitors to Stockdale's (Madden 1860, 3:334). Major Sirr seized papers belonging to Dowdall after the Rising, that are now in the State Paper Office of Ireland (SPOI 620/12/143). Most of the papers are printer's copy, but none of the poetry corresponds to anything in the 1803 *Paddy's Resource* songbook. However, Dowdall's confiscated papers could have been materials intended for yet another collection, or manuscripts that had

been intended for publication in the *Press* in 1798, for Dowdall was also associated with that newspaper.

6. "The Dawning of the Day" had been the title of a seventeenth-century Irish harp tune commonly used for a love song (O'Sullivan 1967, 14). "Shannon's Flowry Banks" perhaps referred to a tune in Bunting's 1796 collection entitled "The Banks of Shannon." The dawning of the day was also associated with the "dawn" of freedom in native Irish poetry. For example, Douglas Hyde's translation of a poem by Antony Raftery prophesying the arrival of the popularly anticipated millennial year of 1829 included these lines: "For it is long since it was said that the bright day would come / When the harp would play to us in the year of the Nine" (Murphy 1972, 21).

7. Thomas Russell's description of Edward Fitzgerald, written in a letter to Russell's brother, illustrates the legendary status he soon assumed among his United Irish colleagues and the people: "It was my fortune to be confined in Newgate when Lord Edward was brought in and I was the only friend who saw him from that time, except his brother a few hours before his death. I had not the good fortune of personally knowing him until after my imprisonment in 1796—so much information, modesty, disinterestedness and virtue I never saw combined. I was with him most of the first night of his imprisonment until I was separated from him by order of the government. I saw him but once after. His death was like his life. He died a hero and a saint" (TCD, Madden Papers, 873/655 I). Russell enclosed a lock of Lord Edward's hair and asked his brother to give it to a person designated by Lord Edward.

This exchange of relics was a common practice among United Irishmen and is yet another aspect of their lives that qualifies the stereotype of them, whether as political reformers or as violent revolutionaries, as motivated only by rationalist sensibilities. After Henry Joy McCracken's execution, Mary Ann McCracken sent a piece of his hair to Thomas Russell, and she later requested Russell to send her some of his own hair before his execution (McNeill 1960, 224). R. R. Madden received some of these "relics" from her when he was compiling his materials in the 1840s. The Madden Papers at Trinity College Dublin contain clippings of the hair of several United Irishmen, including Wolfe Tone, Samuel Neilson, Jemmy Hope, and Henry Joy McCracken (873/335–36). The harper Carolan's skull had been venerated as a relic earlier in the century (O'Sullivan 1958, 117–24).

Bibliography

MANUSCRIPTS

NLI   National Library of Ireland (Dublin)
        Thomas Davis Notes and Letters 1791
PRO   Public Record Office (London)
        Home Office: 100/34–78 (Ireland 1791–1798)
PRONI Public Record Office of Northern Ireland (Belfast)
        Drennan Letters T765 (typescripts of over 1400
        manuscript letters arranged chronologically by number)
SPOI   State Paper Office of Ireland (Dublin)
        Rebellion Papers 620/1–67
TCD   Trinity College, Dublin
        Madden Papers MS873
        Sirr Papers MSS868–69

BOOKS, PAMPHLETS, AND ARTICLES

Adams, J. R. R. 1987. *The Printed Word and the Common Man: Popular Culture in Ulster, 1700–1900*. Belfast: Institute of Irish Studies.

An Address from the Independent Freeholders of the Province of Munster and a Collection of 48 Original Patriotic Toasts drank at a select assembly of freeholders at Corke [sic], January 1754. 1754. London: N.p.

"The African's Complaint on Board a Slave Ship" by "J.C." 1793. *The Gentleman's Magazine* 63:749.

Akenson, Donald, and W. H. Crawford. 1977. *James Orr: Bard of Ballycarry*. Belfast: Public Record Office of Northern Ireland.

The American Republican Harmonist; or, a Collection of Songs and Odes: Written in America, on American Subjects and Principles. 1803. Philadelphia: William Duane.

257

Anthologia Hibernica. 1793–1794. Dublin: Mercier.

Ashley, Leonard, ed. 1973. "Introduction." In *Ballad Poetry of Ireland,* edited by Charles Gavan Duffy. Delmar, Pa.: Scholars' Facsimiles.

Ashton, Robert. [1756] 1826. *The Battle of Aughrim; or, the fall of Monsieur St. Ruth. A Tragedy.* Belfast: J. Smyth.

Barrington, Jonah. 1833. *Historic Memoirs of Ireland, Comprising Secret Records of the National Convention, the Rebellion and the Union.* 2 vols. London: H. Colburn.

Barry, Michael Joseph. 1845. *Songs of Ireland.* Dublin: James Duffy.

Beckett, J. C. 1986. "Literature in English, 1691-1800." In *A New History of Ireland, IV: Eighteenth-Century Ireland, 1691–1800,* edited by T. W. Moody and W. E. Vaughn, 424–70. Oxford: Clarendon.

Benn, George. 1877. *A History of the Town of Belfast from the Earliest Times to the Close of the Eighteenth Century.* London: Marcus Ward.

Bigger, Francis J. 1895. "The Northern Star." *Ulster Journal of Archaeology,* 2d ser. 1:33–35.

——— 1922. "James Porter (1753–1798), with Some Notes on *Billy Bluff* and *Paddy's Resource.*" *The Irish Book Lover* 13:126–31.

Bolg an tSolair: or, Gaelic Magazine. 1795. Belfast: Northern Star Office.

Boswell, James. 1934. *Boswell's Life of Johnson.* 6 vols. Oxford: Clarendon.

Boydell, Brian. 1986. "Music, 1700-1850." In *A New History of Ireland, IV: Eighteenth-Century Ireland, 1691–1800,* edited by T. W. Moody and W. E. Vaughn, 542–618. Oxford: Clarendon.

Bradsher, Earl. 1966. *Mathew Carey: Editor, Author, and Publisher.* New York: AMS.

Brander, Michael. 1975. *Scottish and Border Battles and Ballads.* New York: Clarkson N. Potter.

Breathnach, R. A. 1965. "Two Eighteenth-Century Scholars: J. C. Walker and Charlotte Brooke." *Studia Hibernica* 5:88–97.

Brooke, Charlotte. [1789] 1970. *Reliques of Irish Poetry: Consisting of Heroic Poems, Odes, Elegies, and Songs, Translated into English Verse: with Notes Explanatory and Historical; and the Originals in the Irish Character; to which is subjoined an Irish Tale.* Reprint. Gainesville: Scholars' Facsimiles and Reprints, 1970.

Brooke, Henry. 1793. "Proposals for Printing by Subscription the History of Ireland from the Earliest Times." *Anthologia Hibernica* 2:188–91.

Brown, Malcolm. 1972. *The Politics of Irish Literature: from Thomas Davis to W. B. Yeats.* Seattle: Univ. of Washington Press.

Brown, Stephen. 1919. *Ireland in Fiction: A Guide to Irish Novels, Tales, Romances, and Folk-Lore.* Dublin: Maunsel.

Brown, Terence. 1975. *Northern Voices: Poets from Ulster.* Totowa, N.J.: Rowman and Littlefield.

Browne, Ray B. 1964. "The Paine-Burke Controversy in Eighteenth-Century Irish Popular Songs." In *The Celtic Cross: Studies in Irish Culture and Literature,* edited by R. Browne, W. Roscelli, and R. Loftus, 80–97. West Lafayette, Ind.: Purdue Univ. Studies.

Bunting, Edward. [1796] 1969a. *A General Collection of the Ancient Irish Music.* Reprint. Dublin: Waltons.

———. [1809] 1969b. *A General Collection of the Ancient Music of Ireland.* Reprint. Dublin: Waltons.

———. [1840] 1969c. *A Collection of the Ancient Music of Ireland.* Reprint. Dublin: Waltons.

Burk, John Daly. 1799. *A History of the Late War in Ireland.* Philadelphia: Bailey.

———. 1808. "An Historical Essay on the Character and Antiquity of Irish Songs." *The Enquirer* [Richmond, Va.], 27 May 1808, 1–2.

Burke, Edmund. [1790] 1965. *Reflections on the Revolution in France.* New York: Holt, Rinehart and Winston.

———. 1990. *A Philosophical Enquiry into the Origin of Our Ideas of the Sublime and the Beautiful.* Oxford: Oxford Univ. Press.

Burns, Robert. 1962. *The Songs of Robert Burns and Notes on Scottish Songs by Robert Burns.* Edited by James C. Dick. Hatboro, Pa.: Folklore Associates.

Cassirer, Reinhard. 1938. "United Irishmen in Democratic America." *Ireland Today* 3: 131–37.

Casteleyn, Mary. 1984. *A History of Literacy and Libraries in Ireland.* Brookfield, Vt.: Gower.

Catalogue of the Books, Belonging to the Belfast Society for Promoting Knowledge, with Their Rules, and a List of Members. 1795. Belfast: William Magee.

"Centenary of Father Meehan." 1912. *The Irish Book-Lover* 4:25–27.

Clark, William Smith. 1965. *The Irish Stage in the County Towns 1720–1800.* Oxford: Clarendon.

Collins, William. 1937. *The Poems of Gray and Collins.* Edited by Austin L. Poole. London: Oxford Univ. Press.

Corry, John. 1797. *Odes and Elegies Descriptive and Sentimental; with The Patriot, A Poem.* Newry: Moffet.

Cox, Liam. 1969. "Westmeath in the 1798 Period." *Irish Sword* 9:1–15.

Cronin, Sean. 1964. *Jemmy Hope: A Man of the People.* Drogheda: Sceim na gCeardchumann.

Curtin, Nancy. 1985. "The Transformation of the Society of United Irishmen into a Mass-Based Revolutionary Organization, 1794–96." *Irish Historical Studies* 24:463–92.

Darnton, Robert and Daniel Roche, eds. 1989. *Revolution in Print: The Press in France 1775–1800*. Berkeley: Univ. of California Press.

Davis, Thomas. 1914. *Essays Literary and Historical*. Edited by D. J. O'Donoghue. Dundalk: Dundalgan.

Deane, Seamus. 1986. *A Short History of Irish Literature*. London: Hutchinson.

———, ed. 1991. *The Field Day Anthology of Irish Writing*. 3 vols. Derry: Field Day Publications.

De Charms, Desiree. 1966. *Songs in Collections: An Index*. Detroit: Information Services Inc.

Dickson, William Steel. [1793] 1812. *Scripture Politics*. Reprinted as "Appendix" in *A Narrative of the Confinement and Exile of William Steel Dickson*. Dublin: J. Stockdale.

Dix, E. R. "Miscellaneous Scraps of Songbooks (1797–1829)." Typescript in the Royal Irish Academy.

Donnelly, James S. 1980. "Propagating the Cause of the United Irishmen." *Studies: An Irish Quarterly Review* 69:5–23.

———. 1983. "Pastorini and Captain Rock: Millenarianism and Sectarianism in the Rockite Movement of 1821–4." In *Irish Peasants: Violence and Political Unrest, 1780–1914*, edited by Samuel Clark and J. S. Donnelly, 102–39. Madison: Univ. of Wisconsin Press.

Dowden, Wilfred S., ed. 1983. "Introduction." *The Journal of Thomas Moore*. 5 vols. Newark: Univ. of Delaware Press.

Doyle, David Noel. 1981. *Ireland, Irishmen, and Revolutionary America, 1760–1820*. Cork: Mercier.

Drennan, William. 1785. *Letters of Orellana, an Irish Helot, to the Seven Northern Counties not represented in the National Assembly of Delegates held at Dublin, October 1784, for obtaining a more equal representation of the people in the Parliament of Ireland*. Dublin: John Chambers.

———. 1795. *Letter to His Excellency Earl Fitzwilliam, Lord Lieutenant of Ireland*. Dublin: John Chambers.

———. 1799. *Second Letter to the Right Honourable William Pitt*. Dublin: N.p.

———. 1815. *Fugitive Pieces, in Verse and Prose*. Belfast: F. D. Finlay.

———. [1791] 1844. "Idem Sentire, Dicere, Agere." In *The Irish Rebellion of 1798, with Numerous Historical Sketches Never Before Published*, edited by James McCormick. Dublin: James McCormick.

———. 1931. *The Drennan Letters, being a Selection from the Correspondence which passed between William Drennan and his brother-in-law and sister*

Samuel and Martha McTier during the years 1776-1819. Edited by D. A. Chart. Belfast: Stationery Office.

Drummond, William Hamilton. 1797. *Hibernia*. Belfast: Northern Star Office.

———. 1797. *The Man of Age*. Belfast: Northern Star Office.

———. 1852. *Ancient Irish Minstrelsy*. Dublin: Hodges and Smith.

Duffy, Charles Gavan, ed. [1845] 1869. *The Ballad Poetry of Ireland*. 40th ed. Dublin: James Duffy.

———. 1881. *Young Ireland: A Fragment of Irish History, 1840–50*. New York: Appleton.

———. 1895. *Short Life of Thomas Davis, 1840–46*. London: Unwin.

———. 1898. *My Life in Two Hemispheres*. 2 vols. London: Unwin.

Dunne, Tom. 1982. *Theobald Wolfe Tone, Colonial Outsider: An Analysis of His Political Philosophy*. Cork: Tower Books.

———. 1990. "Popular Ballads, Revolutionary Rhetoric, and Politicisation." In *Ireland and the French Revolution*, edited by Hugh Gough and David Dickson, 139–55. Dublin: Irish Academic Press.

Elliott, Marianne. 1978. "The Origins and Tranformations of Early Irish Republicanism." *International Review of Social History* 23:405–28.

———. 1989. *Wolfe Tone: Prophet of Irish Independence*. New Haven: Yale Univ. Press.

Emmet, Thomas Addis. 1915. *Memoir of Thomas Addis and Robert Emmet*. 2 vols. New York: Emmet.

Emsley, Clive. 1979. "The Home Office and Its Sources of Information and Investigation 1791–1801." *English Historical Review* 94:532–61.

Ewen, David. 1966. *American Popular Songs: From the Revolutionary War to the Present*. New York: Random House.

Fairchild, Hoxie. 1961. *The Noble Savage: A Study in Romantic Naturalism*. New York: Russell and Russell.

Fallis, Richard. 1978. *The Irish Renaissance: An Introduction to Anglo-Irish Literature*. Dublin: Gill and Macmillan.

Farrell, William. 1949. *Carlow in '98: The Autobiography of William Farrell of Carlow*. Edited by Roger McHugh. Dublin: Browne and Nolan.

Fitzhenry, Edna. 1936. *Henry Joy McCracken*. Dublin: Phoenix.

Fitzpatrick, Rory. 1989. *God's Frontiersmen: The Scots-Irish Epic*. London: Weidenfeld and Nicolson.

Foster, Roy. 1988. *Modern Ireland, 1600–1972*. London: Penguin.

Fox, Charlotte Milligan. 1911. *Annals of the Irish Harpers*. London: Smith Elder.

Freneau, Philip. 1963. *Poems*. Edited by F. L. Pattee. 3 vols. New York: Russell and Russell.

Gay, John. [1728] 1969. *The Beggar's Opera*. Edited by Edgar V. Roberts. Lincoln: Univ. of Nebraska Press.

Goldsmith, Oliver. [1760] 1854. "The History of Carolan, the Last Irish Bard." In *The Works of Oliver Goldsmith*, edited by Peter Cunningham. 3 vols. London: Murray.

Gray, John. 1989. "Millennial Vision: Thomas Russell Re-assessed." *The Linen Hall Review* 6:5–9.

Gray, Thomas. 1937. *The Poems of Gray and Collins*. Edited by Austin L. Poole. London: Oxford Univ. Press.

Green, E. R. R. 1970. "Thomas Percy in Ireland." *Ulster Folklife* 15–16:224–32.

Hamilton, William. 1786. *Letters Concerning the North Coast of Antrim, containing a Natural History of its Basaltes: with an Account of such Circumstances as are worthy of notice respecting the Antiquities, Manners, and Customs of that Country*. Dublin: Bonham.

Hardiman, James. 1831. *Irish Minstrelsy; or, Bardic Remains of Ireland; with English Poetical Translations*. London: Joseph Robins.

Herd, David. [1776] 1973. *Ancient and Modern Scottish Songs*. 2 vols. Edinburgh: Scottish Academic Press.

Hewitt, John. 1974. *Rhyming Weavers and Other Country Poets of Antrim and Down*. Belfast: Blackstaff.

———. 1987. *Ancestral Voices: The Selected Prose of John Hewitt*. Edited by Tom Clyde. Belfast: Blackstaff.

Hogan, Ita M. 1966. *Anglo-Irish Music 1780–1830*. Cork: Cork Univ. Press.

Hume, David. 1754–1762. *History of England from the Invasion of Julius Caesar to the Revolution of 1688*. 8 vols. London: A. Millar.

Hutchinson, Francis. 1734. *Defense of the Antient Historians of Ireland and Great Britain*. Dublin: J. Smith and W. Bruce.

Hutchinson, John. 1987. *The Dynamics of Cultural Nationalism: The Gaelic Revival and the Creation of the Irish Nation State*. London: Allen and Unwin.

Inglis, Brian. 1954. *The Freedom of the Press in Ireland, 1784–1841*. London: Faber and Faber.

Jacobs, Rosamond. 1937. *The Rise of the United Irishmen, 1791–94*. London: Harrap.

Jeffares, A. N. 1982. *Anglo-Irish Literature*. New York: Schocken Books.

Johnson, James, ed. [1787–1803] 1962. *The Scots Musical Museum*. 1853 ed. with "Illustrations of the Lyric Poetry and Music of Scotland by William Stenhouse." 2 vols. Hatboro, Pa.: Folklore Associates.

Jones, Howard Mumford. 1937. *The Harp That Once: A Chronicle of the Life of Thomas Moore*. New York: Holt.

Jordan, Hoover. 1975. *Bolt Upright: The Life of Thomas Moore*. Salzburg: Salzburg Studies in English Literature.

Joy, Henry. 1794. *Belfast Politics*. Belfast: H. Joy and Co.

————. 1817. *Historical Collections Relative to the Town of Belfast: from the Earliest Period to the Union with Great Britain*. Belfast: George Berwick.

Keating, Geoffrey. 1723. *Foras feasa ar Eirinn [The History of Ireland]*. Translated by Dermod O'Connor. Dublin: James Carson.

Killen, John. 1990. *A History of the Linen Hall Library, 1788–1988*. Belfast: The Linen Hall Library.

Kinsella, Thomas, ed. 1986. *The New Oxford Book of Irish Verse*. Oxford: Oxford Univ. Press.

Landreth, Helen. 1948. *The Pursuit of Robert Emmet*. New York: McGraw-Hill.

Latimer, W. T. 1897. *Ulster Biographies, Relating Chiefly to the Rebellion of 1798*. Belfast: J. Cleeland and W. Mullan.

Leadbeater, Mary. 1986. *The Annals of Ballitore*. Edited by John MacKenna. Athy: Stephen Scroop.

Lee, John. 1780. *A Favourite Collection of the So Much Admired Old Irish Tunes, the Original and Genuine Compositions of Carolan the Celebrated Irish Bard. Set for the Harpsichord, Violin, and German-Flute*. Dublin: N.p.

Leerssen, Joseph. 1986. *Mere Irish and Fíor-Ghael: Studies in the Idea of Irish Nationality, Its Development and Literary Expression Prior to the Nineteenth Century*. Amsterdam: John Benjamins.

Lyons, F. S. L. 1971. *Ireland Since the Famine*. London: Fontana.

Lysimachia. A Poem Addressed to the Orange or Break-of-Day Men in the Counties of Armagh and Down. 1797. Belfast: Public Printing Office.

McCormick, James. 1844. *The Irish Rebellion of 1798, with Numerous Historical Sketches, Never Before Published*. Dublin: James McCormick.

McCullough, Norman V. 1962. *The Negro in English Literature: A Critical Introduction*. Devon: Arthur Stockwell.

McDowell, R. B. 1940. "The Personnel of the Dublin Society of United Irishmen, 1791–94." *Irish Historical Studies* 2:12–53.

————. 1979. *Ireland in the Age of Imperialism and Revolution, 1760–1801*. Oxford: Clarendon.

————. 1986. "Reform and Reaction, 1789–1794." In *A New History of Ireland, IV: Eighteenth-Century Ireland 1691–1800*, edited by T. W. Moody and W. E. Vaughn, 289-338. Oxford: Clarendon.

MacGrath, Kevin M. 1948. "Writers in the 'Nation,' 1842–45." *Irish Historical Studies* 6:189–223.

McHenry, James. 1824. *O'Halloran; or, the Insurgent Chief, An Irish Historical Tale of 1798*. 2 vols. Philadelphia: Carey and Lee.

McHugh, Roger, and Maurice Harmon. 1982. *A Short History of Anglo-Irish Literature from Its Origins to the Present Day*. Totowa, N.J.: Barnes and Noble.

McNeill, Mary. 1960. *The Life and Times of Mary Ann McCracken, 1770–1866: A Belfast Panorama*. Belfast: Blackstaff.

MacNeill, Maire. 1990. *Maire Rua: Lady of Leamaneh*. Edited by Maureen Murphy. Whitegate, Co. Clare: Ballinakella.

Macpherson, James. 1857. *The Poems of Ossian, to which is prefixed a preliminary discourse and dissertation on the aera and poems of Ossian*. Boston: Phillips, Sampson.

McSkimin, Samuel. [1849] 1906. *Annals of Ulster, from 1790–1798*. Belfast: William Mullan.

Madden, R. R. [1842] 1858a. *The United Irishmen, Their Lives and Times*. 1st ser., 2d ed. Dublin: James Duffy.

———. [1843] 1858b. *The United Irishmen, Their Lives and Times*. 2 vols. 2d ser., 2d ed. Dublin: James Duffy.

———. [1846] 1860. *The United Irishmen, Their Lives and Times*. 3 vols. 3d ser., 2d ed. Dublin: J. Mullany.

———. 1887. *Literary Remains of the United Irishmen of 1798, and Selections from Other Popular Lyrics of their Times*. Dublin: James Duffy.

Maddyn, Daniel Owen. 1842. "Character of the Right Honourable Stephen Woulfe." *Dublin Monthly Magazine* (July–Dec. 1842) 2: 278–95.

Mason, William. 1759. *Caractacus*. Dublin: P. Wilson.

The Masonic, or Sentimental Magazine. 1792–1795. Dublin: Jones.

Maxwell, W. H. 1845. *History of the Rebellion in Ireland in the Year 1798*. London: A. H. Baily.

Michelburne, John. [1705] 1841. *Ireland Preserved; or the Seige of Londonderry*. Dublin: N.p.

Miller, David. 1987. "Presbyterianism and 'Modernisation' in Ulster." In *Nationalism and Popular Protest in Ireland*, edited by C. H. E. Philpin. Cambridge: Cambridge Univ. Press.

———. 1990. *Peep O' Day Boys and Defenders: Selected Documents on the County Armagh Disturbances 1784–96*. Belfast: Public Record Office of Northern Ireland.

Mitchell, Arthur, ed. 1976. *Ireland and Irishmen in the American War of Independence*. Dublin: Academy.

Moore, Thomas. 1808–34. *Irish Melodies*. London: J. Power.

———. [1817] 1843. "Lalla Rookh." In *Poetical Works of Thomas Moore*, 27–98. Philadelphia: Crissy and Markley.

———. 1818. *National Airs*. London: J. Power.

———. 1824. *Memoirs of Captain Rock, The Celebrated Irish Chieftain, with Some Account of his Ancestors, Written by Himself*. 3d ed. London: Longman, Brown, Green.

———. 1831. *The Life and Death of Lord Edward Fitzgerald*. 2 vols. London: Longman, Rees.

———. 1843. *The Poetical Works of Thomas Moore*. Philadelphia: Crissy and Markley.

———. 1853. *Memoirs, Journal, and Correspondence of Thomas Moore*. Edited by John Russell. London: Longman, Brown, Green.

———. 1858. *The History of Ireland*. New York: E. Dunigan.

———. 1983. *The Journal of Thomas Moore*. Edited by Wilfred S. Dowden. 5 vols. Newark: Univ. of Delaware Press.

Morgan, Sydney Owenson, Lady. 1862. *Memoirs: Autobiography, Diaries, and Correspondence*. 2 vols. London: W. H. Allen.

Murphy, Maureen. 1972. "Carleton and Columcille." *Carleton Newsletter* 2, no. 3: 19–22.

"The National Library for Ireland." 1921. *The Irish Book-Lover* 13:16.

Neal, John and William. [1724] 1986. *A Collection of the Most Celebrated Irish Tunes Proper for the Violin, German Flute or Hautboy*. Edited by Nicholas Carolan. Reprint. Dublin: Folkmusic Society of Ireland.

A New Song in Praise of the Sporting Plowman, with 1. The Negro's Lament 2. A Drinking Song. 1793. Belfast: N.p.

Nichols, John. 1817–58. *Illustrations of the Literary History of the Eighteenth Century, consisting of authentic memoirs and original letters of eminent persons*. 8 vols. London: Nichols and Bentley.

Noonan, J. D. 1913. "The Library of Thomas Davis." *The Irish Book-Lover* 5, no. 3:37–41.

O'Broin, Leon. 1972. "R. R. Madden, Historian of the United Irishmen." *Irish University Review* 2:20–33.

O'Callaghan, John Cornelius. 1841. *The Green Book, or Gleanings from the Writing-Desk of a Literary Agitator*. Dublin: O'Gorman.

O Casaide, Seamus. 1920. "A Rare Book of Irish and Scottish Gaelic Verse." *The Bibliographical Society of Ireland Publications* 3:59–70.

———. 1930. *The Irish Language in Belfast and County Down 1601–1850*. Dublin: Gill.

———. 1935. "Thomas Moore and Robert Emmet." *The Irish Book-Lover* 22:8–9.

O'Cathaoir, Brendan. 1990. *John Blake Dillon, Young Irelander*. Dublin: Irish Academic Press.

O'Conor, Charles. 1753. *Dissertations on the Antient History of Ireland, wherein an account is given of the Origine [sic], Government, Letters, Sciences, Religion, Manners and Customs of the Antient Inhabitants, to which is Subjoined a Dissertation on the Irish Colonies established in Britain with some*

Remarks on Mr. MacPherson's translation of Fingal and Temora. 2d ed. Dublin: Faulkner.

O'Donoghue, D. J. 1892. *The Poets of Ireland.* London: Paternoster.

O'Flaherty, Roderick. [1685] 1793. *Ogygia, seu rerum Hibernicorum chronologia.* Translated by James Hely. Dublin: W. McKenzie.

O'Halloran, Sylvester. 1778. *A General History of Ireland, from the Earliest Accounts to the Close of the Twelfth Century.* 2 vols. London: A. Hamilton.

O hOgain, Daithi. 1990. "Folklore and Literature: 1700–1850." In *The Origins of Popular Culture and Literacy in Ireland: Language Change and Educational Development, 1700–1920,* edited by Mary Daly and David Dickson, 1–14. Dublin: Univ. College Dublin and Trinity College Dublin.

O'Kelly, Francis. 1935. "Wolfe Tone's Novel." *The Irish Book-Lover* 22:47–48.

O'Leary, John. 1886. *How Irishmen Should Feel.* Dublin: A. and E. Cahill.

O'Neill, Francis. 1910. *Irish Folk Music: A Fascinating Hobby.* Chicago: Regan.

———. 1913. *Irish Minstrels and Musicians, with Numerous Dissertations on Related Subjects.* Chicago: Regan.

O'Reilly, Vincent. 1924. "Books from the Libraries of Wolfe Tone and William Sampson." *The Recorder* 2:5–15.

O'Sullivan, Donal J. 1958. *Carolan: The Life, Times, and Music of an Irish Harper.* 2 vols. London: Routledge and Kegan Paul.

———. [1927] 1967. "The Bunting Collection of Irish Folk Music and Songs, 1796." Reprint edition of Bunting manuscripts with commentary. Vol. 5, *Journal of the Irish Folk Song Society.* London: William Dawson.

Paddy's Resource: Being a Select Collection of Original and Modern Patriotic Songs, Toasts, and Sentiments, Compiled for the Use of the People of Ireland. 1795. Belfast: N.p. [This edition was re-issued in Philadelphia in 1796, with the only change being that the phrase "People of Ireland" was replaced by "All Firm Patriots."]

Paddy's Resource: Being a Select Collection of Original Patriotic Songs, for the use of the People of Ireland. 1796. Belfast: N.p.

Paddy's Resource, Being a Select Collection of Original and Modern Patriotic Songs Compiled for the Use of the People of Ireland, to which is added Arthur O'Connor's Address. 1798. New York: R. Wilson.

Paddy's Resource; or, The Harp of Erin, Attuned to Freedom, Being a Collection of Patriotic Songs Selected for Paddy's Amusement. 1798. Dublin: N.p.

Paddy's Resource, or The Harp of Erin, Attuned to Freedom; Being a Collection of Patriotic Songs, Selected for Paddy's Amusement. N.d. [1803?]. Dublin: N.p.

Paine, Thomas. 1925. *The Life and Works of Thomas Paine.* 10 vols. New Rochelle, N.Y.: Paine National History Association.

Pakenham, Thomas. 1972. *The Year of Liberty: The Great Irish Rebellion of 1798*. London: Granada.

Parsons, Lawrence. 1795. *Observations on the Bequest of Henry Flood to Trinity College Dublin with a Defense of the Ancient History of Ireland*. Dublin: Bonham.

Penny Readings for the Irish People, compiled by the editor of *The Nation*. 1879. 2 vols. Dublin: T. D. Sullivan.

Percy, Thomas. [1765] 1876. *Reliques of Ancient English Poetry: Consisting of Old Heroic Ballads, Songs, and Other Pieces of Our Earlier Poets, Together with some New Pieces*. Edited by J. V. Prichard. 2 vols. New York: Thomas Crowell.

The Political Harmonist; or, Songs and Poetical Effusions, Sacred to the Cause of Liberty. 1797. By "A Cosmopolite." 4th ed. Dublin: William Porter.

Pollard, Mary. 1964. "John Chambers, Printer and United Irishman." *The Irish Book-Lover* 3:1–22.

Pollock, Joseph. 1779. *Rights of Ireland Asserted, in the Letters of Owen Roe O'Nial*. Dublin: N.p.

Porter, James. 1796. *Billy Bluff and the Squire; or, A Sketch of the Times*. Belfast: N.p.

Power, John. 1866. *List of Irish Periodical Publications (Chiefly Literary) from 1729 to the Present Time*. London: J. Martin.

Proceedings of the Dublin Society of United Irishmen. 1795. Philadelphia: Thomas Stevens.

Rafroidi, Patrick. 1980. *Irish Literature in English: The Romantic Period (1789–1850)*. 2 vols. Atlantic Highlands, N.J.: Humanities.

Ramsay, Allan. [1724–1737] 1740. *The Tea-Table Miscellany: or, A Collection of Choice Songs, Scots and English*. 4 vols. 10th ed. London: A. Millar.

———. [1725] 1974. *"The Gentle Shepherd: A Pastoral comedy."* In *Poems by Allan Ramsay and Robert Fergusson*, edited by A. M. Kinghorn and A. Law. Totowa, N.J.: Rowman and Littlefield.

Report of the Committee of Secrecy of the House of Commons. 1799. London.

The Report of the Secret Committee of the House of Commons, with an Appendix. 1798. Dublin.

Rogers, Cornwell B. 1949. *The Spirit of the Revolution in 1789: A Study of Public Opinion as Revealed in Political Songs and Other Popular Literature at the Beginning of the French Revolution*. Princeton: Princeton Univ. Press.

Russell, Thomas. 1796. *A Letter to the People of Ireland on the Present Situation of the Country*. Belfast: N.p.

———. 1791–95. Journal and Memoirs of Thomas Russell, 1791–95. Edited by Christopher Woods. Unpublished typescript of 251 pages.

Ryan, Desmond. 1939. *The Sword of Light: From the Four Masters to Douglas Hyde 1636–1838*. London: Arthur Backer.

Sampson, William. [1794] 1806. *A Faithful Report of the Trial of Hurdy Gurdy; Tried and Convicted of Seditious Libel in the Court of the King's Bench on the Testimony of French Horn*. New York: B. Dornin.

———. 1832. *Memoirs of William Sampson, an Irish Exile*. London: Whittaker.

Sampson, William and Thomas Russell. 1794. *Review of the Lion of Old England; or, Democracy Confounded*. Belfast: Northern Star Office.

Savage, John. 1856. *'98 and '48: The Modern Revolutionary History and Literature of Ireland*. New York: Redfield.

Seymour, Aaron. [1816] 1970. "A Memoir of Charlotte Brooke's Life and Writings." In *Reliques of Irish Poetry* "by Miss Brooke." 2d ed. Dublin. Reprint. Gainesville, Fla.: Scholars' Facsimiles and Reprints.

Shepard, Leslie. 1962. *The Broadside Ballad: A Study in Origins and Meaning*. London: Herbert Jenkins.

Sigworth, Oliver F. 1965. *William Collins*. New York: Twayne.

Simpson, Claude. 1966. *The British Broadside Ballad and Its Music*. New Brunswick, N.J.: Rutgers Univ. Press.

A Sketch of the Life of Samuel Neilson of Belfast, Ireland: Editor of the Northern Star and Member of the Irish Directory. 1804. New York: Bernard Dornin.

Snyder, Edward. [1923] 1965. *The Celtic Revival in English Literature 1760–1800*. Reprint. Gloucester: Peter Smith.

Songs on the French Revolution that took place at Paris, 14 July 1789. Sung at the Celebration thereof at Belfast, on Saturday, 14 July 1792. 1792. Belfast: N.p.

The Spirit of the Nation. 1843. Dublin: James Duffy.

The Spirit of the Nation. [1845] 1981. Dublin: James Duffy. Reprint. Wilmington, Del.: Michael Glazier.

Stewart, A. T. Q. 1977. *The Narrow Ground: Aspects of Ulster 1609–1969*. London: Faber and Faber.

———. 1976. " 'A Stable Unseen Power': Dr. William Drennan and the Origins of the United Irishmen." In *Essays Presented to Michael Roberts*, edited by John Bossy and Peter Jupp, 80-92. Belfast: Blackstaff.

———. 1986. " 'The Harp New-Strung': Nationalism, Culture, and the United Irishmen." In *Ireland and Irish Australia: Studies in Cultural and Political History*, edited by Oliver Macdonagh and W. F. Mandle, 258–69. London: Croon Helm.

Taylor, John. [1791] 1984. "The Trumpet of Liberty." In *The New Oxford Book of Eighteenth-Century Verse*, edited by Roger Lonsdale, 782–83, 855. Oxford: Oxford Univ. Press.

Taylor, W. C. 1833–1839. *History of Ireland, from the Anglo-Norman Invasion till the Union of that Country with Great Britain.* 2 vols. New York: Harper.

Teeling, Charles Hamilton. [1828] 1876. *History of the Irish Rebellion of 1798: A Personal Narrative.* Glasgow: Cameron and Ferguson.

Thompson, R. ed. 1793. *A Tribute to Liberty: or, a New Collection of Patriotic Songs, entirely Original . . . together with a Collection of Toasts and Sentiments Sacred to the Rights of Man.* London: N.p.

———. 1794–1795. *A Tribute to the Swinish Multitude: Being a Choice Collection of Patriotic Songs.* London and New York: N.p.

Thuente, Mary Helen. 1985. "Violence in Pre-Famine Ireland: The Testimony of Irish Folklore and Fiction." *Irish University Review* 15:129–47.

———. 1989. "The Folklore of Irish Nationalism." In *Perspectives on Irish Nationalism,* edited by Thomas Hachey and Lawrence J. McCaffrey, 42–60. Lexington: Univ. Press of Kentucky.

———. 1992. "The Literary Significance of the United Irishmen." In *Irish Literature and Culture,* edited by Michael Kenneally, 35–54. Gerrards Cross: Colin Smythe.

Tone, Theobald Wolfe. 1826. *Life of Theobald Wolfe Tone, Founder of the United Irish Society.* Edited by William T. W. Tone. 2 vols. Washington, D.C.: Gales and Skaton.

Upton, Sonneck. 1964. *A Bibliography of Early Secular American Music.* New York: De Capo.

Vallancey, Charles. 1770–1804. *Collecteana De Rebus Hibernicus.* Dublin: T. Ewing.

Vance, Norman. 1981. "Celts, Carthaginians, and Constitutions: Anglo-Irish Literary Relations, 1780–1820." *Irish Historical Studies* 22:216–38.

———. 1990. *Irish Literature: A Social History.* Oxford: Basil Blackwell.

Walker, Joseph Cooper. 1786. *Historical Memoirs of the Irish Bards; interspersed with anecdotes of, and occasional observations on the Music of Ireland; also an historical and descriptive account of the Musical Instruments of ancient Ireland, with an appendix containing . . . the ancient Musical Memoirs of Cormac Common; the Life of Turlough O'Carolan; An Essay on the Origin of Romantic Fabling in Ireland; and Select Irish Melodies.* London: T. Payne.

Webb, Alfred. 1878. *A Compendium of Irish Biography.* Dublin: Gill.

Welch, Robert. 1980. *Irish Poetry from Moore to Yeats.* Totowa, N.J.: Barnes and Noble.

———. 1988. *A History of Verse Translations from the Irish 1789–1897.* Gerrards Cross: Colin Smythe.

Wilson, Charles Henry. c. 1780–90. *Select Irish Poems, Translated into English.* Dublin (?): N.p.

————. 1782. *Poems, Translated from the Irish Language into the English.* London: N.p.

————. 1804. *Brookiana.* 2 vols. London: R. Phillips.

Windele, John. 1829. "Memoir of the Late Mr. Callanan." *Bolster's Quarterly Magazine* 3:280–97.

Winstock, Lewis. 1970. *Songs and Music of the Redcoats: A History of the War Music of the British Army, 1642–1902.* Harrisburg, Pa.: Stackpole Books.

Woods, Christopher J. 1990. "The Place of Thomas Russell in the United Irish Movement." In *Ireland and the French Revolution,* edited by Hugh Gough and David Dickson, 83-100. Dublin: Irish Academic Press.

————. 1991. *Journals and Memoirs of Thomas Russell.* Dublin: Irish Academic Press.

Yeats, William Butler. 1954. *The Letters of W. B. Yeats.* Edited. by Allan Wade. London: R. Hart-Davis.

————. 1961. *Essays and Introductions.* New York: Macmillan.

Zimmermann, Georges-Denis. 1967. *Songs of Irish Rebellion: Political Street Ballads and Rebel Songs, 1780–1900.* Dublin: Allen Figgis.

Index

271

Song and Tune Index

TUNES

WIDENER UNIVERSITY
WOLFGRAM
LIBRARY
CHESTER, PA.

THE HARP RE-STRUNG
was composed in 11 on 13 Goudy Old Style
on a Mergenthaler Linotron 202,
with display in Goudy Handtooled,
by Partners Composition;
printed by sheet-fed offset on 50-pound, acid-free Natural Smooth
and smyth-sewn and bound over binder's boards in Holliston Roxite B
with dust jackets printed in 2 colors
by Braun-Brumfield, Inc.;
and published by
Syracuse University Press

Syracuse, New York 13244-5160

Richard Fallis, *Series Editor*

Irish Studies presents a wide range of books interpreting important aspects of Irish life and culture to scholarly and general audiences. The richness and complexity of the Irish experience, past and present, deserves broad understanding and careful analysis. For this reason, an important purpose of the series is to offer a forum to scholars interested in Ireland, its history, and culture. Irish literature is a special concern in the series, but works from the perspectives of the fine arts, history, and the social sciences are also welcome, as are studies that take multidisciplinary approaches.

Selected titles in the series include: